A Chateau of One's Own

Restoration Misadventures in France

SAM JUNEAU

summersdale

A CHATEAU OF ONE'S OWN

Summersdale Publishers Ltd
46 West Street
Chichester
West Sussex
PO19 1RP
UK

www.summersdale.com

Printed and bound in Great Britain

ISBN: 1-84024-641-3
ISBN 13: 978-1-84024-641-4

A Chateau Of One's Own

SAM JUNEAU

Dedicated to Bud, Blue, Grim and Oak
and in loving memory of Hill

Contents

Acknowledgements

There are many ingredients that go into writing a good book. Equal parts inspiration, hard work, luck and perseverance. But there are some individuals who make it possible. I would like to thank the publisher of Summersdale, Stewart Ferris, who, from the beginning saw the entertainment possibilities of our unlikely adventure. His wonderfully skilled and dedicated staff made the book all that it could be, especially Jennifer, Sarah and Carol who spent countless hours teasing the best story out of a hapless, rollicking undertaking. Any joy and clarity comes from them, all the mistakes are mine.

I want to thank the cast of characters that make up the book, especially our French neighbours Jehan-Claude and Marie-Christine who faithfully and generously helped us find our way through the maze of maintaining and beautifying the chateau. And to my colleagues in television who gave me work when guests at our bed and breakfast were few and far between; a special thanks to Suzette Knittl at NBC News, Lisa Zeff at ABC News Productions and Judy Bishop and Diane Petzke at Court TV. And the Irish gang, Tom, John, Andrew and Richard as well as Marion and Dennis who all lent a hand when we most needed it. And warmest thanks to my mother, Annette, for sending me to Europe in the first place so that I could fall in love with France for the first time many years ago. I am grateful too for the instinctive generosity of Jim and Nydia and Marcella who made our lives easier.

And finally, I want to thank my dear wife, Bud, whose patience and care have made our life and the story of this book an exceptional thing.

CHAPTER ONE

'It Will be Lovely...'

We are sitting quietly behind a vast and elegant seventeenth-century chateau. We have just poured the last of many glasses of a rich, not overly sophisticated, Loire Valley red wine. There is half-melted bleu d'Auvergne cheese curling over the edge of a yellow plate. Laid casually within arm's reach is the manna of the local *boulangerie*.

The chateau spreads out behind us in stately languor, dominating all around it. It is 10.30 p.m. and the sun only now decides to drift down, sprawling tendrils of light into the forest just beyond. The men have been working on the property for the better part of the day. The gardener brings the richest bounty of tomatoes we have ever dared to desire. The beekeeper unloads a few jars of honey taken from fastidious and well-fed bees in the woods. These are our neighbours. This is our chateau.

The Château du Bonchamps resides in all its grandeur in the broad, never-ending river valley of the Loire. It is the seat of noble and almost-noble families going back to 1507. There have been six owners since this time. We are the sixth. Most of our predecessors have served as minor vassals of the Plantagenet dynasty of Anjou. Yes, those Plantagenets, that dysfunctional, ruthless ruling clan made famous by Peter O'Toole and Katharine Hepburn in *The Lion in Winter*, the kings with big appetites and a fondness for ruling Britain and France. We are comforted by the fact that Richard the Lionheart and Eleanor of Aquitaine are buried nearby. The climate is mild, the summers long, the days even longer. We do not serve the Plantagenets. Just the bank.

We have always loved the country house. We have hungrily devoured countless hours of period dramas where the house is often the primary and most interesting character. How many times have we wanted to meet Darcy and the other characters from *Pride and Prejudice* just to spend time at their splendid country houses? How many times have we soaked up the immensity of *Brideshead*'s Castle Howard? So, here we are. Delighted and sometimes crushed by the getting of what we asked for. Here we are, drinking wine alongside a half-millennium-old forest, behind a massive castle that some visitors have too generously likened to Versailles. Château du Bonchamps was meant to be our salvation.

Like the violent scratch of a needle across an old record, a guest hurries down, out of breath and red-faced. Our reverie pauses.

'I'm afraid there is a leak in our room. I think it is coming from the bathroom above,' the rattled Dutchman explains.

'Let me take a look,' I say.

I've heard it before. I am sure I will hear it again. The thing about the chateau is only emergencies are dealt with. And there are infinite circumstances that can set off an emergency, especially in the summer, when our home turns into a bed and breakfast and guests roam the grounds while the building plots its next 'incident'. The chateau has surely seen many changes over its lifetime. I think it is safe to say Richard and his lions did not have to run a guest house.

We pad quickly up to the Poplar Room. All the rooms are named after trees on the property. A bit quaint but appropriate. The chateau is embraced by thousands of exquisite trees of all shapes and sizes, young and old. The most spectacular array is a set of twenty-odd sequoia trees in the shape of a 'V'. To enter the grove is to enter nature's cathedral. The thick, bulky, tremendous waists of these giants stretch skyward in endless arcs.

I accompany the Dutchman into his bathroom and there is in fact a leak from above. Drip, drip, dripping onto polished marble floors.

'Hold on. I will check upstairs.'

'That's good. But please know, it is not a problem for us. We love your house. I just thought you should know,' he kindly offers.

I run up another flight of stairs and burst into the bathroom in the Oak Suite. I was sure the friendly English family there had left for the day. Evidently not. There, in all her splendid womanness, is an early thirty-something mother and her three-year-old child, both as nude as the day they were born. They are in the bathtub doing what people do on holiday; namely, lounging in the bath. The toddler is throwing water everywhere. The ceiling is not exempt from the sweet thing's earnest attempts to express herself.

'I am so, so sorry. Please excuse me. There was a leak,' I explain sounding like a 15-year-old in the first throes of puberty. I stare briefly, unable to help myself. I recover and step out of the bathroom, red-faced and stammering again, 'There was a leak.'

The contented mother understands and is not in the least perturbed.

'It's really OK. We are making a terrible mess, but we will clean up when we get out.'

'Fine. Fine, please take your time.'

I trot downstairs to my curious Dutchman.

'I've found the leak. Just a bit of mess from playtime with baby in the tub. I will have it cleaned up *tout de suite*.'

'That's good. I just wanted you to know. Like I said, we love your chateau. It will be really lovely when you finish the works.' His words are meant to comfort, but they hit an especially sensitive nerve. The house has been 'finished' now for two years. We have not undertaken significant works in all that time. Just disaster relief.

I hesitate and refrain from reacting. I want to yell, 'For Christ's sake, can't you see all of the work we've put into the thing already? Do you know how hard we've laboured to bring it to this level? Do you realise we've spent everything we have to make your room comfortable?'

Instead, I assent, 'Yes, it will be lovely.'

CHAPTER TWO

Origins of a Specious Venture

We are first-time homebuyers. But unlike other couples starting out, our first home is a massive seventeenth-century chateau in the French countryside. Five years ago, this hulking French creation became our lives for the near future. Possibly forever. Or so we hoped.

Visitors often arrive at the front door of our chateau with a look of incredulity and awe. The first question to pop from hitherto speechless lips is usually, 'So, did you inherit this place?' Impossible, they imagine, a young couple foolish enough to buy such a beast. An old friend of mine recently met me for lunch after a long absence. I was sporting a nice, large, shiny silver watch that my wife Bud had given me, and he noted, 'That's quite a large watch. Overcompensating for something?' I paused. 'You should see my house.'

I don't believe every family should buy an unwieldy carcass of refined stone, plaster cornices, endless windows and a centuries-old forest. But I do believe everyone should have a 'chateau', a grand or modest dream that they can call theirs. A chateau of one's own.

Several years ago, we took stock of our lives. Most families in the States and the UK today have two parents working 40 to 50 hours per week, drowning in credit card debt, struggling with a sizeable mortgage, juggling costs for university, worrying about the quality and availability of health care, and dealing with all the other struggles that come with modern life. Combine this with an average commute of 45 minutes a day and the puny reward of a few weeks' holiday, and today's family is, to say the least, living a truly harried life.

As we peered down the road of our respective careers (TV producer and fashion designer), we realised we weren't completely happy with what lay ahead. We were climbing steadily in modestly stimulating jobs, fighting gamely in the hustle of modern urban existence. We couldn't help but feel that there had to be something better than the daily grind, something that would give us more time for each other and for our future children.

It was at our wedding that we realised what this something better would be.

★★★

We were married happily in a nineteenth-century castle one hour due west of Dublin. That's where my wife Bud (short for Brigid) is from. There's not a whole lot to recommend her part of Ireland except for a few hills and a picturesque mountain range called the Slieve Blooms. But there is a lovely Georgian bed and breakfast stood at the foot of these Irish mountains, named Roundwood House. A destination in its own rights, we chose it as a base for throwing together the last-minute details of our wedding that would take place across the mountains at Kinnitty Castle.

I called the owner of Roundwood from our cramped apartment in New York to enquire about availability. Always on the alert for authenticity, I asked the owner a fairly presumptuous, American-style question.

'Hi. I'm calling from the States. We're looking for a B&B not far from Kinnitty. But I need to know whether or not your house is 'genuine', not overly modernised.'

Frank, in unflappable deadpan, didn't miss a beat. 'Often we are accused of being too authentic.'

I knew we'd found our place to stay.

I won't rattle on with details about the wedding. Weddings always tend to be the same, with the climax coming at the beginning of the marathon – namely, when two enthusiastic souls say 'Yes'. But the event bore fruit in more ways than is normally expected from the union of two.

Frank and Rosemarie had run Roundwood House for some eighteen years when we met them. They managed to raise six beautiful and smart children while living just outside the mainstream. Frank found the world of nine-to-five too constricting. Rosemarie's attention to detail and boundless patience with guests is what made the thing go.

We were enchanted by their devotion to a dream that was solely created and maintained by them. Not a bad way to spend a life.

We realised that this was the very solution we'd been searching for. What could be better than shedding all of our mundane day-to-day concerns, moving to Europe, and opening our very own chateau bed and breakfast? It would be an escapade of a lifetime.

We had no idea what we were getting into.

★★★

And so our journey began.

We searched almost endlessly in Ireland, but as we looked, prices went up, and our hopes drained away. Three years after our wedding we still hadn't found our 'country house'. We did, however, give birth to our baby, Blue. She was a girl born on an island, in a village, at a crossroads – that is Manhattan, in the West Village, at the intersection of Fourteenth and Hudson. With the birth of our perfect baby girl – her only fault was that she breastfed 42 times a day – our dream to own a chateau and live in the country became even more pressing. Like so many parents, we considered our careers less important than our growing family, and we thought opening a bed and breakfast would allow us the freedom to spend countless hours together. Shortly after Blue's birth we decided to head across the great pond to visit Bud's family. We thought it would be good for the Irish, especially Bud's mammy, to see Blue in all her infant glory. Luckily, Blue did have eyes to match her name, and a solid disposition.

While we were back in Ireland, we took the opportunity to continue our property hunt. We were having awful luck in our pursuit, and an incident involving an estate agent in Limerick led us to other greener, pastures.

Long known as 'Stab City', Limerick was a beaten and desperate town and its surrounds were only slightly better than the city itself. I arranged the meeting by Internet so the agent knew nothing of our background (specifically 'rich' Americans coming from New York City). This kind-looking, solicitous gentleman suffered from a fairly common disease. For the sake of argument, one might call it 'greed'. We met at a pub in central Limerick and set off in his late-model Mercedes.

'I wanted to let you know, the price of this house has changed slightly,' he began.

'What do you mean?'

'Well, I know the listing said £250,000, but the owner wants £350,000,' he ventured tentatively.

If I had a sliver of sense, I might have excused myself from the car right there. But hope springs eternal.

We drove well into the countryside, down twisty lanes and around impossible curves until we arrived at the house. Set majestically on a hill, surrounded by a few stately trees, the mansion seemed perfect, if not at all ideally situated (no one, and I mean *no one*, holidays in Limerick). Even at the new price, the mansion's distinguished eminence seemed well suited to our oversized ambitions.

According to the agent's details the house had five bays, three storeys, extensive ruined outbuildings, lovely plaster mouldings in the main entrance hall and a generosity of space and proportion befitting a proper-sized country house. But upon further inspection, our hearts sank.

'Where are the fireplaces?' Bud queried.

'They were stolen by travellers,' our host said.

'And the floors? Why is there plywood everywhere?'

'They were rotten. The owner replaced them with what you see.'

Bud pulled me aside and whispered, 'Sam, there are no mouldings. This is really a shell.'

'Just hold on. Maybe it gets better.' Unlikely. No windows on the second and third floors. The roof was pitted and marked by large holes. To all these astonished remarks, the agent wearily responded that the 'tinkers', Ireland's home-grown gypsies, had stolen all the loveliest features.

This we had heard many times before in Ireland. It's a nice story, but utterly false, as we would soon find out. We made a hasty retreat after considering the cost of making this overpriced rabbit warren habitable. At the end of the road, we ran into the owner-farmer, who had just built a brand-spanking-new bungalow.

After a few pleasantries, the farmer asked, 'What do you think about the house?'

'Well, it's missing a lot of features. The building is nice but we think there's too much work,' I answered.

'Well, my sister wanted the oak floors for her new house down the road. And we sold off the fireplaces a few years back to pay for the upkeep.'

Upkeep? Apparently a vague word meaning different things to different people.

Tragically, this was the way of many Irish country homes – a crime that no law in Ireland defines as such. Of course, the 'big house' was detested for centuries because it embodied the perceived and real maliciousness of foreign landlords. But I always believed the Irish should be proud of these masterpieces despite a sordid history. Irishmen designed many of these homes and certainly all were built with the craft and skill of local Irish labourers. The neglect and indifference to these homes has persisted. Thieves were not primarily responsible for the systematic dismantling of Ireland's country house; the blame lay with modern owners and practical, pragmatic farmers.

On the drive back from our dispiriting visit, Bud made her true desires clear, once again.

'Sam, you know I want a country house. But this is too much. You couldn't give away some of these old houses ten years ago. Now, just when we're looking, the prices are going up, the market is skyrocketing. Maybe that's a sign.'

We drove along in silence for a short time. I gazed out the window as clouds gathered over the hills in huge clumps of black and grey. It wasn't raining but there was always the threat of rain. The clouds formed massive columns and lurched toward the car.

I didn't really know how to respond to my wife. The more we looked, the more I doubted we could ever find what we were looking for.

'Don't get too discouraged. A few bad visits can't make or break our plans. It's an exciting thing, this thing of ours.'

'I don't know what we're trying to do. I know I want to live in the country. And I want to live in Europe, not necessarily Ireland. And the way prices are going, it may not be possible for us.'

'For the time being, the only thing we *can* do in Europe is buy a house and run a business. I haven't found a lot of jobs in Ireland, not for me at least. You know, we found all those houses in France. Seems like a good deal. I don't quite understand why the big houses are so cheap there, but we should check it out,' I ventured.

'I'm open to that. Who knows, we might just fall in love with the perfect house.'

Famous last words, as they say. So, on a whim, fresh from the wounds of another failed house visit, we set off for France. Whimsy is never a good rationale for anything.

This decision to search in France had been brewing for a while. With nearly 40,000 castles dating from the Middle Ages to the nineteenth century, it appeared to be the land of opportunity. It seemed too good to be true. The decision made sense on a primal level, too. My family came to New Orleans, Louisiana a couple of hundred years ago from France to set up shop in the New World and start a new life. I am Cajun, and grew up in the swampy, mosquito-infested environs of the Big Easy. According to family legend, my ancestors were trappers, criminals and all-round brigands. Only in a Cajun family would this be a source of pride.

The most intriguing features of my home town and Cajun culture in general include the extraordinary spicy food and a hidden love of suffering. It's on the latter point that my Cajun background and my wife's Irish roots conjoin. If there is an arduous, painful way to do something, we will discover and pursue it with single-minded determination. Delighted we can keep up the tradition.

We returned to Bud's family home to say brief goodbyes. Everyone at the house seemed surprised by our abrupt change of plans. But we were on a mission. Nothing could stop us now. And so we set off for France, cutting our visit 'home' short by a week. We slipped into our cramped rental car and secured Blue in her seat. We bid adieu to Bud's family. I made a 13-point turn to reposition the car.

'Make sure you drive on the right side of the road!' Bud's mother said.

'Do you mean the right side or the left side?' I teased.

'You know, the correct side, the left side.'

'No problem.'

We have had this conversation every time we've visited Ireland. Bud's mother is scared to death I will forget and drive like an American. She has reason. I've made this mistake several times now.

'I'm excited about our trip,' Bud said as we started down the lane. 'I don't know what to expect, but I have a feeling it will work out. We need a change.' Then, without blinking an eye, Bud reversed direction, 'Do you think we're doing the right thing?'

'I'm not sure, but for now, all we can do is look.' I said.

'It's just it's such a big thing – the move, the language, starting a business. Can we make it work?'

She had a point. We'd never bought a house, we'd never started a business and we spoke very little French. I came to a roundabout and had to think twice about which direction I was entitled to take.

'I think it can work. What have we got to lose? Let's say the house and the B&B don't work. Then we sell. Even if we sell for less than we buy, it's OK. We'll work again. Save more money,' I said.

'I know, I know. I just want our children to grow up in the country like I did. And I want us both to spend time with them. Those are my concerns.'

This really was the nub of our move. We had long lamented the extended hours and rigidity of our jobs. As it was, I rarely saw my wife and daughter. To us, simply unacceptable. We wanted time together.

'I just worry sometimes, that's all.'

This was one of many such exchanges but the truth was, we felt there was only one solution. We simply had to make a move. Our mission was grounded firmly in a dream. The choice is always easier when you feel you have no choice.

And so, that last-minute trip to France on a dreary, inauspicious January day is where our story truly begins. After years of searching, we found ourselves sitting in a rundown French café in the Loire Valley, waiting for the man who would change our lives. Like the revered Frank and Rosemarie, Philippe the estate agent would be dropped into our laps by providence. Often, I've noticed, seemingly random intersections can change the path of one's life. Damn them and bless them at the same time.

CHAPTER THREE

All's Well that Begins Well

Our slightly hunched, congenial estate agent came through the door followed by a gust of wind and rain that frightened the quiet inhabitants of the Café des Sports in Loudun, in the Loire Valley, about an hour or so south of Tours. We meekly introduced ourselves as Philippe brushed large shards of dandruff from his blue sport coat.

Philippe explained the situation, as he saw it. Ten minutes from the café, he had discovered a genteel aristocrat trying to sell a delightful nineteenth-century chateau with 30 acres and a pool. Madame's house was small by chateau standards but well appointed and basically ready to live in immediately. We all hopped into our rental car and started down the road. Butterflies fluttered with abandon in our anxious bellies.

Just around the bend on a small country road, the chateau loomed ahead on a hill. It was composed of red brick and 'tuffeau', the white, porous limestone found in the Loire Valley region. Tuffeau is not particularly tough but quite malleable, as far as stone goes. You can shape it and carve it and define it pretty much as you wish. A lovely decoration.

The house had a great sense of verticality, dotted on top with graceful spires touched with zinc weathervanes. Each window was surrounded by a delicate confection of laced stone carvings and glass. The main entrance door was carved to within an inch of its life, heads and horses and dogs sprouting all over, the door thick with life and a keen 1800s Romantic imagination. We arrived in front of it expectantly. Philippe made the usual polite and formal introductions in the normal French way. I added, '*Bonjour, madame. Nous sommes désolés de vous déranger.*' Good day, Madam. We are sorry to bother you.

'*Bonjour,*' she replied. 'We can speak English if you like.'

Our hostess was dressed in a fine pink and black cross-hatched Chanel suit. Her black hair was pulled tightly back into a ponytail which rested just above her shoulders. She was thin and vaguely glamorous. She wore black stockings which ended abruptly and remarkably in rubber boots. The chatelaine let us into a grand, panelled entrance hall. A vast and handsome staircase of oak rose to our left. Two large and comely salons, or sitting rooms, broke off to the right. We could see an immense fire burning in a monumental tuffeau fireplace.

'You will see here a beautiful staircase. You like, *non*?'

'Yes, very beautiful,' Bud answered.

'And here you will see a parquet floor in perfect condition. It is nice, *non*?'

We ambled through the hall and into the first salon with similar comments and affirmations all attesting to the worth and beauty of the chateau. We came to a stunning dining room with an oak-sculpted buffet that smartly served the eating area and the kitchen at the same time. A Renaissance reproduction, the buffet was covered with carved heads of nobles and peasants alike with hidden drawers to stash utensils and other sundries. A great breakfast room for our hoped-for guests.

Again, 'Splendid, *non*?'

'Yes, very impressive.' And so on for 15 or more rooms.

Finally the attic with large oak beams supporting a heavy but well-maintained slate roof.

'This is *charpente*. In good condition. Do you like?'

At this point, I noticed something odd in our chatelaine's countenance. As we all looked up at the massive vaulted wood beams protecting this bourgeois jewel, I stole a glance at her noble Gallic nose which started out wide and came to a very precise, decisive point. Our gracious hostess enquired several more times as to the pleasantness of her house, and each time her left eye twitched almost imperceptibly. Her mouth was fitted tightly around clenched teeth.

I would like to think it wasn't because of our bearing or lack of nobility. Her body, her mouth, her teeth spoke clearly: regret and hesitation. We could see it in her eyes – she needed to sell the house badly. The whole dance was surpassingly uncomfortable. Normally, the agent shows you around while the owner sits discreetly in another room patiently awaiting the verdict. It's tough for today's aristocrats, who hang on to the family dowry by fingernails and ingenuity until, one day, the luck just runs out. It is a story we had encountered several times before but never so poignantly as on this day.

Of course, we did feel stabs of guilt as we visited, inspected and, in some way, transgressed the private spaces of this faded noble. We couldn't help feel the common pang of loss as she displayed the family patrimony. Perhaps the sadness of the transaction could be softened by a fresh flow of greatly needed cash.

The grounds were well sculpted in a modified French Baroque style. Every hedge and flower was well tended, and small topiaries sat here and there forming gentle patterns on a vast stone terrace. To the rear of the house, small limestone hills rose up to a couple of dozen metres, topped with spindly, anaemic trees. In ages past, men had carved enormous caves into the tuffeau hillside. To this day, Frenchmen live in these caves, where they store wine and grow mushrooms. This chateau's cave meandered back into the hill, disappearing into darkness. There were many rooms fashioned out of this ubiquitous stone, some smooth, some rough and pockmarked.

'So, Bud, what do you think?' I asked as Bud fed Blue on a worn green bench at the foot of a cave.

'It is perfect. Except for one thing. Did you see that road? It's very busy.'

'Yes, but it's far enough to be safe. *Non?*' Philippe offered hopefully.

'I just fear for the cats. I think it's too close.' Ah yes, the cats. The real reason for moving to the countryside. Bud had rescued each and every cat from daily peril and certain death on the mean streets of New York. Her charge and moral responsibility in life was to care for these abandoned strays.

Alas, the house sat on a hill overlooking a minor but busy road. Normally a selling point for a B&B in the Loire Valley, this road posed a problem for my wife and her 15 cats. I argued that the property was certainly a step up from the one-bedroom, 600-square-foot apartment in New York which we currently called home. The only apparent plus of the apartment was its cheapness, rent-controlled under some ancient New York socialist scheme. (And the jokes were sometimes funny too, spilling every weekend, and some week nights, from the comedy club Dangerfield's beneath us.) The relatively modest rent had allowed us to save for the big chateau in the sky.

The cats could enjoy the freedom of the back of the house, I argued, to no avail.

'It's just too close. We'll have to look elsewhere.'

Bud has many qualities but flexibility as regards the cats is not one of them. She is usually extraordinary in her tolerance for risk. What other wife would move husband and child to a foreign country with no safety net, only basic language skills and a smallish handful of money? Our financial livelihood and uncertain future in a faraway land caused little or no ruffle in this bird's feathers. But the cats. That was another story. Bud wouldn't be satisfied, so we made plans to meet Philippe again.

Unlike the Irish agent, Philippe was refreshingly honest. When we asked for renovation cost estimates, he offered what seemed to be realistic quotes and suggestions for how one might do the work. He pointed out defects and directed our attention to future concerns. At first I thought Philippe was up to something. Why would he be so forthcoming? It appears this is the way of agents in France. What a wonderful tonic in a property world sometimes infested with cunning.

The next day, Philippe ambled through the same café door and sat in our small booth with a handful of tattered papers. We all ordered *cafés* and prepared to discuss the week's progress. The locals eyed us as they drank preprandial cocktails in preparation for lunch. It was mid-morning after all. One fellow in blue overalls and worn, thick black boots slopped with manure uttered a few words as we prattled on. I heard '*anglais*' and '*acheter*', '*maisons*', and '*tout*'. It seems we, the English, were buying all the properties to be had in this small corner of the world.

'What did you think of the chateau yesterday?' Philippe asked hopefully.

'Well, it's a little close to the road and a bit noisy,' I answered.

'But it is a *beau* chateau, *non*?'

'Yes, very much so, but we have fifteen cats who need a safe place to live,' Bud said.

In an argument we had heard before, Philippe naively suggested, 'But we have many cats in France. Can you take some of these? Ones that can live near a road?'

Just a week earlier, Bud's mother had said the same thing. Why fly 15 cats from the States since there are plenty of cats in France? Logical, but slightly missing the point. Undaunted,

Philippe showed us a few other houses from his stack. None appealed in a way that would push us to assume a potentially crushing debt. A bit exasperated, Philippe pulled out a postcard.

'Well, there is this one. Very nice and large but needs a lot of renovation.'

My eyes widened. I managed to blurt out in an uncontrolled spasm, 'Now, that's more like it!'

Looking back, one could finish the sentence by, 'Now, that's more like it… if you had no sense, a longing for stress and a Napoleonic complex.'

The postcard was an aerial shot of an immensely handsome, gargantuan structure vaguely in the Louis XIII style. This is to say, it had a central structure with two arms, two wings actually, in the shape of a large 'U'. Surrounded by trees and a captivating little garden folly in the back, the chateau looked like a place that just might draw people to the middle of nowhere. And the windows. Fifteen bays. As a long-time amateur of the grand old country house, I had made it a habit to count the number of bays as a measure of the greatness of the estate.

'You see here in the 'fiche technique' that it is large, as you like. The facade is fifty metres long with a great hall, as you say in English, of forty metres.'

'Sam, that's much too big.' Bud knew well my tendency to bite off more than I could chew. Undeterred, I eagerly read every word in the particulars of this latest wonder. The size, the sheer grandeur of the place made my heart beat at an excited pace. A 50-metre facade. That's only a bit less than a full city block in Manhattan. More than half an American football field. Or almost half a standard football pitch. The house was composed of more than thirty rooms totalling about 15,000 square feet.

'Bud, the place is perfect for the B&B. Listen, you can have a chateau like this with 15,000 square feet, that could hold 15 to 20 one- or two-bedroom apartments in the same building, for the *same* price as a one-bedroom apartment – you're telling me it's not worth a visit?' I was shaking.

Bud was nonplussed. 'Sure, we can take a look, but I'm telling you it's too big.' I was convinced with absolute certitude that she was wrong, but for now my eyes sat like saucers on my awestruck face.

A real lightning bolt, as the French would say. Stunning. The price, 3.5 million francs (this was pre-euro), or approximately £360,000. I practically grabbed poor Philippe by the collar and dragged him to the car.

Bud said simply, 'It's really too big.'

It was now 11 a.m. Our flight was set to leave at 6.30 p.m. from Paris, three hours' drive from the chateau. One last visit before our return to the Big Apple. We set off on our hour-and-a-half journey to the Château du Bonchamps. Feeling the giddy pressure of an imminent sale, Philippe phoned his partner, Laurent. They would drive up together and give us directions. We would all meet at the castle sometime after noon.

We arrived in the small, somewhat tired village known as Châteauneuf-sur-Sarthe, with its handsome bridge across the river. It was modern but constructed in a medieval,

Romanesque style complete with wide Roman arches and wrought-iron railings. To the right of the town, we could see the spire of a Romanesque church poking up above the new-build bungalows and nineteenth-century '*maisons bourgeoises*'. Just over the river, someone had had the audacity to plonk a 1960s motel complete with neon sign and brown shingles.

It appeared to be a small town, worn around the edges. Most of the shops were closed, forever, save a bank, a couple of insurance offices and a glasses shop. The French have extraordinarily good taste in eyewear.

Our baby girl Blue was upset. We had dragged her all the way across the Atlantic to Ireland, then France and now to yet another house. Her crying was unnerving and the rain didn't help. If we had wanted rain like this, rain that fell sideways, we would have stayed in Ireland.

There was one town beyond Châteauneuf called Juvardeil. This was the town of 'our' chateau, the official mailing address. A pleasant nineteenth-century hamlet, Juvardeil had one church, one *tabac*, a *boulangerie* and a gentle river. It was considerably more promising than Châteauneuf. The houses were older, more sixteenth- and seventeenth-century. The church was mid 1800s, but well preserved and graceful, perched there above the river.

In times past, the town would have belonged to the chateau. We stopped briefly in front of the church and read about the history of Juvardeil. The Romans had founded the town in the second century and Gauls refortified it in the seventh century. Most significantly, General Bonchamps was born in Juvardeil.

Philippe's directions were less than clear to us in our excitable state and we could not find the chateau. We stopped at the *bar-tabac* for information. Dark, a bit seedy, stained yellow from years of filter-less cigarette smoke, the bar nevertheless seemed like a nice respite on a dreadful day. A reasonably attractive woman with black hair to her waist sat behind the bar dragging strongly on a Gitanes. At the end of the bar, a red-haired villager sat over a small glass of red wine. The floral wallpaper tugged away from weeping walls. An assortment of candies and treats as well as cigarettes and cigars lined the makeshift shelves. Formica chairs filled the small space. Ancient wood beams drooped lazily from the ceiling, witness to better days long ago.

'*Bonjour.* I am looking for the Château du Bonchamps. Do you know it?' I said hopefully.

'*Non,*' the barman responded. I detected a slight wince as I spoke my broken French. Not an uncommon response when I launch into the language of Racine.

The bar's sole red-headed denizen, whom I immediately dubbed 'Monsieur le Rouge', rose from his lunchtime cocktail. 'I can show you if you drive me home,' he muttered.

We all left the warm *tabac* and squeezed clumsily into our hire car. Monsieur le Rouge sat in the front next to me while Bud sat in the back cuddling Blue. We set off down the road. To the left was a homely little country lane scarred with holes. At the entrance to the lane, we found a set of outbuildings and former farmhouses that at one time had serviced the chateau.

'It's there. Now, can you bring me home,' our guide demanded with a hint of a slur issuing from a face that looked like a burst tomato sitting uncomfortably on his thick neck.

We did our agreed duty and drove him ten minutes to his small stone farmhouse, then returned and started up the lane. Blue had settled down into a comfortable sleep as we moved from barely paved road to dirt lane. At the entrance of the estate stood a dozen or so Lebanese cedars, from the early 1800s by the look of them – massive with thick trunks and long branches that splayed across the road like an opened hand. We drove by them and continued on for a few minutes. I noted my odometer – 500 metres from the cedar guardians to the house.

'Far enough away from the road for the cats?' I asked Bud.

'We'll see. I still think it's too big.'

'Be open. Think big and good things will happen.'

The rain continued. The car's windows were fogged up but we could faintly make out the straight, stately lines of the roof of the chateau. As we approached the house, a vast woods appeared to our left and a muddy, barren field to our right. A bit closer and we saw the north wing of the chateau. We rolled by the front and continued to the end of the chateau for what seemed a very long time. A 50-metre facade indeed. Not bad. Countless rows of windows, shuttered for the winter. The place was immense. In a state of restrained delirium, I thought to myself *finally, my own little Versailles*. The chateau was awe-inspiring.

Philippe and Laurent were parked out front awaiting our arrival. I stopped, jumped out of the car and tapped on their window. In 15 seconds, I was soaking wet.

'Do you have the key?' I enquired.

'No, we do not have a key but we will find a way in,' Philippe said.

As we scrambled around the exterior of the chateau, Philippe told us the owner's son, Jehan-Claude, spelled in the old style, but pronounced 'Jean-Claude', worked as a bus driver in Angers. He took on this new métier just after the chateau – a home for handicapped adults – had closed four years back. Since 1969, the chateau had served as home to more than 30 adults with Down's syndrome. After almost 30 years, the institution was forced to shut its doors due to lack of funds.

We all searched frantically in the rain for an *entrée*. Philippe's sidekick Laurent scurried around, industrious if not entirely effective in refined Parisian loafers, camel-hair coat and exceptional eyewear, which did not serve him well in the torrential downpour.

After twenty minutes, I happened to pass a locked shutter and noticed, by chance, an open window. *Voilà!* We commandeered a bench from the back of the house and propped it against the old chateau walls. Philippe and his colleague mounted the bench, looking like two fussy lovers daintily arranging flowers. The two figures appeared miniscule against the stone walls of this grand structure. This window, like the hundred or so others, measured two and a half to three metres high. I tended to be useless in these situations, so I let the 'men' work. Finally, they broke two wooden slats of the shutter. Laurent put his small hand into the crevice and gingerly unwound a bit of wire that held the shutter closed. We were in!

We all climbed through the window hastily. The rain blew into the house as if someone had tossed a bucket in. The place was dark and sealed, coffin-like. No electricity. The shutters and doors throughout had been locked and secured with wire.

Jehan-Claude, however, had left this one window open behind the closed shutter in order to create a cross-vent to dry out the place. If not for this housekeeping, we would never have seen the house. One small, responsible act and Jehan-Claude's life, and ours, changed forever.

The next 45 minutes were a whirlwind of confusion and wonder. We darted from room to room, endlessly prying open shutters for light and bumping into old furnishings, which were the only inhabitants now of this monstrous space. I frantically snapped pictures, the flash illuminating too briefly the object of our desire.

Throughout the chateau, France's finest tradesmen had left intricately carved plaster mouldings with delicate ceiling rosettes and fleurs-de-lis. Handsome marble fireplaces could be found in each room in an endless stream of elegance. To say we were on sensory overload is insufficient. The vastness of the space was simply incomprehensible. If you've ever visited the Metropolitan Museum of Art in New York or the National Portrait Gallery in London... well, it wasn't that big. But close.

Mixed in with these wonderful details were slices of a not-so-glorious past. The interior of the place was covered in 1970s wallpaper. Particle-board doors were stuck in doorways where once oak-carved doors from centuries prior had stood. The place felt institutional in the worst sort of way. A bit like the hotel in 1970s horror movie *The Shining*, but especially decorated for neglected inmates. But we could fix all that, no problem, I thought, only half-believing my own assertions.

Our plane was leaving in a little over three hours, the exact amount of time it took to get from here to there. We jumped into our cars and took a quick tour of the outbuildings. The stables, chicken houses, piggeries, horse-washes and garages formed an exceptionally large complex almost equal in size to the chateau. Large white wooden doors stood guard over the buildings' mysterious contents. The outbuildings looked exactly like the buildings at the head of the lane: stone covered in '*crèpi*', or sand finish, with tuffeau decoration and red-brick accents along portals and gateways. The roofs were in poor condition, composed of slate, with dilapidated gutters and chimneys with crumbling bricks poking out here and there.

We only had 45 quick, meaningful minutes at the chateau, in the dark and howling rain. As we drove to Paris, we spoke quickly and heatedly.

'Bud, we have to buy that house.'

'It's too big. There is so much work to do. And did you see all that wallpaper? And what happened to the doors? They're all new. I want our house to be our home, cosy and comfortable for Blue and any others that might come along.'

'We can make it warmer. And the size of it allows us to grow the B&B. We can add more rooms and houses as we have money.' Americans – always on about growing something or other. Bigger is better, more is more.

'We don't have that much money. We have just enough to cover the down payment, some renovations. But we still have to buy furniture. And those bathrooms! They are the worst sort of institutional things I've ever seen. It's like an insane asylum.'

Childishly optimistic, I persisted. 'But it is impressive. People will want to come, to stay. We can do well and support ourselves.'

'Sam, you don't know what a renovation like this involves. Granted, you *can* change a light bulb, but that's about it. We'll have to hire so many workmen, pay so much money. And the B&B thing is by no means certain. That will take time.'

I hate it when she's right. 'Stop thinking like a culchie.' Oops. Not the right thing to say. I intentionally used the word in Irish for a country bumpkin. Honestly, I have nothing against country people. But I thought the word would ring a few bells with Bud. It just slipped out. Luckily, Bud is comfortable in her country roots. Always the more mature, sensible part of the equation, she simply said, 'OK. You'll see. We are going to choke on this house.'

I couldn't understand her objections. The conflict centred on two minor details: the size and the cost.

The asking price was well beyond our meagre resources. Philippe told us the chateau could be had for about 20 per cent less than the asking price or about 2.9 million francs. This came to about £300,000 at the time, plus fees and government taxes. Persistent, I pointed out again that this was the price of a modest closet in Manhattan or London. Of course, the difference was you could make a living in these cities. The B&B might never bring in sufficient income to cover the loan. A specious venture at best, disastrous at worst.

We had managed to pull together about $170,000 in our time in New York. Our life's savings. At 33 years of age, not terribly bad, but far from sufficient. If we could make a sizeable down payment while maintaining my *current* income, all would be good. But buying the house meant taking the plunge of leaving a reasonably lucrative living in New York for the unknown vagaries of life in the French countryside. No guaranteed earnings, just sweat, equity and perseverance.

I'd worked in news my entire career, a career that began at age 25. I was now a television producer making documentaries. I had worked for a number of news networks covering the White House, international affairs, daily national news, plane crashes and any other newsworthy event that might bring in a few viewers. My most recent documentaries were good and salacious – *Extreme Fighting* and *Models on the Côte d'Azur*. Not particularly highbrow, but fun nonetheless. I never intended to go into television. Yet not everyone in television was vapid and mean. Most, but not all.

Things had improved over the years and now I was doing something where I determined the hours, often the subject matter, where I travelled and how much I spent on each project. I worked moderately hard but turned out one-hour docs quickly. My compensation weighed far above my exertion.

Until we had Blue, Bud worked as a fashion designer, a pattern-maker for a mercurial, high-end designer who made $200 T-shirts for waifs. Bud brought in a good bit too. Not rich, but not poor. We were frugal in a way that would allow us to save one full income a year.

The idiocy and wonder of the whole endeavour rested in the simple fact that we were planning to leave two sought-after jobs in the world's busiest city for the uncertainty of a 'simpler' country life and the slim rewards of the hospitality business. However, the jump from a one-bedroom, 600-square-foot apartment to 15,000–square-foot chateau on 40 acres was a substantial move up.

As I sped on down the autoroute toward Charles de Gaulle airport, weaving in and out of lanes like a drunken sailor, Bud sat quietly in the back feeding Blue for the entire trip.

We both slipped into the quiet of our own thoughts, mulling over the possibilities and challenges, manipulating our prospects each in our own way, to our own liking. Then we hit Paris, and the vaunted Périphérique. This dreadful concoction of roads and connections forms an almost perfect ring around the City of Light. That's all we could see, lights. Red lights. The entire Périphérique was one enormous car park.

'Damn! We're going to be late. Can you look at the map and find a better route?'

Bud looked hurriedly at the map. The black and red and blue lines formed a jumble of confused options. We were dead still on the ring. It appeared our current route was in fact the best route despite the lack of movement.

We edged forward 15, 20 metres at a jog. The car was filled with tension. Our tiredness, the difficulty of travelling with baby, the vision of the chateau playing aggressively in our heads. Too much. We stopped again. I glanced furtively at the clock every ten seconds as our plane's departure loomed. There must be an easier way to go about things. But we are Irish and Cajun. Nothing was meant to be nor will it ever be simple. We love suffering. It is our calling.

At last, the ring opened up at our exit to the airport. I pressed the accelerator and we sped toward the chaos of Charles de Gaulle. After two wrong turns and a misread sign, I pulled into the car rental car park. We piled out of the car, like a clown car, bodies and bags and babies cast about willy-nilly. I didn't bother to sign the car out properly and left it in front of the check-out office.

We ran to the security check-in. 'Can I see your passports, please?'

'Of course.' I searched my pockets. Then our bags. The nappy bag, the baby, Bud. No luck. I looked at Bud in disbelief. If there is a hard way to do something, we will find it and pursue this path with fidelity and consistency.

I ran back to the car. The passports were stuffed protectively in the rear seat pocket. I gathered my booty and fled. The attendant was waiting, patiently. We trundled onto the plane and collapsed in heaps, like a sack of spuds. Blue slept. Then Bud. Then me.

The seven-hour flight back left us more time for reflection. The chateau seemed, to me, like a good starter house. Think about it: if offered the chance to take on a limitless old property in middle-of-nowhere France, wouldn't you do it? The price: just over three million francs with no proper income in sight. And all you had to do was leave a sizeable income on the table. Just walk away with no retirement at the ascending peak of your career. An easy decision... *non*?

CHAPTER FOUR

The Fowl Smell of Success

We returned to our tiny apartment in New York and the task of understanding what we were about to do. The only thing pushing us forward, stretching us beyond our primal fear, was the hectic clamour of New York and the difficulty of raising our firstborn in a cantankerous city. The scarcity of resources, the limited space, the astronomical property prices, the unattractive blandness of living in the suburbs all pointed to a new life in the country. The move to France was very attractive.

The chateau's qualities surged to the front of our minds as we entered the dark, dirty entrance hall to our apartment building. After the assaults of JFK Airport, the near-death experience of driving from there to our building on First Avenue, and the pungency of the fetid East River, we were left to unlock our depressing metal front door. The building was erected in the late 1940s. The stairs were caked in years of mud, paint flaked off the walls and a high ceiling was weakly illuminated by one bulb. We walked into our apartment, bags and baby Blue in tow.

Our 'living space', about 600 square feet, consisted of a small dining area (littered with seven cat litters), a slightly larger living room, a bedroom and something that, in the most generous of compliments, could be called a galley kitchen. Boxes were stacked throughout the apartment touching plain white ceilings. Our view, if it could be called such, looked out onto the roof of the Dangerfield's comedy club beneath us and beyond that onto a brick wall. There were four large, newly installed windows that did allow a fair bit of light in. The bathroom had last been remodelled in 1951 (we had found the receipt) and comprised a small toilet, tiny shower and chipped porcelain sink.

To note merely that our potential move would be a big change is like saying death makes one less active. I would venture to say that our move from First Avenue in Manhattan to Château du Bonchamps in the Loire Valley would be the largest square footage adjustment in history. The chateau harboured many rooms that were larger than our entire apartment. We were aching to get out.

Bud still felt the castle was too big. Our desperate failure to find an affordable house in Ireland did give her pause. We argued about our capabilities, our limits. Would we have enough resources, financially and physically, to take on something so immense? Could we, after all this time of searching, really make the move, truly dive in and cut ourselves off from what we had been so diligently toiling at for so many years? In the end, though, why does anyone make a change? Why do people leave the security of a conventional life with benefits and a steady salary? This is where Bud and I agreed. People change their lot because they are not really happy. We ourselves were not satisfied with the life we had created. In light of our current unhappiness with life in the fast lane, we made a non-refundable deposit of 230,000 francs (£24,000) on the Château du Bonchamps.

Soon after we paid the deposit and settled back into our grotty hovel for the time being, I received a call. It was RTE, Ireland's national broadcaster. Earlier the previous year, I had applied to be head of a new 24-hour news channel on the Emerald Isle. The slightly incomprehensible voice on the other end of the line informed me that I had made it into the final round for interviews.

Bud and I debated and demurred and finally decided that I would go. The trip was fully paid for by the kind taxpayers of Ireland. I could visit the chateau again in France and really see what we were about to buy.

The interview went well. Of course, my mind was elsewhere, in France. I always perform better when I know I have an out, another option. During the interview, I kept telling myself that I was moving to France and assuming my rightful place as ersatz nobility, reclaiming my patrimony after a few centuries of respite in Louisiana.

The hard part came when I had to show my scant knowledge of Gaelic and that obscure Irish pastime, Gaelic football. Deadly subjects for a man brought up on twangy

English and baseball. I hardly knew the name of the prime minister or even how to pronounce what they called their leader. I think they say 'Taoiseach'; sounds like 'tea-shuck', or thereabouts. Not promising. The France option was looking better every moment.

Once again, I hopped on a cheap flight, this time from Dublin to Belgium, hired a car and headed down to the chateau. The irony did cross my mind: buying cheap, cattle-carrier, no-seats-assigned airline tickets because it is what I could afford, while planning to buy a grand estate? Foie gras taste, hamburger budget.

I found my way to the town and to the chateau without incident. The sun was bright, the day cool and crisp, the full glory of spring waiting to burst forth, a bit of hope in the air. I turned tentatively down the long, slightly mangled entrance road, passing the enormous trees. I felt a little nauseous as I drove along. The implications of the task at hand – the endless work, the difficulty of leaving the US behind, all the fears of creating an entirely new life abroad – weighed heavily on my racing mind.

I inched my way around the front of the house. The chateau looked tired. Every window and door was surrounded by that ever-present tuffeau. Again, I could see just how much was crumbling, torn off by winds, storms, freezing and thawing. Balzac once famously said that tuffeau was good for only 150 years.

I could see now, clearly, all the doors and windows were a sort of putrid brown. I thought defensively, the chateau was more than 300 years old: nothing a few licks of paint couldn't fix. Oh, and the bank account of a Saudi prince. I could see small chunks missing from the large and imposing pediment perched squarely in the middle of the roof, erected in one of the final renovations of the 1850s. Moulded purely from tuffeau, it was adorned with large rosettes, pilasters and a chunky, wide cornice. Placed prominently in the middle was a grand heraldic feature with the letters 'N' and 'A' imposed on the universal Masonic symbol of a carpenter's rule. Philippe had told us the letters signified two families, Nepveu and Abrams, united by a couple blessed with the chateau in the mid nineteenth century. It was this same family who played host from time to time in the 1860s to Napoleon III, the last emperor of France. I was delighted with the 'N'. No one need know the name 'Nepveu'. Guests could be informed of the role the great Napoleon (sans the 'III') played in the history of our chateau. I ambled around the outside of the house, a new feeling of pride welling up as I thought of my many hours searching for my own little domain. In the weeks since our last visit, Philippe had faxed reams of information to us, whetting our appetites to learn more about the castle.

I had spent hours studying a dry yet informative book called *Country Houses of Ireland*. The author's outlines always included the number of bays, storeys, a description of the interior, special features and a short history. The book was enough to put the most studious architect to sleep but I squeezed immense enjoyment out of this effete pursuit. My pipe-smoking role model might have written about the object of our own affection as follows:

'Château du Bonchamps. A vast seventeenth- and nineteenth-century chateau in the Louis XIII style. A large central edifice comprising a gallery of 40 metres and salons built in 1684. The owners, obscure minor aristocrats, chose to enlarge the main building in the mid 1800s with two unwieldy and rather tall wings joined by said gallery. Immense pediment placed on the central building with the letters 'N&A' transposed over Masonic symbolism. More than 30 rooms, 156 large double windows in the French style, 22 marble fireplaces. A splendid wood-carved library with oak mantelpiece. Plaster rosettes in the main gallery and throughout salons and bedrooms. A large outbuilding complex to the south-west of the main house comprising stables, servants' quarters, chicken coops, dog kennels. 30,000 square feet of French provincial hubris. A particularly handsome '*plan d'eau*', or pond, in front. 40 acres of woods and prairies with dozens species of trees as was the custom from the early 1600s to the present. The property was the seat of the de Sibille fiefdom commencing in 1507. Main house constructed in seventeenth century, seized during the revolution in 1793 and passed down to 1969. Napoleon III visited Bonchamps several times in the early 1860s. The family fell on hard times after WWII, closing down a large portion of the north wing of the chateau. Up until recently, run as an association for Down's syndrome adults.'

As I stared at the great pile like a deer caught in the headlights, I noticed a figure a couple of hundred metres up the drive at the outbuildings. I couldn't quite make it out, but it appeared to be a man in work clothes hovering around a bush. I started up the lane to meet this trespasser.

'*Bonjour,*' I said.

'*Bonjour,*' a soft voice returned. I was surprised to realise the voice belonged to a woman.

I explained myself in my poor, yeoman's French. Translation: 'I am Sam. I want buy chateau. I went to America.' I might as well have said, 'Hi, I am a brash American. Was your father a collaborator in the war?'

'I am Madame Pernod, the daughter-in-law of the owner. I was cutting some flowers,' she said. Ah, this was Jehan-Claude's wife, Marie-Christine. Philippe had told us about the couple and their unsuccessful attempts to buy the chateau. She was clipping away at a very old, lovely chrysanthemum tree.

'How long have you lived here?'

'We live down the road but worked here for eight years,' she said. Then, quite suddenly, 'We wanted to buy the chateau from my father-in-law.'

'What happened?'

'Well, my father-in-law has a new wife, a second wife, and she wants the money. He must sell to keep the estate from his first wife, Jehan-Claude's mother.' At this, her eyes glistened and a small tear formed in the corner of her eye.

'*C'est triste,*' I managed.

'*Oui, c'est triste.* Would you like some flowers?'

'Yes. Thank you.'

With that, she fashioned the most perfect little bouquet of flowers I had ever seen. She handed them to me and we started toward the chateau.

'I understand you will stay in the chateau tonight?'

'I would like to.'

I had arranged with the owner, through Philippe, to stay the night. Marie-Christine let me in to the *galerie*, a long hall for hanging paintings. It was dark and dank. She turned on the electricity for one wing and started the hot water in case I wanted a shower. She pointed out old mattresses and blankets from the institution. I thanked her and saw her to the door.

Two months after we had put down the deposit, here I was. Two months of arguments and exasperation. I didn't know where to begin. I scurried around counting the rooms, trying desperately to notice details and take stock of the vastness of the chateau.

It was much as I had remembered, but worse. It seemed every square inch of wall was covered in that ghastly 1970s wallpaper. Not classic, vintage paper, but mouldy coverings from arguably the worst fashion period in the history of the world. The vinyl coverings were blighted with browns and oranges and sick greens, unfit for a French chateau. For what seemed like hours, I could not find a bathroom. In the end, there were two. Thirty-odd rooms and two bathrooms. The chateau had come to reflect the character of four years' abandonment. Neglected, makeshift, forlorn.

I finally stumbled upon the kitchen; hideous and semi-industrial, stainless steel and white tile everywhere, massive functional appliances and brown and white machine-made floor tilings. Not the quaint French country kitchen we'd really wanted. There were plenty of other negatives too. As Bud had noticed, it seemed the institution had replaced all of the doors on the first floor with cheap particle board. I glided through rooms in a daze. Titillated by all the possibility, anxious at the same time by the scope of work needed. Mould, damp and darkness met me at every turn. And that wallpaper.

Amid this tour of decorative tragedy was the odd bright spot. The fireplaces were sumptuous, mostly marble and carved with colourful slabs of emerald, burgundy, grey and black. Each one presented beautifully against well-plastered walls. The main stairs had a solidly crafted wrought-iron banister and polished steps with a large art deco stained glass window in the central part, impressive if a bit odd in a seventeenth-century chateau.

It seems the old family, the Nepveus, had money until roughly World War I or II, then just flat ran out. You could see they continued to make additions and refinements up until the 1920s. But as the *Ancien Régime* slipped into the past, the aristocrats and grand estates slipped with it. People moved to the cities to find work, society moved on. Cheap workers, *domestiques*, became scarce and the houses suffered. The monster hulks of former times were left to decay like discarded carcasses. Why had I gone back? What did I hope to find in this once elegant, now defunct world?

The north wing had a servants' staircase handsomely carved of oak and ascending four flights into the vast *grenier*, or attic. The final stairs in the south wing were made of walnut. I couldn't see the banister as it was covered with two thin walls of plasterboard.

As it grew dark, I decided to end my melancholic tour and go into town for a bite to eat. I rolled down our long lane and onto the main road. Along the two or three kilometres to Châteauneuf, I passed through a small gully and was immediately struck by a putrid, all-encompassing smell. *Incroyable.* It took my breath away and I quickly breathed through my mouth. Must be the scent of an active countryside, I thought.

A couple of minutes later, in Châteauneuf, I found a handsome country restaurant along the banks of the River Sarthe, in a nineteenth-century *maison bourgeoise* that may once have held the local notary public or town doctor. It was covered in sprouting ivy and decorated throughout in slightly dated though appealing floral prints.

'*Bonjour,*' I proudly asserted to the hostess. Always greet the owner and acknowledge his or her presence. This appears to be a universal necessity of daily life in France. The French tend to be formal and respect of this custom can bring many good things. It is a custom that allows the owner of the restaurant, shop or bar to know that you recognise their proprietorship, respect their place and are willing to proceed on their terms. More importantly, the simple hello is a clear acknowledgement that they deserve the greeting. Simple yet remarkably effective human courtesy.

'Bonjour, monsieur. Est-ce qu'on prend un apéritif?'
'Oui, merci. Un kir, s'il vous plaît.'

I sat down, scanned the menu and ordered quickly. I started, like a good Frenchman, with a *kir*, a champagne-raspberry cocktail, to clean the palate. This was followed slowly by a pot of *'rillettes'*, a local confection of coarse pork pâté. I spread the mixture expectantly on a baguette, remembering my first experience of this delicacy from my studies 12 years ago in the region, near Tours. At the time, I was a student of Georgetown University in Washington, DC. I was enrolled in the School of Foreign Service, Bill Clinton's alma mater. One of the more onerous requirements for graduation from this particular school was the need to pass a proficiency exam in a language other than your own. I had started my college career with French, detested it, dropped out of all my French classes and was left to scramble at the end. I headed off to Tours for three months the summer after my class graduated. I managed to just barely pass the proficiency retake through the help of a very attentive local French girl and a few bottles of wine. My first experience of Europe. So the infatuation truly began.

The *rillettes* were deeply satisfying despite being a heaped dose of pork fat mingled in with thick shreds of pork. My next course offered another sensory onslaught with small, perfectly rounded medallions of rare duck, complemented by small rinds of duck fat hugging the edges of these tender morsels. Heaven.

As I ordered chocolate-slathered profiteroles, the maîtresse stopped by my table.

'*Ça va?*' she proffered.

'*Oui, tout va bien.*' We continued in French.

'Are you visiting the area. A tourist?'

'Not really. I am buying a house near here.'

'Yes? Which one?

'Do you know the Château du Bonchamps? Near Juvardeil?'

'Château du Bonchamps?'

'Yes, Château du Bonchamps.'

'The chateau at Juvardeil?'

'Yes, it's big, with woods and a pond.'

I think my French was not so bad that she did not understand me. She simply couldn't believe what I was saying.

'Do you know it?' I said.

'Yes, my husband and I looked at it to buy.'

'Really? What happened?'

'Oh, too many works. The place is falling down.'

This seemed to be the consensus among in-the-know French property buyers.

'What will you do with it?' she asked, a small, in-the-know smile crossing her lips.

'We want to run a *chambre d'hôtes*.'

A burst of laughter popped out and she managed, '*Bon courage!*'

Very comforting. Of course, everyone knew what a Sisyphean challenge Bonchamps presented. It seemed all the locals and indeed all the French who had viewed the house realised it was a lost cause. I felt slightly foolish.

I waited for my *café* but it didn't arrive. Not for the first time, I felt ignored, unloved even, as I waited patiently for this coffee. My usual dining experiences told me coffee arrives with the dessert. Not in France. In France, the coffee is another course, the fourth or fifth, never to be taken with the dessert. It should be savoured as the *digestif* that it is – after the dessert, by itself, perfect in its substance, serving its proper purpose to excite the body into digesting a rich meal.

My new friend offered me a cognac on the house, probably overcome with compassion for my chosen lot. The four-course meal confirmed the urgent necessity to move to a place that treated eating as a solemn ritual. London and New York and other modern-day gastronomic centres offer delightful culinary creations these days, and some might say France is no longer the centre of power in the food world. But I would say a good French country meal is still unparalleled in Western civilisation. The goodness of it is indigenous, it grows from the *terroir* and the people who will not tolerate bad food. While the very best of British or American food is excellent, the key to a true gastronomic society is to have the best food available all the time at all levels of eating. This is food art. *Vive la France*.

I finished a small bottle of exquisite Côtes-du-Rhône and drove back to the chateau. As I was driving, something struck me. Roughly two kilometres out of town, again, a smell worthy of the eighth ring of Dante's *Inferno* engulfed the car. I had noticed it on our first visit but ignored the nuisance in a rush to embrace my chateau. Here it was again like a bad rash. This was unmistakable. Not quite sulphurous, but invasive, like rotting flesh. I had once made a documentary on death scene investigators in New Orleans. During my time on the beat, I filmed a number of autopsies. An unforgettable, unique smell that makes grown men cry and hardy souls faint. This was like that. I drove around and found only what appeared to be an abandoned factory. I would have to investigate in the daylight.

Nearing the chateau, I passed a house, a farm really, situated directly across our pond. The farm might have been part of the original estate but had been sold off about fifteen years ago, according to Philippe. The pond was actually a small lake, filled with fish and surrounded by willows, sycamores and oaks. In times past, the estate workers would have used it for laundry and watering the animals around the property that would feed the estate. It currently served the aesthetic purpose of reflecting the image of the castle.

My curiosity got the best of me so I decided to drop in on our neighbours. Maybe they had an idea of where the smell was coming from. It wasn't too late, I hoped, to visit. I entered the farmyard, which was flanked on two sides by large, cavernous sheds and dilapidated stone buildings. These simple, two-storeyed buildings were vaguely in the same style as our outbuildings. Sand-covered stone, slate roof and brick and tuffeau decoration. This, all part of the thousand-acre estate belonging to Bonchamps in the old days.

The yard was illuminated by a very powerful spotlight. One could find here almost any tool or motorised piece of equipment produced in the early to mid twentieth century. As I pulled in, a clamour rose that made my heart stop. I couldn't find the source of the noise but it sounded like ducks.

I got out of the car, took two steps and was blind-sided by an aggressive and determined gaggle of geese. The noise was deafening. One took a chance and poked me in the forearm with his beak. I darted to the front door and knocked. The lady of the house answered, cracking the door open gingerly so I could see just one eye.

I explained my presence and she reluctantly let me in. I entered a small vestibule, then a kitchen where several large men were seated with very serious looks on their faces. One was an extremely large man with the face of a young boy, a bum leg and a slightly turned eye. He appeared harmless if not a little unsettling. They all sported blue overalls befitting local custom among agrarians in France. Ancient leather boots were flung haphazardly around the place like forgotten toy soldiers. A fire blazed up from a monumental stone fireplace.

They offered me wine out of an unmarked bottle and gave me a small glass. I related my meeting with the geese in my broken French. Everybody laughed. And laughed. Several of them made flapping motions and pecked each other on the arm. Meanwhile, my arm was grower blacker from the bruise. Very funny, it seemed.

I told them I was looking to buy the chateau across the way. This was met with general bemusement and curiosity. Now for *the* big question:

'What is the smell around here?' I ventured.

The farmers looked at me, a whiff of Gallic indignation in the air. 'It's probably the cows. We have a cow farm, about seventy, all milk,' the patriarch said. He was a small man, unlike the rest. He had a rounded, stringy moustache and long hair down past his shoulders. As he spoke, his left eye rolled out sideways, spying, I think, the fire, as the other eye fixed me good.

Indeed, the smell of cows was like a musty presence in the kitchen. I looked through a rough doorway and saw troughs and livestock. I suppose having the cows so close lessened the farmer's commute. And the methane gas could warm the house in the winter.

'I think I know cows and this smell is much stronger. The smell is stronger nearer to town, between here and Châteauneuf.'

'Oh, that's the tannery,' the big guy with the peg leg said.

My heart sank like a ton of bricks tossed from a third-floor chateau window. I was in shock, numb. Besides the dreadful putrescence of a pig farm, a tannery ranks as the source of one of the most rotten smells known to man, in my opinion. The farmers explained that occasionally the wind shifts and blows down into the gully where we were situated. I felt hoodwinked. Not only had I bitten off more than I could chew, but now we had to contend with the chemical and biological refuse of a venture that treats dead skins on a commercial level. And to think I hesitated to put down ten per cent on this lovely house.

As I drank more moonshine, the problem grew less important. *Madame* then brought out a large steaming plate of what looked like liver. The farmer told me it was their very own foie gras. Finally, my revenge on those pesky geese. And it was good. I drank and ate foie gras like I was going to prison, slipping into a near coma from the richness and pungency of this makeshift feast.

As I edged my way to the car, the patriarch pulled me aside and whispered,

'Just remember. We have right of access to the pond to water our cows. Never forget that.'

By midnight, I had swerved my hire car back to the chateau and once again entered the *galerie*. I had made no plans concerning where and exactly how I would sleep. I was drawn quite strongly to the library. This, the best room in the house, with its tall doors and intricate wood carvings and miles of old, musty books, seemed like the logical place to set up camp. I dragged two mattresses, somewhat soiled and damp, onto the parquet floors. I had one bulb to light my way. I scrounged a couple of blankets and felt content with my little nest. I opened a window. The air was cool but I needed a remedy for my creeping headache. Too much wine, too little sleep.

Feeling the urge to pee like a racehorse, I climbed a flight of stairs to the toilet in the dark. I did my business and turned on the tap only to be met by a thick reddish sludge from the bowels of an ancient plumbing system. I decided against a shower.

I crawled back into bed and pulled the sheets up. I looked around at the carved oak panelling, or *boiserie*, and contemplated the ancient books that lined the delicately crafted shelves with their handmade glass doors. The ceiling consisted of substantial oak beams, painted with fleurs-de-lis and gold designs. My head filled with pleasant last thoughts, I turned off the light and drifted off to sleep.

I have no idea how much time passed. At some point in the depths of the night, I awoke to the sound of scraping. The sound grew more insistent, followed by the faintest hint of footsteps and a small coo. Disorientated, I eased my way to the wall and switched on the light. I turned around and saw an astoundingly large bird flying directly toward me. I leaped up and ran madly in circles, then into the adjoining sitting room where I ran smack into the iron base of an old bed.

The pain shot up my leg making me forget the pain in my arm from the goose attack of the early evening. Peering warily back into the library, I saw a beautiful white barn owl standing boldly on my bed. I picked up a broom and hobbled toward him. Something warm ran down my leg. I looked down and saw a good-sized gash on my shin, blood streaming onto the wood floor. So, this was it, I would bleed to death in the middle of the French countryside, in an abandoned house, brought to my untimely end by an owl.

After some pause, I shooed and coerced and lightly tapped the stubborn bird with my weapon of choice. He hopped. And stopped. He flew upward in an arc and landed on an old trunk. He stared at me with those wide, unmoving eyes that are sometimes mistaken for wisdom. Unnerving. Finally, I inched my way to the window and circled back around my guest like a caveman, hunched and frightened. One last time, I poked him gently on the bum. He obviously concluded I was insane and flew off into the night. I closed the window, kept the light on and drifted off into an uneasy sleep again. The broom stood guard.

The next day, I set about tending my wounds with a cold compress made muddy by water from rusty pipes. I decided to call Bud with the latest news. I drove my two-door Fiat Punto to Juvardeil and parked outside the church. The Sunday calm of the town comforted my aching head and bruised ego. I made my way back to the *tabac*, Monsieur le Rouge's old hang-out, taking in the genteel, rustic appointments of our new town, the streets covered with *pavés*, or thick cobblestones. In the bar, I ordered a small glass of red wine, a hair of the dog to steel myself for the impending exchange with Bud over the existence of the tannery.

Outside again, I found the lone phone booth in the town, just outside the *tabac*. As I dialled, Monsieur le Rouge stumbled up the main street and disappeared into the bar.

'Hey, Bud. How's it going?'

'Good, good. Hold on, I'm feeding Blue… OK, so what's going on?'

'A good visit, some promising things, some not so.'

'What do you mean?'

'Well, first of all, remember that horrible smell? It appears there's a tannery near the house, just outside Châteauneuf.'

'You're kidding me! No way. Oh, Sam, we can't buy it. That's terrible. We can't have people so close producing smells from the skins of dead animals. How are we going to get our money back?' Bud is a vegetarian. I had dreaded her response knowing her deep empathy with everything living.

'I don't think it's that serious. Maybe it will go away. Maybe they'll fix it.'

'Uh-huh. Just like Dangerfield's went out of business? We've been waiting for the end of that thing ever since we moved here.' She had a point. The comedy club had been a constant source of annoyance and strain in our extended sojourn in New York. We had hoped and fought for the end of this annoyance for six years, all to no avail. We now suffered quietly on the weekends as bad jokes played up through our wooden floors. Duped then, duped again. We had thought the cheapness of both properties meant a good deal. Sometimes you get what you pay for.

'You're right. Well, if we lose the money, it's only $45,000. It's not our whole savings.'

'Sam, that's a lot of money. We can't lose that. But I can't get over that we'll be living so close to a place with rotting animal skins. What are we going to do?'

'Honestly, I think we have to push forward. And hope the wind doesn't blow this way too often.'

'I can't believe this. I told you the chateau was too big and now this. And last night, I was having such good thoughts. Thinking of the children playing, the cats lounging around the woods. I can't believe this.'

'Bud, I don't know what to do. I think we push ahead and hope for the best. I talked to the farmers, the Pasteurs, and they said it's not so bad.'

'They live with cows. Farms smell, how could they know the difference?'

'I know, I know. Can we talk about it when I come home?'

'Of course. But, I must say, that's about the worst news you could tell me. But come home. We'll see.'

Good. An opening. I wouldn't call myself obstinate, but I am stubborn. I wanted the house. We could figure out a plan, a way to sit comfortable with this new-found obstacle. Plus, I didn't want to lose the 35 grand.

'OK, Bud, I'll see you soon. I love you. Give my love to Blue.'

'I love you too. See you tonight. Be safe.'

I slipped back into the car feeling a little emotional. The more we learned, the worse it seemed. But stashed deep inside, somewhere hidden beneath the layers of doubt, the same romantic urge that drove us this far poked its little head up and calmed me for the time being. I still dreamed of roaming our property, stick in hand, with happy peasants working the fields. Too much Tolstoy, I suppose. Yes, that was it, we would be Levin and Kitty with loads of children, happy workers, grain-covered fields, strapping horses and roaring fires. Now, if only we could derail the current course of the story and veer away from what looked like an inevitable remake of *Anna Karenina*'s tragic ending.

I passed by the tannery glumly and stopped at the pharmacy. There I loaded up on vitamin C, water and aspirin. I began the journey back to Belgium. My hangover from the night's revelry subsided ever so slightly. Cheap wine and rich food are one thing. If only I could find a remedy for my chateau-buyer's remorse.

We hadn't even bought the place and already we were filled with the type of existential dread that paralyses the most optimistic souls. But hope sprang eternal.

CHAPTER FIVE

'We're all mad here'

The Cheshire Cat in *Through the Looking-Glass,*
Lewis Carroll

Bud loves cats. Her affliction, I mean calling, can be summed up in the words of French artist Jean Cocteau: 'I love cats because I enjoy my home; and little by little, they become its visible soul.'

For the record, I myself am not particularly fond of cats. I don't dislike them really, but I would choose other companions first. Like wild boar or hyenas. I'm not allergic to them, as so many cat-haters feign. They are just tolerable to me. But I care for Bud and she cares for them. As Bud makes me greater than I would have been alone, we live peaceably together with her cats. All 15 of them.

Certainly, that is a lot of cats. At all times, there were seven litter trays in our tiny flat, demanding a good scooping at least twice a day. The joys of marriage.

In our time in New York, Bud often fostered cats from local rescue centres and shelters. Inevitably, the 'fostering' turned into adoption. Bud didn't exactly hang out with the city's band of cat rescuers but she knew them all. To say they are a *committed* bunch is mild. Wild-eyed, apocalyptic and overzealous are words that come to mind.

It's important to note that all the cats are strays, inbreds, 'mutts' in dog jargon, not pedigree. Sure, by chance, there are a few presentable ones: Grainne the Tonkinese, Angus the Maine Coon. But the majority of the gang are domestic short-hairs. One, Boru, was found on the highway in the Bronx. He is a dark cat with stripes. At the time of his deliverance, he was the tiniest thing you've ever seen. He was stuck on a four-lane highway, shivering and badly scratched. The rescuers stopped 70-mile-an-hour traffic to snatch Boru from certain death. Many of Bud's cats have similarly dramatic stories. Enough already. I don't even like them.

We arranged with the owner of the chateau to move in before the actual exchange or closing, the *acte authentique*. Since we did not have many belongings in our cramped cave in Manhattan, getting all we owned to France would not be much of a problem. I contracted a shipper to bring a container and load our meagre, un-precious worldly goods. One problem solved.

There remained the final dilemma: how on God's green earth would we get the cats to the chateau? Obviously, this would take some planning. There was no question of leaving the cats. Honestly, the idea was never considered.

We called the French consulate in New York to begin the process of sifting through the requirements of cat-shipping. It took no fewer than four transfers to find someone who knew what to do. Bud presented our little problem.

'You want to bring cats to France, yes?' queried the woman on the other end of the line.

'Yes,' Bud said.

'Well, of course, you can put the cat in a bag and bring her on the plane. There is no quarantine.' This is very good news. In Ireland, there is a six-month quarantine.

'OK, but we have fifteen cats – we have to ship them by freight,' Bud pointed out.

'You say how many cats? Five?'

'No, fifteen, *quinze*.'

'What do you want to do, breed these cats?' the woman asked.

'No, they are pets.'

'But why do you have fifteen cats? This is too many, no?'

'Yes, it is a lot of cats. But I have rescued them and want to take them with me.'

'But there are many cats in France.' Ah, yes. Again.

'I'm sure there are and I will adopt some of those too. But for now I want to bring these cats with me.' Bud pushed ahead.

'You will have to come in. I must meet you and give you a dossier.' The woman was helpful and mighty curious.

That afternoon we made our way from our flat on First Avenue and 60th Street to the French consulate on Fifth Avenue. We walked, Blue tucked snugly in the baby sling, passports and cat trivia stuffed in pockets. The French consulate was a beautiful several-storeyed building on one of the most exceptional streets in the world, just down the way from the Metropolitan Museum of Art. The facade was classical, Italianate, like something you might find in Florence. Cut stones formed neat symmetrical blocks and refined pilasters with elegant cornices. As we entered, I told Bud they had recently discovered a sculpture by Michelangelo here. It was simply sitting in one of the reception areas. How exciting, we were moving to a place where Michelangelo was overlooked, taken for granted amongst the infinite splendours that make up *la France*.

We announced ourselves at the front desk and waited patiently as we watched French people and Americans come and go (speaking of Michelangelo). We were escorted through an old brass and wood revolving door to our contact, a Madame Borderon. Of course, she was smartly dressed, outfit complete with a perfectly arranged and colourful scarf. She showed us to her surprisingly messy desk and asked us to sit.

Bud and Madame Borderon repeated the exact same conversation as relayed over the phone. Almost word for word. We came to learn that cats are not held in the same esteem in France as, say, dogs. Cats are more akin to rodents. Madame chuckled as her eyes lit up, no doubt reflecting on the absurdity of the request. But, like a decent bureaucrat, she had all of the forms one might need. Very thorough, these French.

There were roughly 728 things to do. The dossier was about fifty pages. I told Madame Borderon that we were shipping cats, not the famed Michelangelo sculpture. Madame Borderon made sure we all knew this was not very funny.

'Also, you must write a formal registered letter to the Minister of Agriculture. It is a request for the importation of animals. If you have more than three, as it appears you do, you must write directly for permission.'

'Are you serious?' I asked, flabbergasted. My first encounter with the infamous bureaucracy of France. I wondered, silently, if in fact President of the Republic of France Jacques Chirac would look at our dossier and sign it personally.

'Yes, you must.'

As we strolled back to the flat, I shared my thoughts.

'What do you think? It sure seems like a lot of trouble.'

'We can work through it. Would you consider leaving Blue?'

That was that.

At home, we pored over the dossier. It seemed we must make up information sheets on each and every cat: name, date of birth, vaccinations, description, colouring, breed, major surgeries, relationships with other cats, etc. They would all need a check-up and proof of rabies vaccination. And we needed to tattoo or place a microchip with encoded number behind the ear of every feline traveller. Our loan application had been much simpler. For that matter, the *compromis de vente,* or pre-sale contract to buy the chateau, was like a child's colouring book compared to this.

Over the next two weeks we transported two cats at a time to the vet. The complete check-up, microchip and necessary vaccines ran to about $100 (about £55) per cat. After six cats, the vet agreed to come to our cramped apartment to finish up. He made three visits in total; each time we chased, hunted and finally snared a cat or two or three. The vet was a good sport. He got clawed repeatedly and bitten a number of times. Although our cats were apparently domesticated, some still harboured an intense feral quality that made them a bit difficult. Sort of like Bud. The mean streets of Gotham had trained some of these lovelies to fight and defend as if their lives depended on it. Bud has found kindred souls who persevere in adverse circumstances. This is evidently the source of her ability to live with me.

The big day arrived. Our plan of attack had been prepared with Rommel-like precision and intensity. It was the end of May, four months after we had made the deposit on our new life. Bud, Blue and I would fly to France, to the chateau. Bud would stay for the summer and I would return to the States after ten days. Regrettably, I was still gainfully employed. I had to do a shoot on monster trucks in Las Vegas. In the history of Western civilisation, are there two more disparate subjects than monster trucks in Las Vegas and the beauty of a seventeenth-century French chateau? I would return and we would sign the *acte authentique* in late July.

We had our 15 impeccably crafted dossiers on the cats. The French were ready for us and we for them. We'd negotiated with two airlines but Air France gave us the best deal: $1,200 (about £650) for 15 cats each in their own carrier, direct from JFK to Charles de Gaulle. Bud had read all the literature: to drug or not to drug the cats for safe travel (not – because they often have respiratory problems in transit); one cat per carrier or two (one – to avoid fights); water and food in the carriers or not (yes to water, no to food).

We searched the Yellow Pages for a means to get the cats from our apartment to the airport. From her many cat travels and feline interactions, Bud remembered an outfit called 'Pet Taxi'. Only in New York is there a pet limousine service. Bud called Pet Taxi.

'Hi, I need to transport my fifteen cats to the airport,' she began.

'No problem, darling. We got three minivans. What time?' The operator, obviously a long-time denizen of New York, had seen it all. No hesitation, no problem.

We ordered a car for ourselves, too. Three o'clock arrived and we all climbed in. Bud, Blue, Sam and a load of cats. Our perky convoy headed off like a detail for a very important diplomat or head of state: one black town car and three bright yellow minivans.

We arrived at the airport with plenty of time to spare and pulled up to the freight loading part of the airport. There were boxes and crates and animals and forklifts and containers of every size and shape imaginable. The check-in guy was expecting us. He processed our precious cargo without a hitch. Bud said a somewhat tearful goodbye to her 'babies'. She felt as a mother might feel sending her sons off to some horrific and unjust war.

'They'll be fine,' I suggested.

'I know, it's just hard. I worry about every one of them.'

All I could think was that the collective costs of the gang of 15, from adoption to the current day, could refurbish a large country chateau. I did not share this thought.

We boarded our plane without much ado. The flight was uneventful. Blue threw up twice and breastfed every three minutes for seven hours. I tried to watch the film but thoughts of the house, our new life, the finances, the baby, the cats and my job all flew around my head. Were we doing the right thing? Would it work? How would we afford this if I quit my job? Would we be able to start a business in a foreign country? Could we make ourselves understood in French? Would I be able to communicate with the workmen? These and a million other tiny doubts and concerns collided violently as I drifted in and out of sleep.

Bud asked, 'How do you think Io is doing? You know, she's always nervous anyway.'

'She's fine. Don't worry. Io's a big girl.'

Five minutes later. 'What about Angus? I still think he's too big for the carrier.'

'Angus is fine.'

Seven minutes on. 'Dana, you know, is basically wild. She might have a heart attack.'

'Dana has survived this long – in Queens, no less. She will come through.'

So it went for portions of the long, uncomfortable flight. The purity of Bud's focus was admirable.

The plane landed at about half past eight in the morning. We exited in a fog, cramming bits and pieces of our baby's life into the back of a flimsy stroller. We passed through passport control and customs with no problems. Bud glanced at me anxiously as we started toward the car hire counter. I knew what was on her mind. I was worried too. What were the consequences of just one dead cat? I shuddered to think.

We asked the sweet lady at the counter about the whereabouts of the *fret* and the *animalerie*. She said, 'It's simple – just follow the signs for the "*fret*" once you leave the car park.'

We found our car, which was more like a truck really, with room for ten adult, human passengers. It was white and large and unwieldy but sufficient for our needs. Up to this point, all had gone smoothly. Normally, this is a bad sign but I remained optimistic. We were tired and a bit grouchy. I dreaded, quietly, the three-hour trip down to Bonchamps.

'I can't believe this has been so easy,' I whispered.

We followed the signs for *fret* in and around and under a myriad of overpasses and roads and side roads and through terminals and out the other side. We arrived in about thirty minutes at a large structure. Painted on the side in officialese font was '*FRET*'. I parked in the vast car park.

'You wait here. I'll just go see if this is it.'

I jumped down and entered the building. I stammered in broken French that we had 15 cats en route. Was this the building?

The customs agent with an impossibly enormous moustache said, '*Non, il faut aller à l'animalerie.*' You must go to the *animalerie*.

He led me over to a preposterously large map of the entirety of Charles de Gaulle and pointed to a small, unassuming building. 'This is the *animalerie*, here.'

Not quite sure where it was in relation to where we were, I started off again in what I hoped was the general direction of our destination. More overpasses and underpasses and roads and terminals and endless lines of prefab buildings. After an hour and a half, I ended up in the same hangar with Monsieur la Moustache. He laughed, took my arm and led me over to the map again.

When I got back in the car Blue was screaming for no apparent reason. Bud was visibly shaken. We had now been off the plane for two and a half hours and still no cats. We were exhausted, dirty. The night's fitful sleep, the long travel, the fear and preparation for this grand adventure all bore down, crushing my weakened spirit.

'I cannot believe we cannot find the damned cats. I cannot believe we cannot find the damned cats.' I repeated this possibly thirty times as I banged my head against the steering wheel. Bud began to cry. Blue cried more and loudly.

Now the recriminations began. Why did we have to bring the cats? Why couldn't you find homes for these cats? I was certainly not at my best. All of the misgivings and anxieties about our 'dream' lay in our laps as we sat paralysed and mad. I could smell the stink off myself as my head rested on my chest.

I spotted a *gendarme* walking in front of our forlorn truck. I darted out of the driver's seat and nearly tackled the uncomprehending Frenchman. He was startled but soon saw that I was mentally deficient or at least foreign.

'Please, do you know where the *animalerie* is located?' I asked desperately in a madman's melange of franglais.

'Yes, it is just over there. Do you see the roof, just behind that crane?' And there it was, a corrugated roof in the distance; like so many things longed-for, so close and yet…

I got in the truck without saying a word. We were there in about five minutes. We pulled up and jumped out of the truck, all hope and nervousness. It was about five minutes after noon. The animalerie was closed. I grabbed a workman wandering by with a half-eaten baguette and asked him, where is everybody?

'At lunch. Until two p.m.,' he responded, casually, suspiciously.

Of course. France is monolithic when it comes to lunch. All businesses, offices and stores are closed from 12 to 2 p.m. All restaurants are open at the same time. There are and will be no exceptions, ever.

We peered into the small brick building hoping to grab a glimpse of the feline gang. No sign. We stepped back into the truck and chatted idly. Blue was quiet now and we napped briefly.

An official looking man in a white coat and blue work trousers came back at around 2.15 p.m. We greeted him and enquired about the cats. He knew them well by this point. He told us everything was fine. *Tout va bien*.

'All the cats are OK. But you must find an *"expéditeur"* to register these cats,' the vet said.

'What do you mean? An *expéditeur*?'

'He is a man who verifies all imports into the country.'

'Where is this man located?' I asked, about to cry.

'Do you see that building over there?'

Of course. It was the same building we had now visited a number of times. We made our way, this time more confidently, to our old hang-out, the hangar. I parked the van, hopped out, sensing the closing of a very big deal. And more paperwork.

I found Monsieur la Moustache sitting at his desk chomping a baguette with what appeared to be tuna and brie. I realised how hungry I was.

'*Bonjour*, we are back. It seems we must find an *expéditeur* to register the cats.' More accurately, '*Bonjour*, back are we. It seems to him they must find an experience to rule the cats.'

'Eh? Oh, that is me.' Indeed.

La Moustache searched the intricacies of his maze-like desk. He pulled out a thick dossier. 'The most important thing is the value. What is the value of the cats?'

'What do you mean? They are pets. There is no value,' I argued.

'Oh, they must have a value. Everything has a value.'

'I'm telling you, there is no value. They are stray cats found on the streets. They are pets. In fact, they are invaluable.'

'We cannot process this unless you place a value. Are they special cats? Will you breed these cats?' He smirked.

'No. They are all castrated. *Castrés*. Hold on a minute. I'll come back.'

I exited the large metal doors and found Bud sitting patiently in the van.

'Bud, we need to put a value on the cats.'

'A value? There is no value. They are pets.'

'I know, I know. But the guy with the big moustache insists.'

'Well, make up a number. How's one thousand francs?'

'OK, I will try.'

I re-entered the building filled with dread.

'How's one thousand francs?'

'This is OK. I will do the paperwork. Do you have *les dossiers* and the letter to the Minister of Agriculture?'

'Yes, yes.' I was truly joyful.

La Moustache filled out the paperwork, asked the occasional question and offered me a cup of very good coffee. In the middle of calls, a chat with a co-worker and verification with the Ministry of Agriculture, the EU and the United Nations, our man handed me the dossier for signature.

'This will be two thousand francs.' Roughly £200.

'Why? That is greater than the value of the cats.'

'There is a base fee and then a percentage of the value.'

By this point, I would have paid almost anything. I signed, paid and sped off to the *animalerie*.

Bud rushed in and darted from carrier to carrier. Angus had torn his nail and was bleeding a little. Everyone else, a bit shaken but in good health. No casualties. Except possibly for our marriage.

The dutiful vet scanned each cat and looked casually at our brilliantly prepared dossiers. These invaluable documents took a lot of care and attention to prepare. I could have completed a PhD thesis on cat care in the same period of time. He glanced, counted and handed them back.

The vet helped us load the cats into the truck, sniggering, I was sure. The costly pets were stacked somewhat haphazardly one upon the other filling the entire volume of the truck meant for ten adults.

Bud was delighted and our chatting was easy and comfortable. All the pressure and fear of the past 24 hours subsided, replaced by a new giddiness about the final leg of the trip. I pulled out a map and we made our way to the Loire Valley.

It was sunny and mild with a light breeze by the time we reached our destination. The house was illuminated by a brilliant light reflecting off the tuffeau stone. The grandeur of the place stopped us for a moment as we got out of the truck. It was absolutely stunning. Its rows of windows, its height and breadth and width, captivating. The pond was full and fish burst out of the water to send ripples from bank to bank. The ancient trees stood guard in silence surrounding the vastness of this 300-year-old structure.

We sat on enormous, uneven granite steps leading to a glass and oak double door, and bit hungrily into our recent purchases of French bread and pastries.

We looked at each other. We knew now that all the impatience and aggravation and bitterness of the past day was gone. We held unspoken the belief that we have made and would make each other better than we could have been alone. We had, finally, arrived. And so had the cats. Now Dana, Freya, Remus, Po, Honey, Io, Snow, Angus, Cali, Loki, Boru, Tyr, Baldur, Sif and Grainne would settle into full lives befitting the cats of Bud. *Vive les chats*.

CHAPTER SIX

Unsettled

In our mad rush to get the cats to France, we forgot one very important requirement: a bed. Thirty-five rooms, ten or fifteen bedrooms, but no useable beds. And just two bathrooms. Well, not really bathrooms. Actually, there was one room with a toilet and sink. There was another room with a long row of cheap porcelain shower basins fitted brutally into the floor with no shower curtains or dividers. And one unusual tub, small, quarter-sized, with a steep shelf so that the less mobile can sit somewhat upright and receive a bath.

In 1969, the current owner's father purchased the house to provide housing for his sister and others like her who were born with what the French call '*trisomie*', or Down's syndrome. This grew into a home for some thirty patients funded by the state and administered by a dozen or so workers. It closed in 1997 after something mysterious happened.

We have only heard rumours and whisperings of what occurred. From what we could gather there was a lot of consternation around the closing involving complaints from concerned loved ones and some sort of action taken by the French government. At the same time, funds dwindled and a sale became inevitable. There was more but the details remain murky.

Scattered throughout the chateau were the vestiges of this once charitable but sadly deteriorated venture. Industrial-sized kitchen implements, enormous pots and pans, cheap single beds with worn mattresses, the remains of a shower room worthy of a concentration camp, moth-eaten wool blankets and naked bulbs hung from denuded ceilings. The house was empty for four years before our arrival. Plaster bits had fallen here and there revealing old wood laths, or strips, that once secured the plaster. In most rooms large black stains of the dreaded mould shouldered through the offensive wallpaper.

Before we could face the increasingly daunting task of renovating, we had to find a bed. We searched high and low throughout the house for the best mattresses. It was almost impossible to find one without a few springs or lumps of ancient horsehair making its way to the light of day. Finally, we cobbled together three single horsehair mattresses and laid them on the floor in a sunny room in the north wing, next to the communal shower. We were happy to try this for a while. Luckily, we had brought sheets with us.

It was May and sunny. The house was still locked up tight from four long winters. Our second task was to open all of the shutters and let light find its way into dark, damp rooms. There were 156 windows, each with two shutters. Jehan-Claude, had sealed all the shutters in what we learned was his trademark fastidious fashion. I found an old iron wire cutter in the outbuildings and set about opening the house.

As I hurried from room to room, light flooded the once dark, moribund interior. The sun's rays were brilliant and served to highlight all the good qualities of the house. Bud helped me as we discovered things we had not seen or appreciated before – the craftsmanship of a sculpted fireplace, the beautiful swirl of a plaster rosette, the intricate inlay of oak parquet floors. The house, like our hopes, glowed brightly as we steadily banished the darkness. With each opening, the rooms seemed to breathe a sigh of relief, gasping for fresh air and light. The chateau, like a creature waking from hibernation, suddenly came to life.

Just down the road, a young group of workers, the children of friends of ours from Liverpool, Angus, Kate and her boyfriend Leo waited in a 1960s Logis de France by the river. They had travelled from the UK to help with renovations. The trio had kindly offered their services and skills, such as they were. Leo had done some work on building sites while Kate and Angus were relative newcomers to the renovation game. They would live and work in the house, and we would pay them a modest salary and cover their food costs. We promised to pay them a larger, unnamed sum when the work was done.

The three were all in their twenties, eager for a new adventure, but most importantly for us they agreed to work cheaply. It was evident we were amateurs. There is an old adage that instructs the weaker-willed to forego lending money or employing family or friends. *Lend money to an enemy and he will become a friend. Lend money to a friend and he will become an enemy. Employ friends and you will have no friends.*

But then, we were all optimistic.

We received a call from the hotel and Bud headed out to pick up our renovation crew. We had arranged with the owner to buy a red 1981 Ford van for the equivalent of about $100, or £55. The paint was a thoroughly faded red, the shock absorbers non-existent, the seats little more than benches. It was an automatic transmission with four slow speeds. Part of the ceiling was falling in and the tyres were bald. Driving the van felt like an open-carriage ride in the countryside. It sounded like an ailing tractor as it ploughed through country roads. This would be our mode of transport for the next two years. Bud returned in ten minutes with a somewhat motley, though well-meaning, gang of three.

'Good to see you all,' I enthused as they piled out of the truck.

'It's good to be here,' Kate said.

'I can't believe this place,' Angus observed. Leo, Kate's boyfriend, was quiet but appeared to be amused.

'It was a long, uncomfortable trip down, other than that, it was fun!' Angus laughed.

'Well, come in and we'll show you around,' Bud said. Blue clung to my shirt in her little carrier.

We walked the vast halls of the chateau remarking on things to do and hoped-for projects for the future. Bud showed Kate and Leo their room. Angus roamed the corridors looking for a suitably private place to call home. Our three workers moved quietly from room to room, jaws dropped, eyes wide open, gazing uncomprehendingly – at what, I wasn't sure. They were either overly impressed or completely crushed by the task that lay before them.

'Bud, let's relax and have some lunch,' Kate said.

'I could eat a horse,' Angus smirked.

This conversation seemed to animate Leo. He didn't say much, but the idea of a big meal caught his attention.

The new additions were optimistic and brimming with energy. Kate was pretty and had an athletic build, long, curly blonde hair and wide smile. Angus was large and rangy with broad, thick shoulders. In fine Scottish tradition, he was an avid storyteller.

We sat outside at the back of the house, pulled open a few drinks, and laid out a baguette, cheese and fruit.

'So what do you think of the house?' Bud began.

'It's bigger than I thought. But amazing. A lot of work,' Angus remarked.

'I can't believe how large it is. Definitely a lot of work,' Leo finally piped up.

Kate noted earnestly, 'As long as we have enough to eat, it should be fine.'

'I hope you guys do more than just hang out while you're here,' Bud said, a bit too harshly.

'Come on Bud, relax. We'll get the job done. We have a whole year, we've got to have a little fun,' Angus teased.

But of course, they had just arrived, spirits were high. We could afford some frivolity. The youngsters charged off around the property to investigate their new domain.

'What do you think about the lads?' I ventured to Bud. 'They seem enthusiastic. I hope it works out. Leo has done work like this before. I think he will keep the other two in line.'

★★★

So our first week at the chateau began. Bud appeared happy to be here. Her cats were safe, and Blue was relatively happy as long as she could breastfeed on demand and pull the cats' tails whenever one had the lack of good sense to wander near.

We did feel like we had embarked on a tremendous adventure. We had moved a cattery, fashioned a bed, opened countless shutters and engaged close family to start work on the house. There was only one small problem: we had not actually purchased the house yet.

The *acte de vente*, or closing, was set for the end of July. The owner allowed us to move in early as he was not using the house and probably thought it was a good way to secure the sale of a house that had been on the market for four years. This had at first seemed incredible to us. The original asking price, 3.5 million francs or £360,000, was laughable. The more we toured the house, the less we laughed. The chateau had been tempting but frightfully forbidding for the many potential buyers who had passed through its tall double doors. Philippe the estate agent told us there had been many visits, mostly French. However, for them, the dream of owning a chateau – though wild and exotic – is a risk most dare not take.

For many, chateaux are vestiges of a feudal system that was rightfully slaughtered in 1789 during the French Revolution, when several hundred thousand nobles and clergy were guillotined over a period of five years. Chateaux across France were seized, ransacked and razed. Yet the French still revere the families that live in today's chateaux. They rarely admit it, but the chateau owner, whether French or foreign, will always be treated with a touch of awe, a dash of wariness and, quite often, suspicion. The *châtelains* had for centuries taken advantage of the less fortunate. It's an age-old truth that those in power will do many things to keep those without in their place.

Even with all the work to do, it amazed us that the house hadn't been able to find a buyer. We are not architects or engineers, but everything seemed to be sound. The wood frame in the attic, called a *charpente*, was in good working order with no termites, though there were signs of woodworm. But older *charpentes* are made from oak and after 150 to 300 years, without serious attack, they are like steel. The roof was OK. It was relatively old, possibly 15 to 30 years. The thin black slates, or *ardoise*, had gone missing here and there. An ambitious renovator might set upon this task, but certainly not us.

The *crépi* that covered the exterior of the chateau was largely missing on the rear of the house. A good bit of it on the front was dark and mouldy. We thought it made the house look old, distinguished. Others would say '*abîmé*', or dilapidated. The faltering state of the chateau was not aided by the largely crumbling stone cornice on three different levels. This was more serious, aesthetically speaking. There were parts missing, parts in good condition and parts waiting to fall. We had two choices: hire stonemasons to cut, extract and replace the stone cornice; or hire the same stonemasons to create a paste of tuffeau, silicon and sand which they could mould to match the cornice and fill in the blanks. This last choice was cheaper and thus preferable. The exact cost, unknown.

The plumbing and electrics were all good. But two bathrooms were not enough, to say the least. The outbuildings, from what we could gather, were in good order with some patches of new roof.

So much potential. But there is an ever-so-important corollary to this hopeful phrase. So much potential… so much money! Sure, you could put a million British pounds into the beast. We were planning on closer to 600 or 700 thousand francs or (50 or 60 thousand pounds) – with furniture, bathrooms, fixtures, etc. And light fixtures; there were no light fixtures in the entire house. But, thankfully, we only had about a hundred to buy.

In our property search, we had come across another chateau just down the road. It was not for sale, but offered high-end bed and breakfast to paying guests. Philippe had informed us that the chateau was owned by a local count, a noble whose family stretched back to the Middle Ages. Philippe assured us that the count made a decent living with his 15-room hotel. We were curious. And so, a few days after we arrived, we planned a visit to the mysterious count. We loaded up the red van – five adults and a baby.

After 15 minutes of driving we saw signs for the 'Château des Fontaines'. We truly were in the middle of *la France profonde*, the heart of the French countryside. Large open fields of pear and apple trees fanned out over hills and into the near horizon. We passed through a small town with the now common sight of an impressive Gothic church. In minutes we found the beginning of a long lane leading to the count's house. 'Everything is so perfect here,' I noted.

Nobody spoke as I turned into a neatly laid stone lane. On either side, the lawn extended, perfectly cut, to surrounding woods. There was a pond to our left with two regal swans holding court and fishing for their morning meal.

I pulled up to the chateau. We had been told that this was the sister chateau of Bonchamps. It resembled our own with one small difference: it was perfect. There was a long central bay and two wings forming a vague 'U' shape, just like ours. Lilacs and roses and a lovely trellis framed the front of the chateau immaculately.

We piled out of our old banger and made our way to the front door. Perhaps this is what we dreamt of when we decided to buy a castle. I rang the bell and a discreet tune emanated from the great hall. Through the tall, elegant windows, I saw a stout figure arrive at the door. He looked out cautiously at our wreck of a van, probably thinking we were tinkers looking to sell some discarded zinc or newly found floor tiles.

'*Oui?*' He was average in height with a deep tan. His jaw was wide and very prominent. He had a full crop of dark hair and close-set eyes. Not necessarily aristocratic but passably so.

'*Bonjour. Je suis Sam Juneau. Nous avons acheté le Château du Bonchamps à Juvardeil. Nous venons à vous visiter à dire... bonjour,*' I managed to spit out.

'Oh, yes. I heard about you.' He spoke English. A relief. 'I am François de Richelieu. Please come in.'

The 'de' in his name was the sure sign of nobility. He was 'of' a certain place, a fiefdom given to his family in former days. It is a very serious offence in France to add the 'de' to your name without having 'earned' it. 'Earn' is used loosely here; I should say without having received some fiefdom or territory as a token of loyalty from a greater count, lord or prince. Though, I must note, Honoré de Balzac was not born with a 'de' and he managed to pull it off just fine, but the fact that he wrote eighty-something works in a thirty-year period served to allay noble anger at his substantial impertinence.

We all pushed through the door awkwardly, happy to be allowed in. The main hall was a masterpiece. There was wood panelling throughout the length of the gallery with impeccable eighteenth-century paintings in the manner of Poussin. These were positioned gracefully over pieces of Louis XV and Louis XVI furniture, gilded, polished and splendid. François showed us into the main salon. There were paintings of noble faces, more rare furniture, two large, puffy couches and four doors leading out to the rear of the chateau. A large grassy field stretched out of sight framed by tall chestnut trees in very, very straight lines. The French are great planters of straight lines of trees.

We sat knee by knee on the grand sofas and admired the intricately carved marble fireplace. In a large painting over the fireplace, little girls danced lightly on new-mown lawns in front of a vast fountain.

I introduced us. 'This is my wife, Brigid, our friends, Angus, Kate and Leo and, of course, baby Blue.'

He nodded. 'How long are you here?'

'We arrived this week. Just getting settled in.'

'You know, I looked to buy your chateau. My brother has a chateau north of here in Vendôme and it is time for my sister to buy a chateau and have a hotel.'

'Why didn't you buy it?'

'Too much work,' he said dismissively.

'There is much to do,' Bud agreed.

'Yes,' the count continued, 'the cornice is falling, the rooms are *affreuses*, just horrible. No bathrooms. The roof is old.' OK, tell us something we don't know. 'How much did you pay for it?' François asked. My experience of Europeans and especially French is they don't tend to talk about money. The last thing available for conversation. *Indiscret*, as the French say. I was a bit off-balance.

'Well, how much was it when you visited?' I asked.

'About two point five million francs.' He didn't miss a beat. We paid about two point seven with agent's fees. I told him this.

'That is correct. A good price. You should not pay more. Are you rich? Do you have a mortgage?'

Again, surprisingly blunt.

'No, not at all. And we do have a mortgage,' I stammered.

'You will have a very hard time making a living. I have inherited all of this, all the furniture, the house. I have no mortgage and each year I must struggle to bring people to the chateau. I pay so much in advertising, you cannot believe it. You should have bought something smaller, closer to a large town, like Saumur. This is the way to make a living. That is what we arranged for my sister. A small nineteenth-century chateau in the middle of Saumur.' Saumur is a lovely medieval and Renaissance town on the banks of the Loire river about one hour directly east of our chateau. The tourists like it. 'It will be very hard for you,' he emphasised.

Just what we needed to hear. And to think we had arrived *chez* François with hopes of idle chatter and a few introductions.

'Yes, but the house is so grand and there will be many people who would want to stay in a chateau and visit the others in the region.' I defended our honour, feebly.

'But we are too far from the big castles – Chenonceau, Blois, Chambord,' he retorted. 'It is almost impossible. And with a mortgage, there is not much to say. You will buy the house, work on it, be unhappy, suffer through long, dark winters and sell in three years. You will sell for about what you bought it for and leave with nothing. It will be better than now, another foreigner will buy it for a little more. He will do some works.

Then he will be discouraged and sell it for no profit to a French person. This is how it always goes.'

We all sat stunned and offended at his directness, rudeness even. But François had an easy manner. He was not aggressive, just truthful, as he saw it. Obviously he had struggled to hold onto the family patrimony. He knew the vagaries and pains of maintaining a vast estate.

'Yes, but our mortgage is not very large. We will use the Internet to market and pull in foreigners. And hopefully the French will come too.'

What François said next was shocking.

'You will get no French guests. They will not pay for this type of lodging. Eighty per cent of my business is foreign. English, Dutch, American. And the very rare French businessman.'

'Why is that?' I was confused.

'*Les Français sont appauvris.*'

'*Appauvris?*'

'Yes, poor. The nation is poor. People have no money. The taxes are too high. The wages are low. And they are cheap. It is *criminel.*'

Bud and I looked uncomfortably at one another. Help, I wanted to say. Could this be true? But there were so many nice things in this country. What about Dior? And fine Bordeaux wine? And Hermès? Who buys these things?

François showed his impatience. He was obviously a busy man.

'Well, I have some things to tend to. Please do come back. I will show you around next time.'

'You should come visit us and see the house again,' Bud gracefully suggested.

We all stood and bid our *au revoir*. Bud and I were a bit unsteady. We were determined to prove him wrong. François was blunt, very un-French. But then again, the aristocrat always has lived by different rules. I presumed it was part of his act to be shocking and brusque.

We loaded into the van and set off. I looked for a lifeline.

'What do you think about what he said?'

Bud pondered a moment. 'It does worry me a little. But I think he must be wrong. There has to be a market for people who want to stay in a lovely, big chateau in the countryside. Anyway, it's too late now. We've already moved the cats.' She laughed uneasily. I looked in the rearview mirror and was met by uncomfortable glances darting among our renovation team.

The ride back to our chateau was mostly quiet. Bud and I glanced at one another and agreed in an unspoken pact to ignore the count. He was a Cassandra foretelling uncomfortable truths that we, in our hopeful condition, chose to view as lies.

In any case, we had more pressing concerns. The current owner of our chateau had insisted on remaining in the old stable master's house in the outbuildings. We were on the verge of buying the chateau and we had not yet seen the inside of this house. Nor had we seen the other 15–20,000 square feet of the remainder of the stables and outbuildings. As far as we could tell, the *dépendances* consisted of a Tshaped building with a former lodging on each end, one of them being the stable master's house.

Through broken windows we could see a *'four à pain'*, or bread oven, other stone fireplaces, remnants of doors and shutters and windows. But all was locked tight. Jehan-Claude strikes again. Very thorough, that fellow. There were old cars, some American, some French, parked neatly in one of the cavernous stables. It appeared Jehan-Claude and his father liked tinkering. Though mildly interesting, I hoped they would be gone by the time we signed. The date for closing was set for two months' time.

As we poked around the outbuildings, I saw a large figure lumbering down the stone drive. I continued snooping as the figure approached.

'*Bonjour,*' he said, followed by a series of rapidly spoken words jumbled together into an incomprehensible jumble of French. I did manage to catch the words 'live' and 'Pernod' and 'Jehan-Claude'

'*Bonjour, enchanté.*' Nice to meet you.

We struggled for a few more minutes, he trying to decipher my patois and I trying to catch a word or two from his rapid-fire speech. Then he asked me a question, which I knew only because his phrasing ended on a slight shift up in intonation followed by a lifted brow.

'Can you show me?' I suggested.

I followed Jehan-Claude to the chateau and he pointed vaguely. I gathered that he wanted to take the items in the great hall. There were blankets and tables and chairs and beds and varia from the institution days.

'Does your father want these?' I asked.

Jehan-Claude said his father had told him nothing. He had just learned about the sale the day before and wanted to offer his help.

'Yes, please take these things. It would be a great help,' I said.

He left and returned shortly with his flatbed truck. He got to work on the main hall with the energy and verve of a young man, although I assumed he was in his early forties, tall with thick salt and pepper hair, strong, well-muscled forearms and trousers pulled up above his belly button. JC cleared the great hall in under an hour. He was, in a word, extraordinary.

I offered him a drink of water which he gladly accepted. We stood awkwardly in the gallery thinking of something to say that the other might understand.

I couldn't help myself. 'And the outbuildings? Do you have keys?'

'Yes, I do, but we have many things in the *dépendances*. I can clear them out later, a few months after you buy the house.'

Fair enough. Patience was evidently a virtue in France. I was eager to see the buildings because, firstly, I was about to buy the place and secondly, I had plans to rent out the stable master's house that summer. Bud and I had decided to call it the 'Guard's House', thinking this sounded fancy, like our property would need guarding or had needed guarding at some point.

Renting out the Guard's House was part of our assault on the hospitality business in France. After hours spent on the Web, I found a great website with thousands of holiday rentals, ranging from apartments and modest farmhouses to grand chateaux. I quickly reviewed some of the offerings in our area and set about posting our advert on the Internet. The sooner we could make money, the better chance of survival we had.

I cobbled together a few photos and used an aerial shot from a fairly recent postcard of the chateau. A few more photos of the pond and the woods and we had a bonafide advertisement. I set the rental of the Guard's House at 5,300 francs (£550) per week, and put together an impressive description: *The Guard's House is rustic but noble, nestled in the heart of 40 acres of woods and a pond.* 'Nestled' is a word one always finds in these descriptions. *And not just any pond, but a pond where you can enjoy fresh spring water in your daily swim.* Yes, I could see the cows now on the other side of the pond, wading and drinking and occasionally defecating. I did not mean to mislead my clients. I was just excited about the place.

A loaded all our information up and waited for the reservations to come rolling in. A faint doubt flickered in the back of my mind as I considered how I had never actually seen the inside of the so-called Guard's House.

'Sam, you can't rent that house before you see it,' Bud admonished.

'Come on, how bad could it be? Let me just set up the advertisement and we'll see how it goes.'

'That's not the way to build a business. Everything should be checked and cleaned and we'd better be certain it's in good order.' Details, details, I thought. *C'est rien*. But as any good hotelier would tell you, details are the most important thing in a client's pleasant stay.

Within a few days, I had two enquiries, resulting in two bookings from the States and the UK. Each set for two weeks at the end of July, early August. Our first possibility. That was almost 16,000 francs (£1,650) and we hadn't even begun. We hadn't even bought the house. What did François know about this business?

'Sam, I wish you hadn't done that.' Bud frowned.

'We have time. It will be OK. We'll get the lads in there, clean up by the time the guests arrive and we'll have a little money to show for our efforts. We have to get started.'

My long-suffering wife gave in disapprovingly.

I remained at the chateau for the next two weeks, puttering around with Bud, tending to the baby, making trips to the farmer's hardware store in the next town, inspecting our new home and making plans. Meanwhile, I should have been back at my job in New York. Reluctantly, I left Bud, Blue and Bonchamps behind and headed back to the States to work on the monster trucks documentary and a show called *Mean Dogs*.

The title of the latter show was not subtle but it was concise. As soon as I hit the ground in New York, I headed for Detroit to film a group of animal rescue workers on the mean streets of the most forgotten city in America. Race riots in the 1960s had gutted large parts of the city. Other areas were simply left to decay; victims of neglect and poverty. We were aiming to find evidence of illegal dogfighting. The breed of choice: the pit bull.

I spent the day making house calls with the investigators. We all wore bulletproof vests as we caroused the streets looking for the telltale signs of abused animals. We had entered into an altercation with one of the alleged dogfight organisers. This involved considerable yelling, bickering and the threat of bodily harm. Someone hinted there might be a gun nearby. Then we found a dead dog on the organiser's property. This did not bode well for anyone involved. The animal, a pit bull, had been dumped after a weekend fight where he had been on the short end of a mean squabble with a neighbouring dog. We noted and filmed the finding and quickly left. The day had been long and depressing. I found a steakhouse on the outskirts of town. Just as I sat, my mobile rang. The caller ID flashed a number beginning '33'. France. It must be late there, I thought.

'Hello?'

'Sam, it's Bud. Blue had an accident.'

'What happened?' My heart beat almost out of my chest.

'She fell off the bed and hit the bedside table. She cut her chin. I thought it was nothing, but when I looked down, there was blood everywhere.' Bud was calm.

'Where are you?'

'Everything is fine. We're at the chateau. We drove down to Jehan-Claude's house, woke them up and they called the doctor.'

'What time was that?' I was trying to comprehend what had happened, but simply couldn't.

'Around midnight. We went to the doctor and he gave Blue six stitches.'

'My God. Is she OK?'

'She's sleeping now. I think it will be fine. Jehan-Claude and Marie-Christine were great.'

We talked hurriedly of the past few days' events. My heart ached as I thought of my wife with our baby back in the chateau having to deal with the immensity of our project. It made me sad. I refrained from telling her about my day. Guns and mean dogs were not what she needed to hear just now. It would not be the last time we were apart for a good chunk of time. The sacrifice of our bold choice had begun.

Our conversation wound down. Bud said she was tired. It was now about 2 a.m. at the chateau.

'We found a new bed,' Bud stated in an optimistic tone. 'It's horsehair, an old mattress we pulled down from the third floor. It sleeps great.'

'That's good news.'

'Oh yeah – and Angus, Kate and Leo haven't done anything this week. They say they'll start the serious work after they get settled in.'

'Great,' I managed sarcastically.

'Sam?'

'Yes.'

'I love you.'
'I love you too. Kiss Blue for me in the morning.'

CHAPTER SEVEN

Trop Jeune

Wine connoisseurs in France love to mull over the proper time to drink a vintage. One often hears that a wine is *trop jeune*, or too young. The tannins are 'too aggressive' or the alcohol overly pronounced. That perfect combination of year, grape, region and ageing method remains elusive. Most admit it is virtually impossible to determine when the wine is exactly '*mûr*'. I cannot recount how many times I have tasted a vintage in the presence of a self-described wine expert and the words 'It is good but it will be better in five or ten years' come tumbling off moist, red lips. The rule is simple: the only way to know is to open the bottle. The proof is in the glass. As we started to uncork the possibilities of the property, it wasn't clear whether we had vinegar or wine.

I returned to New York after my dogfighting expedition in Detroit and a short trip out to Vegas for the monster trucks. A few weeks later Bud came back with Blue for a week. Our most recent *séjour* at the chateau had by no means been easy or peaceful but it had left us with a great sense of possibility, even hope, despite Monsieur le Comte's dire prognostications. As we settled back into the distinct *lack* of possibility in our one-bedroom apartment in New York, the idea of French country life grew more appealing. The smallness, the dilapidation, the modesty of our apartment cried out for a remedy. We had left the gang in charge to spiffy up the Guard's House, now vacated by Monsieur Pernod, and continue their bone-wearying labour.

Each day, I set off for work, usually not too early. My commute, one of the worst things about making money, was about 45 minutes. My company provided a small shuttle to usher Manhattan workers to small cubicles several miles west in a soulless industrial park in New Jersey, one of the broadcast centres of the mighty NBC News.

At about the same time, Bud would leave our cramped apartment to do errands and take Blue to the park. Anyone who raises kids in the city knows the difficulty of navigating city streets with a baby. Inevitably, Bud would end up at Central Park, several blocks from our apartment. Among nannies of New York's elite, protocols were established as young children fought for limited space and maximum usage of swings, slides and sandpits. She dreamt of our new house with its generous woods and orchards.

One evening, a few weeks before the final signing of the *acte de vente* and the arrival of our first guests, we received a call. I answered the phone.

'Hello?'

'Sam, it's Kate.' The three of them had been working away at the chateau for some time now. Their latest project involved stripping, sanding, patching and painting the 39-by-4-metre-wide main gallery. Things were advancing, with no major problems.

'Hi Kate.'

'Sam, we have a problem. Leo, Angus and I finally got into the Guard's House today. It's a disaster. There is brown, mouldy carpet everywhere. The sink is broken, the bathroom is a beige nightmare. It needs painting. Plus, Jehan-Claude told us his father plans to stay there the week before you come over for the signing. I think the guests are arriving that week?'

'That's terrible! I can't believe this. Let me talk to Bud and we'll figure out a plan. How are things otherwise?'

'OK, but it's lonely here. Since we don't speak the language, there's nothing to do except work.'

'Hang in there. I will call you back.'

I humbly shared the news with Bud.

'Well, he can't stay there. We've rented out the house.'

'It's his house until we buy it.' Hard to argue with that.

'Sam, why don't you call the clients and arrange for them to stay in the chateau for the first week and move into the Guard's House for their second week?'

'OK, but we have no proper beds and the bathrooms are dreadful.'

'Maybe I can go over there early, buy some beds and work with the gang to get everything ready,' Bud suggested hopefully. 'On second thoughts,' she continued, 'I still think it's a bad idea to rent the place out. Can't you cancel?'

'They've already paid the deposit and made plans to be there at the end of July. I can't cancel now. We have to move forward. How bad could it be anyway?'

With that muttering of wilful denial, we made plans for Bud to venture back to France to get things in order. Blue had already racked up more frequent flyer miles than any two-year-old should have to endure. I would join them in a couple of weeks so we could actually buy the house.

While Bud made her way back to Juvardeil, I called our beloved clients and told them the news. They could stay in the chateau for the first week. Then we would help them with the changeover. They said it was no problem. The woman who had innocently booked 'her dream of life on a seventeenth-century chateau estate' would be delighted to experience life in the chateau, she said.

Bud's early return was utterly futile. Jehan-Claude had the keys to the Guard's House and was protecting the contents. A couple of days after her arrival, Monsieur Pernod, JC's father, arrived to install his family in the disputed Guard's House. That afternoon Bud met the owner and saw the Guard's House for the first time.

Another phone call. 'Sam, we have a problem.'

'Yes, dear?'

'I saw the Guard's House today and it is unrentable.'

'Come on, Bud. Won't the guests think it's quaint and rustic?'

'Only if they are barn animals.'

I left the next day. I had been in the middle of scripting *Mean Dogs* so I completed the first two drafts and submitted them to my boss for approval. All appeared to be fine, so I gave the scripts and tapes to my editor and offered a few words of encouragement as he would be starting the project alone. I told him I was heading off to buy a chateau and would be back in a week. Somewhere in there I promised him a week at the chateau for his solo efforts on our project.

There is something very nice about a long plane flight – putting aside the clichés of small seats, bad food, long lines, motion sickness, stale air and smelly bathrooms. We would have to make this transatlantic flight many times over the coming year. Alone with seven hours stretched before me, I thought of the changes we were making, the things we would leave behind. This was the beginning of the end of our life in America. In a few days, we would sign the contract of sale. No turning back now. Leaving America was a little death. I mourned quietly. In my heart, I hoped this adventure would bring better things. More time with Bud and Blue and hopefully a whole brood of other little ones. Fresh country air, a slower pace of life. If I focused on the good, all would fall into place.

A day later, I arrived at the chateau. Bud and the gang had been busily preparing two large suites for our guests, who were set to arrive that very day. Bud had bought a few oak-carved beds, side tables, linens and other accoutrements that would make our clients comfortable. I inspected the rooms with her. We spoke hurriedly and impatiently of the coming catastrophe.

I made my way to the Guard's House and introduced myself to the owner. The years had been unkind to Monsieur Pernod. He sported a thatch of grey hair, a large belly and a deeply lined face presumably from years of worry and many a bottle of wine. Monsieur Pernod told me he was retired from the French army, where he ran the heavy machinery in Algeria and on mainland France. His manner was generous and open. I thanked him for letting us move in early. Great for the cats, I said. He invited me into the Guard's House for an aperitif and my first glance at my first big mistake.

Yes, indeed, it was bad. The decor had been updated in the late 1970s, then again possibly in the early 1980s. Not good years for design on a tight budget. The kitchen was a do-it-yourselfer with a stainless steel sink, no counter space, a battered old fridge and no cabinets. The walls were covered with that tattered ubiquitous wallpaper. Damp seeped through one wall. I used the bathroom and spied a brown and avocado bathroom suite with a leaky shower head. Upstairs there were long strips of brown, worn carpet not fastened down and curling at the edges. The dining room was handsome, though, with old wood panelling and a *trompe l'oeil* frieze up above. Nevertheless we had our work cut out.

The workers seemed to be in good spirits. I think they were delighted to have some activity and companionship. They had truly begun renovating, and had made their way through about three and a half rooms, pulling down old wallpaper and prepping the walls for paint and minor replastering. They were neat and seemingly efficient. Finally, some good news.

But the weight of things that weren't working began to get me down. The looming fiasco in the Guard's House, the work that lay ahead, the anxiety over financing such a project. Just after my visit to the 'dream' rental house, Bud, Kate, Leo and I decided to take a walk in the forest.

The woods spread out vastly behind the chateau. Sometime in the nineteenth century, so M. Pernod told us, the owners had created a *parc anglais*, a somewhat organised yet wild pleasure park. They had planted oaks and plane trees and poplars and Roman pines and sequoias and *tilleuls*, or lime trees. Now their hard work had borne fruit, creating a massive canopy of beautiful trees. There were quite a few fallen trees and these engulfed the paths every so often. As we walked, I could only think of the work to be done on this part of the property alone. It would take years to clear the debris and clean up the paths. I tried to push these thoughts aside and enjoy our jaunt.

In the distance, we could hear Angus's voice echoing against the old trees. We rushed back toward the house to find him standing in the clearing with a plunger in his right hand, sweat dripping down his red forehead.

'Sam, we have a problem.'

'What's up?' I asked, thinking, *please stop. Please.*

'The toilet in the guest suite is blocked. I've been trying to unblock it for the past hour.'

'Let's take a look.' My heart sank as I pictured our first guests arriving at the chateau only to find the one and only toilet blocked.

I peered cautiously into the small room. The bowl was full, luckily with no sign of recent human activity. The water was clear but unmovable. I took the plunger and started my ownerly duties. In minutes, a black sludge bubbled up to the rim. I turned the water off. This only aggravated the situation. The hellish brew began to bubble up over the side of the toilet onto our newly polished wood floors.

By this time, both JC and his father had been alerted. They arrived in minutes. JC took the tool from my hand and set about the task himself with focus and purpose. After 30 minutes, he suggested we call a plumber.

An hour later, Monsieur Mocques arrived in a tidy white van. Mocques had serviced the chateau for years now. He knew the toilet and seemed to know the problem so JC thought we should leave the man to do his work, which we did. When he surfaced his hands were immaculate, overalls in order, no sweat on his brow, but the toilet was miraculously fixed. Bud and I darted up the stairs and were met by what appeared to be the mess of all messes. Masses of thick goo, water and white paste were caked around the foot of the toilet. JC noted, somewhat unnecessarily, that Mocques was good but he never cleaned up after major surgery.

After a feverish display of courageous cleaning up, we finished our first major 'renovation' by placing a clean roll of toilet paper next to the shiny porcelain toilet. Ah, the glamour and rewards of chateau life. I had gone from producing a documentary for a major American network to toilet-boy in a matter of hours. How the mighty had fallen. At that moment, we heard a car pull up to the front of the house.

I charged downstairs and saw our first guests picking their way around the front of the chateau. The couple, in their late thirties/early forties, was followed closely by two teenaged children. They shyly approached the main door. As I went out to greet them, I noticed my trousers were soiled and my shirt slightly torn from my exertions with regards the toilet.

'Hello. So nice to see you. Please come in,' I offered pleasantly, leading them through the main door. Bud whispered in my ear, 'I hate to say it, but you smell.'

Ignoring this brief *remarque*, I led our lambs into the main gallery, then through the library and up to their suite. The gang had thoughtfully cleaned and tidied the main living areas, leaving the renovation mess behind closed doors.

'Can we swim in the pond?' the older girl asked.

'I think so. We'll have to take a look later today,' I tentatively responded.

The guests seemed pleased with the suites. I ventured carefully to the toilet door. All clear.

'This is your toilet,' I said proudly, as if there were some merit in having a toilet. If they only knew. 'As you know, you will stay in the chateau this week and switch over next week to the Guard's House. I'm terribly sorry, again, but we are in the process of finalising the sale and the owner insisted on remaining here up to the actual closing.'

'That's fine, we are excited to be here. In fact, we think it's great that you're letting us stay in the chateau when we only booked the Guard's House.'

Perfect. Open, forgiving guests. These new creatures gazed around wide-eyed and sheepishly looking, I hoped, at the enormity of the place while possibly searching for more signs of the 'luxury of former centuries', as presented in my not-too-truthful Web brochure. The mum and dad were fit and tanned, neatly if not fashionably dressed. They brought with them two daughters who appeared only slightly bored as we took the tour. They all had an openness and curiosity that the best Americans have. They asked polite questions while keeping their distance and had no problem showing their enthusiasm when they felt it.

'There is one thing. We will have to share the kitchen. Perhaps we can work out some sort of schedule. Normally, we are done at around 6 p.m. Does that work for you?'

'Definitely,' the mum replied cheerily. 'We're late eaters. Just show us where to put the food and we'll stay out of your way. Could we eat early in the morning?'

'No problem.'

Our first night of cohabitation went smoothly. We prepared a meal, fed the troops and vacated the premises in time for our guests. We left the kitchen clean and laid out implements. They ate in the grand dining room next to the oak-carved library. Cheap wallpaper aside, this was in fact a nice room – large and airy, extremely well-lit by four very tall double French doors, and in the middle of the east-facing wall sat a deep burgundy marble fireplace with a gargantuan gilded mirror perched on top of the mantelpiece.

The next morning I awoke fairly early, washed my face and started down to the kitchen. Everything was in good order. I could see a few discreet crumbs sitting innocently on the stainless steel counter top. Good, our guests had eaten, I thought to myself. But what was this? Folded neatly next to the crumbs was a white piece of paper. I unfolded it slowly, my heart beating rapidly.

Sam,
Everything is fine. We were just wondering if you could leave the washroom empty of debris and trash for the mornings.
Thank you.
Martha

Behind the main kitchen was the *arrière cuisine* for storing goods and washing dishes. I rushed in.

There, like a drunken pyramid, were a few dozen bottles of beer. The room smelled like a brewery and looked like a tip. I believe I had had one beer the night before and Bud drank none as she was breastfeeding Blue. I was furious. All of the worry and planning and careful orchestration of eating schedules and my foul-up of letting the Guard's House in the first place became apparent with this one annoying act of carelessness.

I leaped upstairs. Bud was dressing Blue.

'Bud, we have to talk to the gang. There are beer bottles everywhere in the kitchen and the guests had to wade through them to eat breakfast.'

'I can't believe that!' Bud practically shouted. I could see a slight reddening along her neck, creeping toward her cheeks. She was angry. 'I told them to put their stuff outside. It makes sense, though. Angus told me yesterday that they drink occasionally after work. I hope this doesn't become habit.'

I was furious too. Not only had we made a mistake but now the mistake turned into humiliation. It was just plain embarrassing. My blood boiled as I thought of ways to confront the offenders. Around 10.30 a.m., the lads found their way to the kitchen. I had been unaware of the hours they worked.

'Hey guys, please don't leave your beer bottles stacked here. You know we have to share the kitchen with the guests.' I remained calm. I knew too we had many months ahead and I just couldn't stomach a confrontation at this point in our employer–worker relationship. There were simply too many things on our plate. Avoidance seemed the best path on this day.

'Oh, sorry. We were trying to be neat. We'll get rid of them,' came the groggy reply.

We left it at that. I apologised later that day to our guests. No worries, they assured me. 'It's just that we have the girls and they were asking how people could drink so much beer.' They were more than gracious. The work crew was very diligent about removing their bottles after that.

That day around lunchtime, we loaded up a hire car and started toward Alsace. Monsieur Pernod lived on the border of Germany and France about six hours north-east of the chateau. It was decided that we would meet there at the *notaire*'s office to sign the deed. The *notaire* in France is a quasi-governmental figure who ostensibly serves the interest of both parties in any property transaction. He or she will register the deed, officially make note of any liens or mortgages, check the property boundaries and generally assure the legal transfer of ownership for the French government and the parties involved.

Unlike in the States or Britain, none of the parties involved has a private solicitor. All rely equally and faithfully on the *notaire*. All this takes about six to ten hours of work on his part, maximum. The fee: around seven per cent, paid by the buyer, possibly a punishment for being successful enough to buy a house in the first place, added blithely to the five to seven per cent take for the estate agent. Astounding.

It was good for us to get away from the chateau for a day or two. It was ironic – we had only just arrived and already we were seeking refuge. We drove throughout the afternoon and by early evening, we were tired. We found a simple hotel to break up our journey, setting off again early the next day. In a few hours, we arrived at the *notaire*'s office. There sat the *notaire*, a translator, Monsieur Pernod, his French-German wife and Philippe. We tumbled in, baby in tow, only slightly rumpled from our travels and recent ordeals at the chateau.

We shook hands all round and got down to business. The signing felt anticlimactic, a mere formality. I had arranged a decent loan with an English bank at a good rate. We were set to pay the loan off for the next 25 years, based on my salary in America. The only hitch being that I planned to quit my job in the next six months and rely on our meagre savings and income from the chateau. Minor details.

All went smoothly. The *notaire* read the entire deed of sale including full stops and relevant laws governing the sale, which took about two hours. We all sat patiently. Bud and I were eager to sign and the Pernods seemed just as eager to offload the white elephant as quickly as possible. Blue squirmed and squawked at her unnatural confinement. We thanked one another, each party feeling like they got the better part of the deal. Who was right?

Monsieur Pernod offered one small piece of advice before hastening out the door, as if reading my thoughts. 'With a house like this, it is necessary to find a way to do the work and repairs by yourself. Otherwise, you will go broke.'

Just what I needed to hear. I am lucky if I can manage to change a light bulb on my own. I knew he was absolutely right. Yet somehow I refused to believe him. Denial is a powerful and wonderful thing.

The day was still young so we decided to drive straight to the chateau on our way back. The weight of our acquisition sat like an obese, needy teenager in the car.

'Do you think we did the right thing, Bud? Will it work out? Please tell me it will,' I pleaded.

'I think so. There is so much potential.'

'But we only have so much money. And the monthly repayments alone, not including maintenance and utilities, are 2,500 euros a month. That's a load of money.' Bud and I were readjusting to talking in euros after the switch over. Euros were nice because they were like dollars – the rate of exchange was about the same with dollars a little stronger by the time we signed the papers.

'Well, it's too late now. Let's just look ahead and hope for the best. And you need to learn how to hammer a nail.' Bud smiled.

We slept fitfully in the chateau that night, and arose early the next morning. My train to the airport left at 10 a.m. I had to leave my struggling family and our not very hard-working worker bees so that I could go back to work, make the mortgage, and finish *Mean Dogs*. Our guests were still firmly settled in the south wing. They would move to the Guard's House a few days after my departure. I could only imagine what further troubles this would bring. At the train station, I said goodbye to Bud with a small tear in my eye.

'What's wrong?'

'I'm just sorry to leave you here to deal with the chateau by yourself.'

'It will work out. The guests seem nice and Leo, Kate and Angus are ready to help out. As long as we can keep them on the straight and narrow.' She laughed.

'Take care. Call me when you get ready to move them over to the Guard's House.'

I trudged three thousand miles back to our dark apartment, a commute worse than anything I could have entangled myself in stateside.

A few days later, Bud restrained herself from relating the full details of the changeover. When presented with the Guard's House, our long-suffering guests simply said, 'We don't do musty carpets.' So that was that. They held out in the chateau, sharing the kitchen with four other people and a baby whom they didn't know. The beer bottles had magically disappeared but the aftertaste remained.

A month after my return, Angus called me at the apartment. Bud was on her way back to New York, as planned.

'Sam, we have a problem.' I was used to this phrase by this point in my hotel-running career.

'What is it?'

'The new guests have arrived and they are furious. The guy wants to speak to you.'

Fifteen minutes later, he called.

'Hello?'

'Yes, Mr Juneau, this is Mr Givens. We have rented the Guard's House. We've come all the way from Manchester to stay at your house. I am calling to complain. We want our money back. The house is a disaster, the water is sometimes brown and the beds are uncomfortable.'

'Other than that, is everything OK?'

I truly felt sorry for him. He had paid his money and expected a peaceful, luxurious, quiet time with his family in the French countryside. I would be angry too. Sure, I had made a mistake and rented out the Guard's House too soon. But we could work something out amicably.

'What do you mean, "OK"? It's just not on. My kids go out into the garden and there is cat shit everywhere. How could you rent a place out in this state?'

My feeble brain scrambled to think of something comforting, something professional to say.

'Well, first of all the cat shit is going to hurt no one. I can have one of the workers pick it up but there is no need to

overreact. You could eat cat shit and it wouldn't hurt you.'
It seemed like a sensible thing to say at the time. I was just
stating facts. I couldn't really defend the house itself so I
chose to defend the cats' honour instead.

'I can't believe you are saying this. We are leaving today.
We want our money back. I've called a lawyer friend in New
York and he will expect a cheque for the full rental amount
in the morning.'

'OK. I'm terribly sorry,' I said, adding, 'Enjoy your time in
France. And please clean the house before you leave.' This
may have been perceived as a bit cheeky. But I knew, despite
appearances, our team had spent a lot of time cleaning the
house. I simply wanted our guests to leave it as they found
it. This really set him off.

'The only way to clean this sodding mess is to burn it to
the ground,' he snorted.

An old adage informs wine lovers it is better to drink a wine
too young than too old. But in the same way some vintners
will 'serve no wine before it's time', the chateau and Guard's
House were not mature enough to receive guests. Neither
was I. Maybe there is something to be said for waiting for
the right moment. How long would it take, though? Five,
ten years? The thought depressed my naive soul.

CHAPTER EIGHT

Moving Experiences

People who know things say moving house is a traumatic experience. One of the most traumatic things, in fact, a person can do. Losing a close friend or family member is up there, as is losing one's job, divorce and even marriage. Yes, marriage can be traumatic too. I saw this on a list once of life's most difficult things. All these things deal with loss. The loss of one's home or nest, the loss of something dear or beloved, the apparent or real death of something that was a part of our lives. Let's face it, life is sometimes difficult.

The months back in New York, after that first summer in France, crept by slowly as we sat in limbo, not quite gone from the big city and not yet settled in the chateau. The dramas of the great cat move adventure, the purchase of the house, and the fresh, stinging failures of the Guard's House weighed on us. We never faltered in our resolve to make the move. It's just that the impending loss of everything familiar bore down on us. Of course, it was our choice, but we were giving up our careers, our friends in the States, the routine of our lives. So two contradictory but strong feelings battled within – excitement for the future and a small bit of sadness as we left the past behind.

We returned to France once more over the December holidays. The chateau was unbearably cold with no respite in sight. Even if we could afford to heat the thing, it was impossible to get it warm. The ceilings were too high, the heating system too weak, the thick stone walls that served to cool the house in summer now collaborated with the damp weather to keep the cold in. The renovation crew had made good progress stripping wallpaper. They had even repainted the Guard's House and the great hall in the chateau, which was 40 metres long, five metres high and four metres wide. It had been pink; now it was a rich dark, royal red. It looked great but the gang was freezing and underpaid. Mutiny at the chateau looked imminent.

Meanwhile, back at the office in New York, there was a persistent rumour that my show was about to be cancelled by the network. The ratings had been decent and the documentaries were well made and entertaining. But my network was the underperforming stepson of a bigger network that didn't really tolerate underperformance. It seemed like heads might roll again after previous bloodlettings.

This suited us just fine. I had something lined up, something that I desperately wanted to do. Maybe I would get a severance and we could finally make the break and run for France. As for my colleagues, fear and loathing hung in the air like a putrid smell.

One morning I made my daily 45-minute trek out to the studios a few miles west of Manhattan. The first thing I heard as I sat down in my cubicle was, 'Sam, today is the day. I think you're next.'

'What do you mean?'

'Four people have been fired. The show is cancelled.'

Our show had once had as many as 35 producers, a whole gang of associate producers, and half a dozen seniors as well as production people, engineers, editors and a couple of reporters. Since we had bought the chateau, those numbers had been brutally whittled down to eight producers and a handful of support staff and one or two senior people. To say the network was poorly managed is like saying the *Titanic* had had a leaky tap.

I used to think of these almost monthly firings like guerrilla warfare in suits. Executives and human resources people would be seen hovering around our boss's office. Hushed conversations would spill out occasionally from closed doors. Then the boss or one of the human resources people would wander out and toss a career hand grenade into the neatly spaced cubicles. There were usually three to six casualties at once. Producers would stumble around, dazed and confused. It was all a bit cruel. It would have been better to cancel the show outright and send all these hapless souls out into the world to fend for themselves at once. As it was, we never knew who would get it next and when. Some people cried while others were just pissed off. Some of the younger kids had never been fired. If you stay in TV for longer than three years, you will have been fired or your show will have been cancelled. It's just the nature of the business. But dragging it out like this was gratuitous.

There was an electric buzz going around as first one, then two, then three and finally four people were fired. My beleaguered friends and co-workers reported the same thing. The show would go into reruns, production would stop. Everyone would go. I called Bud.

'Bud, they're cancelling the show.'

'No way. Well, I guess it's about time. They've been threatening for months. Now we can move.'

'Let's see what happens. I'll call you when the execution is over.'

I was thrilled and excited. Now, no more excuses. We would pack up and go. I had greatly resented being at the mercy of someone else. Who has the right to determine my fate? Whether I can support my family or not? I had looked down the TV road and seen a future filled with just these types of disappointments, this type of prolonged treachery. Feckless executives making decisions that took no account of human factors or loyalty or even quality. Decisions made for the sake of making decisions. Decisions that affected our lives and families.

My good friend Keith – a lively, smart, kind Lithuanian Jew from Queens, New York – was called into the boss's office. I could see him sitting there shaking back his long mane of black, unkempt hair. Keith was a producer like me. He had a book deal and could take or leave our current gig.

No fear there. He knew the cardinal rule of television, and corporate life: always, always have something else lined up.

Keith sat in the office joking and joshing with the boss. He came out ten minutes later.

'What happened?'

'Don't tell anyone this, but they're keeping two producers to do updates and shoot the occasional new story. They asked me to stay.'

'That's great. You're staying, right?'

'No way. I have that book to write. And they've been screwing us around for too long. I'm outta here.'

'Good for you.'

Out of the corner of my eye, I could see my boss, tall with a fashionably shaved head and killer spectacles, loping down the corridor.

'Sam, can you come into my office?'

'Sure.'

I walked to his office, my heart beating rapidly against my chest. Why was I nervous? I had made plans, Bud was ready to go, we had bought the chateau. My life flashed before my eyes. I sat down. My boss sat across from me and looked me straight in the eye.

'Today is the day. The network is cancelling the show.'

'It's about time.'

'It's true. But there's one catch. We want you to stay on, to do updates, hang around, produce new stories from time to time. We're keeping two producers and we want you and Keith.'

I had feared the firing but had actually wanted it. It would have been perfect. Don't quit, just get thrown out, take

125

a little pile of money and leave. No hard feelings. Better things ahead. Now this.

'That's an interesting turn of events. Why did it take them so long to make a damn decision?' I was frustrated, flattered and confused all at once.

'They didn't know what to do. There was a lot of pressure from the top. They wanted change for change's sake. Do you want the gig? Same money, less work.'

'I have to talk to my wife. As you might know, we bought that chateau in France and we've been waiting for the right moment to take the plunge.'

'OK, but I have to know in the next ten minutes.'

'Got it.'

I strolled back to my desk and told Keith the news. We laughed.

'I'm supposed to give him an answer in ten minutes too,' Keith snickered.

'It looks like we're both going to tell him no. What a rush! This is great.'

I called Bud.

'So, this is the last day for the show. They're firing everyone, like I said.'

'Did they let you go yet?' Bud asked.

'Well, not quite. Even though they're closing the thing down, they want me to stay.'

'What?' Panic in her voice.

'They asked me and Keith to stay. Can you believe it? The only time I want a show to get cancelled and they tell me to stay. Unbelievable.'

'We're going. Tell him no.'

And that was that. Bud was ready. I was too, but leaving that money on the table was hard. I had worked my whole life to find a gig where the pay was reasonably good and the work easy. With some misgivings, I ambled back into my boss's office.

'So, what's it going to be?' he asked.

'Well, first of all, I want to say I've enjoyed working with you. You've been a great boss. Thanks for all the support.' This sounded a little unctuous and servile, but what I said was true. My boss was great and laid-back and smart. It was his bosses that I despised, their fear and bad decisions. 'But I'm going to France with my wife and kid. Thank you for the offer. It is flattering. But one of the reasons I bought the place in France is so morons like your boss would not determine my fate.'

'Fine, understood. It's been great working with you too. I wish you the best of luck. Maybe I'll come visit. Some day.'

'We would love to have you.' I felt empowered and in control of my own destiny. It's a rare thing when you can move on and leave something substantial on the table and say, I simply don't need you, I don't need this job. Like that old silly country and western song from the seventies, 'Take This Job and Shove it'.

I returned home early that evening. We would pack and leave. Why delay?

Over the next two months, we packed and packed some more and made arrangements to leave. There were myriad minor and major details to take care of. Final rent; cancellation of gas and electric and phone; booking a moving company. Most of this went smoothly. Some nights we would sit up and talk of our new adventure. The next day, to add a little extra spice to our chaotic lives, Bud found out she was pregnant. We were overjoyed. All the little niggling things took a backseat to this new life growing now in Bud's belly.

Then a call came from a good friend in Cape Cod. Bud had spent summers during university cleaning houses in this beautiful part of the country. This was how she had paid for her studies, and she had made friends along the way. One of her former clients, Cynthia, knew we were heading out soon.

'Bud, I have an acquaintance – our gardener, actually. He is French. I told him we had friends moving to France and he is interested in talking to you about employment. Do you think you'll need a gardener or handyman?' she said on the phone one afternoon.

'We hadn't thought about it. But the property is quite large and we could use some help in the beginning.'

'I should tell you, he's very capable and experienced. But he does like the drink a bit.' Alas, a recurring theme in our lives.

'What do you mean?' Bud was sceptical.

'Well, it's nothing bad, just that he is French and he likes to have some wine at lunch. He's fond of whisky too.'

'I suppose it can't hurt to meet him. Where is he now?'

'He's here in Cape Cod. I will set everything up. You can come stay with us and meet him at our house.'

It's odd how people come into our lives. Here was a friend from Bud's former days as a maid, inserting herself into our plans with the best of intentions and changing how things would unfold.

We hired a car, packed up Blue and started off for Cape Cod. We both thought a handyman might be good, just to help get us on our feet. Plus, vainly, we liked the idea of employing a caretaker on our new estate. We envisioned a life in the country full of workmen and servants who could tend to the estate and help us maintain a life that we were not accustomed to, but one that we hoped for. We were already planning to assume our place as lord and lady of the manor. Self-deception is a very powerful tool.

We arrived in Wood's Hole, Massachusetts, a sleepy, cosy, beautiful little enclave at the western end of Cape Cod. The town was tiny, home to a major oceanographic institute filled with scientists, local workers and some summer holidayers. It was rumoured that the town was composed of 600 couples in summer and twice that number in winter. Bed-hopping appeared to be the local sport during the slow season.

We pulled up to Cynthia's house, an early-1900s shingled dwelling surrounded by trees and a pond. Lovely.

'It's so nice to see you,' Cynthia said. Bud hugged her old boss and we settled in on the porch for a cocktail. Cynthia was a serious, pragmatic woman who knew what she wanted, with shoulder-length grey hair, thick glasses and long, elegant fingers. Her movements were abrupt and clipped as though she was displeased with something and wanted to get on with things. But she could not have been any more kind or generous. Bud had formed a genuine friendship with her despite their age and social background differences.

'Hercule, the gardener, will come by any minute now,' she said.

'Great. We're looking forward to meeting him.'

Cynthia offered us drinks and we moved out to a vast wooden porch overlooking a smooth, oval pond. We chatted about local gossip and life in the big city. Bud and she reminisced about summers long slipped past. Cynthia laughed quiet, persistent laughs, muffled with her hand. It was good to see Bud enjoying memories that I was not a part of. Sometimes it seemed we had been together forever. This reminded me that we had both, at one time, maintained separate lives.

Ten minutes later, a 1960s pickup truck pulled into the yard. From the porch, we could see a medium-sized, fit, handsome guy get out of the truck. Hercule looked to be about forty, deeply tanned with a thick head of hair and a weathered Gallic face. He wore a tweed sports jacket and tan trousers with loafers.

'Hercule, this is Sam and Bud. They're the ones I told you about.'

'Very nice to meet you.' He had the slightest French accent but spoke perfect English. This was a good start. He could translate for us in tight spots and help us get things done.

We chatted idly about the property, about his work experience. Bud breastfed Blue as she squirmed in her arms. Hercule's eyes widened like saucers. But he was kind and gentle and seemed to have loads of experience. He told us of former clients – an estate in Palm Beach, a massive property here in Wood's Hole – and his life as a gardener. His former bosses were way out of our league but we pushed ahead. After about half an hour, Bud pressed him.

'So, if you were to come work for us, what kind of salary would you be looking for?'

'I think about 2,500 euros per month. I think that's fair and I spoke to my brother in France and he says that's what the going rate is.'

We both stifled an almost uncontrollable gasp. This was far, far beyond our means.

'That's too much, I will tell you right now.' Bud didn't miss a beat.

'We can talk about it. I realise you would be giving me a place to live. I am open. The important thing for me is to get back to France. It's been almost twenty years.'

We arranged to call Hercule in the coming week with our answer. He could certainly help us and having him around might even increase our chances of getting the B&B up and running sooner. Or so we rationalised.

Bud called Hercule later that week and we offered him the job. At 24,000 euros a year (£16,500) or 2,000 a month. For some reason, this sounded better than 30,000 a year. It was just as bad and far beyond our resources. But we were insecure and needed help. Our first mistake. We found out later that the average salary for a good, professional handyman in France was far less than this; around 16,000 (£11,000) a year. And Hercule was simply a gardener. But, coming from New York, where everything is triple the price, we thought the salary seemed reasonable at the time. Hercule accepted the offer but requested that we pay for the transport of his beloved pickup truck. He said it would be used for work around the property. This would be another $1,000 (£540) on top of our own moving expenses. At the time, we thought we had enough money, so we agreed. We have never been accused of being canny entrepreneurs.

The movers arrived and placed everything we owned into a large metal container, ready for shipping across the pond. Hercule would follow several weeks later.

In early April, almost a year after we had moved the cats and bought the chateau, we arrived at our new home. Kate and Leo had been working for the same period of time. Angus, the youngest, had left early, tired of the work and feeling underappreciated.

They had made great progress. Walls had been stripped; false partitions torn down; the gallery, Guard's House, dining room and several bedrooms painted. The day before we arrived, Leo and Kate also left the chateau, exhausted and discouraged. It seemed that no matter how much work they did, there was always a greater amount to be done. The stress of the work, the crushing size of the project, weighed heavily on them. We gathered that things were not well for them in paradise. There were the language problems, the loneliness of country life in the winter, the isolation of being in a culture not your own. The unhappy couple packed their things, drove to the train station and left our beaten-up van in the car park.

MOVING EXPERIENCES

We found the van at the train station and made our way to the house. Our first days back at the property left us wandering around, once again, in a daze. We made to-do lists and explored the rooms again. Jehan-Claude was now living just up the road in a former farm building that had once belonged to the estate. It was a year after we had bought the place, but he still had the keys to our outbuildings.

This was something we would have to sort out, but for the time being it was OK as JC had been most helpful to the worker bees.

Spring had begun in the Loire Valley. A nice metaphor for the true start of our venture. The trees were sprouting new leaves, flowers poked up after a long, dormant winter. The birds sang us awake every morning as we gathered our thoughts and prepared for the new day. In our first weeks at the chateau, we felt the days warming and lengthening. We absorbed the smell of possibility around us. This set us on an optimistic path and helped us to put aside the true scale of work that lay ahead.

Each day we left the chateau early and visited the local *boulangerie*. The divinity of French bread and pastry is well established. But to experience the gifts of the local baker day in, day out was to realise why exactly we had moved in the first place. Every trip brought a sweet assortment of crusty bread with a chewy centre, fresh tarts and the odd eclair. Like our French neighbours, we made this trip at least once and sometimes twice a day, giving our day a sense of order and regularity. The trip to the bakery made us focus on the importance of every day's meal, the rhythms of everyday life.

We had found in the big city that eating was simply an errand, a tiresome means to an end, to be taken care of quickly and with as little fuss as possible. Here in France, the eating seemed, at least for us, to be the means *and* the end. You would get at least two hours for lunch each and every day while fitting in the errands and other mundane necessities around these essential acts.

Our daily rituals were punctuated from time to time by a trip to the weekly market in our small town. It is true that in parts of America, including New York City, and throughout England and Ireland, the farmers' market does in fact exist. In many cases, these markets were resurrected after long neglect and urban and suburban flight. With a new generation of families with disposable incomes, smart people came up with the idea to recreate the weekly market. These are authentic in the sense that they tend to cultivate local produce and rely on small landholders and family farms to supply the weekly goods.

The small-town market in France never went away. This isn't to say that French city-dwellers don't live modern, harried lives like the rest of us. The late-night *supermarchés* and the Wal-Mart- or Tesco-type monstrosities do exist in France. All arranged to cater to the needs of frantic modern lives. But alongside this clearly new arrangement is a vital, thriving network of tens of thousands of small country markets where most French families get at least some of their weekly produce. This is one of the myriad reasons we moved to France, to Europe, in the first place. We were looking to get back to basics. And we took full advantage of its goodness.

Our own market was a simple affair. Each week, it was filled with seasonal fruits and vegetables, tasty-looking but highly imperfect as all home-grown things tend to be. You would not often find the perfect, unblemished tomato, plump and red. It might be oblong or fat with tiny scars. But the taste was true tomato-ness, tangy-sweet and luscious. There was always a van full of meat, freshly slaughtered calves, half and whole pigs, mouth-watering sausages and *boudin*, a blood sausage that I had also found in my native Louisiana. We often frequented the cheese man, or *fromager*. He was a local farmer who specialised in goats' cheeses and a thick-rind, creamy, mouldy concoction that reminded us of the divine Gorgonzola of Italy mixed with peppers.

You could also buy a mattress or a pair of shoes or a polyester jumper, roller skates and a pair of cheap sunglasses. I presumed these were all made in China. So much for authenticity. The live fowl always fascinated me too. Every week, several farmers would set up with a selection of savoury birds including geese, turkeys, ducks, chickens, pigeons and pheasant. You certainly wouldn't enter a Marks and Spencer and negotiate with the butcher the ins and outs of butchering your own fowl followed by an in-depth discussion of preparation.

One day we ventured toward the turkey stall with friends who loved animals. Tom, a tall, rangy man with light hair and steely blue eyes, approached the farmer and asked him the price of the turkey, the one with the broken wing.

'Twenty euros,' the farmer replied.

'Sounds good. We'll take her,' Tom responded happily. 'We want to take her home and help mend her wing and make her a pet.'

The farmer stopped in the middle of placing the turkey in a hessian sack. He looked at Tom.

'What?' he barked.

Tom said, 'Yes, we want to help this bird. We keep turkeys as pets.'

The farmer yanked the bird out of the sack and placed him back in the cage.

'What are you doing?' a baffled Tom asked.

'You cannot buy my turkeys for pets. They are for eating.'

'What do you care what we do with the animal? It is the same money for you.'

'No turkey for you. They are for eating. No pets.'

Tom persisted but with the same result each time. Pets were not on the menu. With tradition comes certain ways of doing and being that cannot be questioned. We all shuffled off only slightly disillusioned with our quaint, French country market.

Within a few weeks of our permanent arrival, I sent out an e-mail note to friends and family alerting them to our official move. Most wished us well and promised, or threatened, a visit in the near future. One e-mail came back from our old sources of inspiration, Frank and Rosemarie of Roundwood House, which prompted us to think about our needs for the coming summer of work. We had met their son Richard on our visits to Roundwood. After a few correspondences back and forth, we arranged for Richard and his friend Andrew to stay with us for the summer. They would receive room and board, a small stipend, and a chance to experience France while working on the property and helping us get started. We mentioned this arrangement to other old friends in Ireland and soon we had four strapping Irish lads aged 15 to 18 lined up for the summer. We all made last-minute plans. The boys would arrive in two weeks and stay for three months. It seemed like a great plan. All parties were duly excited and looked forward to a fruitful summer. On our tight budget, especially in light of the imminent arrival of Hercule, the extra help seemed a logical, economical and productive way to proceed. Unfortunately, no one warned us that teenage boys eat their equivalent weight in food each day.

Meanwhile, Hercule arrived, ready to work and eager to sort out the incessant problems of the chateau. His room sat on the third floor of the north wing of the chateau. This afforded our new employee privacy and quiet. We agreed Hercule would use the kitchen with us. His movements were discreet and the first month went off without a hitch.

At nine in the morning exactly one month after our arrival, a large truck laden with a huge metal container parked at the front of the chateau. Apparently, the contents had caused some sort of stir at port in Normandy. Customs had held up the delivery for about ten days. When the container arrived, the seal was broken, which seemed to indicate tampering or entry into the container. The truck driver told us this was because *les douanes*, or customs, had investigated the load.

Simply happy to have received our shipment, we did not question the driver's word. Hercule, Jehan-Claude and I started unloading.

'It looks like all of these boxes have been punctured, opened. Do you see all these tears?' I asked.

'I think it is the customs, as the driver said,' Hercule replied.

'But why would they open *all* the boxes? Wouldn't they do a spot check?'

'I don't know. I will ask.'

Hercule walked over to the driver and they discussed calmly. The driver assured Hercule that this was standard, although he seemed a bit nervous, a little too eager to help unload the boxes. It was almost as though he wanted to help out so he could tidy up, reposition and close up the randomly scattered boxes in the container.

After a few hours, the container was empty. We had carefully placed some 150 boxes throughout the chateau. Packing peanuts and paper and stuffing were left strewn in the container, not so much from our messiness but from a recent ransacking on the docks of Normandy. It appeared for the moment that all was here. I signed the documents saying we had received delivery and everything was in good order.

Over the next week, we slowly unpacked and placed our humble possessions throughout the massive chateau. Quite honestly, we had very little of value save a computer here, a bit of cutlery and silverware there, books, kitchen utensils and the like. One day I opened our box of videotapes and video equipment. The box was virtually empty except for a few cords, connectors and a couple of black tapes in their original packing. I searched in a few nearby 'office' boxes looking for our personal videotapes. These included the videos of Blue's magnificent birth. She was born two years earlier in a birthing centre, in a tub. The event was the highlight of our lives so far. The tapes were missing.

'Bud, I can't find the tapes from Blue's birth. Have you seen them?' I asked, somewhat panicky.

'No. I'm sure they're around, though.'

'I can't believe this. I placed them very particularly in the box with the video cords. They're not there.'

'You'll find them. Keep looking.'

Bud wasn't too worried so I continued my quest. Throughout the next few days, it became clear the tapes were gone. As I said, we really had nothing of any monetary value, but in the whole scheme of things, these tapes were the single most important material possessions we owned.

'Bud, I can't find the tapes. I think they're gone.'

'I can't believe it.' Bud's eyes welled up. 'Why would someone take those ones? What was written on the tapes?'

Then it struck me like a flash of lightning.

'You know what, all the birth tapes were labelled "Blue Tapes".'

Some miscreant, some violating desperado thief had probably mistaken the birth tapes for 'blue', or pornographic, tapes. Someone somewhere along the long journey from New York had entered the container, rummaged through our things, found nothing of real value. Yet, for kicks or sexual curiosity, they had taken the only things that really mattered to us. Irreplaceable things that were valueless in one sense, yet invaluable.

We felt like our lives had been desecrated. The least of the violation was the fact that the tapes showed Bud nude and heavily pregnant, wandering around the birth room in full birthday suit just waiting to pop. Bud was not modest or shy. The real offence came from the taking of the tapes.

I once came upon a small quote from a writer who had spent years as a patient in psychoanalysis. He wittily described the ups and downs and dramas of his stern, Freudian analyst who acted more as drill sergeant than confidant or comforter. At his final session, the sometimes insensitive taskmaster-cum-analyst shared these words with our sensitive hero:

> 'So you see… in retrospect…' he went on, and stirred, rose, on the sofa, trying to force his full authority on his disobedient frame. 'In retrospect, life has many worthwhile aspects,' he concluded quietly, and then we had to stop. He sat looking ahead, and a few minutes later, with a goodbye and a handshake, I left.

In a very real sense, the mundane and anticlimactic feel and tone of this pronouncement is calming, liberating even. No matter what difficulty or pain or violation or displacement life throws at us, in the end, it can be affirmed, life has many worthwhile aspects.

We had chosen to leave our friends and family and jobs and lives and former aspirations for the great unknown of life in a foreign country. We were immigrants. We had gathered all of our belongings and set off for greater opportunity – not the chance to work, like most immigrants, but the chance to live a more authentic life. And, with our first steps toward a different path, we were robbed.

We went to bed that night still quite upset. We spoke of many things. All the little changes, the little losses, in our lives weighed heavily. I had effectively quit my job; we had moved, deserting our cosy, rundown apartment; we had left a life back in the States; and we had said no to everything that was. After a bit of whingeing, our talk turned to plans for the bathrooms and paint colours and the beauty of the woods in the spring. Then, imperceptibly but defiantly, we said 'yes' to the future at the Château du Bonchamps. Like life in general, the chateau had many worthwhile aspects.

CHAPTER NINE

Sowing

Didier arrived at the front door of the chateau in his neat, small, colourfully painted artisan's van. It is a nice touch in France that workmen – skilled workmen at least – are referred to as 'artisans'. In English, the word refers to a skilled manual worker or craftsperson. Its Latin origins translate as 'skilled in the arts'. It's nice to think of your plumber, painter or carpenter as an 'artist'. Reassuring. Not always accurate, but a comforting thought.

I had spent the past few weeks looking for painters and other workmen to start whipping the chateau into shape. I collected three or four names each for plumbers, painters carpenters and *plâtriers*, or plasterboard workers. This was our first *devis*, or estimate, for paintwork.

I shouted, *'Entrez!'* Our first potential painter came directly into the great hall. I went to meet him, happy that my poor French could lure someone into the house. Didier had long hair just below his shoulders, kind, searching eyes, a fleeting smirk, and stood at just over five feet. We shook hands in that French way that is not firm and manly in the English-American manner but a bit tepid and nonchalant. It consists, usually, of touching hands briefly and wagging one's arm from side to side. Often I manage only to get hold of a couple of fingers before the whole thing is over.

I offered Didier a drink but he seemed keen to begin the tour.

'Can we start in the south wing?' I asked.

We headed down the full length of the gallery and started up the south wing stairs. Our Liverpudlian workers had completed the gallery, these same stairs, the one bedroom on the ground floor, the dining room and the main stairs. Thankfully, they had also well prepared the first-floor bedrooms by scraping wallpaper off and filling in some holes in the plaster.

Didier and I slowly made our way around first one, then the second bedroom, aiming to go all the way through the ten large rooms on the first floor. After about three or four, Didier's eyes started to glaze over.

'There is much work to do,' he said, somewhat unnecessarily.

'Yes, but it's pretty straightforward. Sanding, painting.'

'Of course, but do you want the doors painted, the radiators, the ceiling, everything in the room?'

In my inexperience, I had not thought of all these details. Didier explained, logically, that all of these things are done at extra cost. I started to get scared.

'And there is much plaster work to do,' he added helpfully.

'You can do this?' I asked, pleaded.

'Yes, but there will be a surcharge.'

'Fine.'

Things were looking bleak for our little budget. We had briefly, every so briefly, considered doing some of the work ourselves. But it was clear, from my very few and sporadic attempts at minor renovation jobs, that I had absolutely no skill nor inclination to do the work. As the former owner, Monsieur Pernod, had indicated, this was unfortunate. One must learn to do repair jobs if one is to own a chateau, he had admonished. *C'est la vie.* Not possible under current ownership.

We finally made our way through the warren of bedrooms and small adjoining dressing rooms, many of which would become bathrooms. By the time we reached the second floor, Didier looked punch-drunk and utterly overwhelmed. As was I. Luckily, the second floor consisted of only two rooms and two bathrooms with a nice view over the pond to the front of the house, the outbuildings to the south side of the house and the woods to the rear. We stopped to admire the pond. An elegant grey heron landed majestically in the shallows on the north side of the pond and began his daily fishing expedition. He picked the hapless perch out here and there with ruthless efficiency and boundless grace.

Didier and I retired to the front of the chateau with a small aperitif before his departure. We sat at a white, rusted wrought iron table and chairs, looked out over the pond, watched the sun slip slowly behind the trees in the distance. It is always odd dealing with workmen. In one sense, you have all the power, the power of the purse. You are paying, you should be in charge. Yet the artisan always gives the impression it is he who deigns to alight on your property and do the work, as if he is dispensing a favour. We, the grateful payer-owners, are happy to have the harried, always busy workmen. But you are dealing with your house, your home, a very vulnerable spot, and you don't want to be taken advantage of. The stories of cowboy builders and the weak position of foreigners ordering work abroad played heavily on my mind. I thought of the predatory heron.

'I will have to come back and get precise measurements,' Didier noted casually.

'Perhaps you can go around by yourself and take them, yes?'

'No problem. I will be back at the end of this week.'

'Then you can meet my wife, Brigid, and talk about colours.'

I liked Didier. There was something kind and open and honest in his face that inspired me to want to hire him. There was at the same time something slightly discomfiting about his appearance that I couldn't quite get my head around. It wasn't anything serious, just irrational. It would have to wait. Bud would meet him too and give the verdict.

***

It was early June. The boys from Ireland had arrived, Hercule the gardener was beginning to wander the property looking

145

for something easy to do and Bud was plumply pregnant. We had made a few visits to the midwife in Manhattan to confirm everything was OK. After the move, we had been so frazzled that further care and trips to the doctor were ignored. This was fine with Bud as she has an inherent distrust of the medical establishment. Of course, she always says, you'd want a doctor in case of a broken leg or accident, but for pregnancy, most things go smoothly and normally, so why intervene? Let the baby grow and go his course, eat well, avoid the obvious bad things like alcohol. A simple philosophy but it worked beautifully for Blue, our firstborn.

Bud had been immensely busy in the months leading up to and surrounding the move. She is a designer by trade and has a great sense of colour and harmony. How she decided the colour scheme of the chateau came to her in a typical Budian way. She is great at taking other people's ideas and making them her own. I think it's in the DNA of fashion designers to search far and wide for something new and good and unique, modify it and make it one's own. Her choice of colours came from a somewhat unlikely source. In fact, French design purists might be horrified at Bud's idea of what today's chateau should look like.

By now, many people know the infamous story of America's expert of domestic bliss and decoration. Martha Stewart's rise and fall and rise again is well documented. Regardless of the rumours surrounding her, we have both enjoyed her work greatly. Bud and I would sit some days and watch the precision and focus of Martha's homemaking on her television show. There was something about her singleness of purpose, her dedication to perfection, her good taste that served as a soothing balm to the half-hearted and frenzied modern world we lived in. She's sort of Nigella Lawson meets Anthea Turner.

Martha brought something to American culture that was sorely lacking – authenticity. She made real things with her own hands and created objects that in some deep way struck a resonance in the hearts of millions of Americans. She had touched upon something essential and profound.

Like many design icons, Martha had turned her sharp business eye to the masses. So Martha did a deal on her home furnishings line with Kmart, the Carrefour or Tesco of America, and Bud found Martha's paint colours at Kmart in Soho.

Let's call it Martha meets chateau. Chateau Kmart chic. Bud fell in love with Martha's pastels. She felt these would create a light, airy effect in the massive, well-lit chateau bedrooms. Nothing Victorian or neo-Gothic or dark or old. Fresh and light and free. She chose light yellows and the palest of greys and robin's egg blue and some darker, earthier tones for larger rooms. Of course, as is the fashion, every colour seems to have a name that is almost edible, like Sea Oats, Heavy Cream, Pudding Mould, Sourdough, Bee Palm Red, Oat Straw, Cornmeal, Quaking Aspen, Dill Flower, Buckwheat, Quince Blossom. A lot of oats and straws.

I can't say Bud was being a purist. She simply liked these colours, liked the lightness of it all, and, just maybe, the pastels and softness of the scheme was a violent reaction to what we came to call *bordello chateau*. There is a tendency in French chateaux, an authentic, reproductionist tendency, to match pillowcases, drapes, toile, wallpaper and all prints in an explosion of flowers, fawns, nature scenes and jolly peasants. The typical French chateau room, if it makes a pretence to be a chateau at all, greets the visitor with a riot of prints that could blind an unsuspecting soul. Old-world, the *châtelain* might argue. Garish, one might respond. Sensory overload. Tiresome.

We were trying to be purists in all of the essential ways – leaving the original structure intact, highlighting original features, using mostly original materials. But in this one, albeit important matter, Bud just couldn't capitulate to the tired, clichéd, mostly tasteless remakes of yesteryear. Call us heathens, but so it was. We would find over the coming months that the young French and northern European visitors (mostly Dutch and Scandinavian) loved Bud's taste while the older French were simply baffled and disappointed.

Once the rooms were painted, Bud planned on putting up drapes throughout the chateau. At first, I didn't particularly see the need for drapes, given the cost, but Bud pointed out that the vast windows, without dressing, looked like gaping holes. Bud had worked strenuously to keep costs down by sourcing the fabric in New York. Most things in Manhattan were amazingly expensive but if you knew where to look, you could find a rare bargain. In harmony with her pastels, she chose Irish linen in ivory, subtle greens, light yellows and white. One day in the city, she had found a wholesale manufacturer of Irish linen, turned on her brogue and pleaded poverty. She managed to buy hundreds of yards of fine linen for around $1,200 (£650) and craftily arranged with a Chinese sewer in Midtown Manhattan to sew the drapes. Each hanging measured around two to three metres.

We had visited the sewer's shop and were only slightly taken aback by rows and rows of industrial machines spewing out the latest fashions for New York's top designers. But Bud was desperate. Faced with so many windows, she had to damp down her misgivings and get the job done. So, for about the price of one professionally fitted pair of window treatments, Bud fashioned miles of curtains.

As we waited for Didier's *devis*, we talked to Monsieur Mocques, the local plumber. He was happy to fit the bathrooms and we knew his prices were exceptionally fair. There was one small problem – he was booked solid until late autumn. We hadn't foreseen this. Of course, we would wait for this kind, fastidious man who knew the chateau so well. His help with our first guests had saved our skins. He gave us verbal prices of around 500–1,000 euros (£345–£690) for each of the eight bathrooms. And he would let us buy the *installations*, or fittings, so we could avoid the normal 25 per cent mark-up when the plumber supplies the goods. We sat tight.

We had delayed too long in contacting the artisans. Overwhelmed and underequipped with poor French, I dallied and delayed until most of the good workmen were *débordés* until the colder months. We weren't aided by the fact that everyone, every single human in France, artisan or not, took their holiday from late July to early September.

When we bought the house, we hadn't put much thought into a schedule. I think naively we planned on opening that very summer. Now with news that the work would not commence, earnestly, until autumn, we were left to plan and talk and dispute the coming invasion.

Anyone with the minutest experience of renovation knows two things: it always takes longer than expected and a budget is just a suggestion. These immutable laws caused us a bit of grief and not a little worry. We had escaped New York with about $100,000 (£55,000) – but this was for everything – bathrooms, paint, carpentry, furniture, tiling... simply everything. Oh, and we had to live on this until the business got up and running. We had set ourselves a nearly impossible task.

As we collected a few more *devis* and waited for the summer to pass, I spent the days with the lads from Ireland and the French gardener from Cape Cod. They certainly did most of the work, and I served an advisory role. Unfortunately, Hercule had also assumed this role for himself. It appears his plan was to oversee the work crew and make sure things were done right. Funny, we had planned on him doing some work. On the odd day, I dug in and helped with pruning, replanting, clearing brush and nettles, cleaning out outbuildings and knocking down temporary 1970s walls that split up large bedrooms. We mowed the lawn and strimmed and hedged and trimmed and sprayed weeds. The days were long at Bonchamps. The boys seemed to delight in the work, their first time away from home for an extended period of time. In the evenings we would all sit at the back of the chateau round a large wooden table and eat and drink and talk about the day's events together. Bud was occupied mostly with Blue and caring for our new unborn baby, so delighted in the lively chatter of these late, sun-filled evenings.

Andrew became the de facto leader of the boys. He was 17 and had worked at the Irish Roundwood House with Richard, the owners' son (also 17), for several years now. He and Richard were always great on offering advice on how things were done at Roundwood and what might work best. Andrew struck us as a very mature teenager. He had a thick head of red hair, a nice smile and a quiet conservative manner. Every evening before dinner, he would take a shower and come down in his slippers. The others teased him and his old-man ways lightly, but they respected him. Our two other charges – John, 15, and Tom, 18 – were sons of close friends who had helped Bud financially in tight times through college. They were not as used to hard work as Richard and Andrew but they were strong and eager. The four worked well together. Always something to do. And they performed admirably. Occasionally, they would all slip into the local town and play pool and drink beer. But because they were young, it never seemed to affect their work.

Meanwhile, Hercule continued to 'oversee' the work and drink secretly during lunch, which at forty-odd years of age *did* affect his work. I would meet with him each afternoon to talk about the day's progress. Inevitably, he smelled of alcohol. As the weeks of the summer wore on, Hercule began to take Fridays off. He would inform us, usually on Thursday, that he had worked a long, hard week and he was owed a day off.

'I can't stand that Hercule is taking off Fridays while the boys work so hard,' Bud said one evening.

'I know. I don't know what to do.'

'Well, we need to set him straight. He has to work like the others or he's out of here.'

'I will try to talk to him. It's awkward, though.'

'I know, but we're paying him five hundred euros a week. That's a ton of money.'

She was right. Hercule made almost double what the four boys made put together. Of course, we paid for the boys' food as part of the agreement. It had seemed like a good deal at the time. However, the boys' feeding costs seemed to be about double the mortgage for each month they were with us. No one told me that teenage boys consume their weight in food every day. But we did enjoy having them greatly and they brought life and passion to the once moribund property. The work they did would set the property on a good course for years to come.

I caught up with Hercule one day on his two-hour lunch break.

'Hercule, we have to talk. Bud and I are a little concerned about your work schedule.'

'Is there a problem?'

'We feel the Fridays off just aren't working for us.'

'You know the work week in France is thirty-five hours?'

'Yes, but that's the official line. We are giving you a place to live for free and you're your own boss for most of the day.' I was truly uncomfortable talking to Hercule about this. I didn't want to be argumentative or alienate our self-styled *maître de maison*.

'Yes, that is true, but I am working forty to forty-five hours a week.'

I couldn't really argue with this unless I pointed out that the boys were doing most of the work and he was doing most of the supervising. When we hired the gardener we hadn't expected to be offering early retirement. I think this is how Hercule saw the gig. How could I denigrate his work ethic and two-hour lunches without completely offending him? It was clear, I was an inexperienced lord of the manor.

It's surprisingly hard to be the boss, to be responsible for a grand estate. I realise there won't be much sympathy for someone in my position. But the chateau and the boys and the gardener and a couple of cleaning ladies we hired from the local town, along with the worries, the renovation, the anxieties about the business, the baby, the coming baby – all this did bear down on us.

In the heyday of the chateau, in the late 1800s, the owners, the Nepveu family, would have had about 15 to 20 full-time workers. Stable boys, gardeners, groundskeepers, foresters, nannies, cooks, groomsmen, carriage drivers, maids and a head butler would have all lived on the property working every day from dawn til dusk. The housebound workers would have lived on the second floor, in the *chambres de bonnes* or *domestiques* quarters while the rougher outdoors lads would have stayed in the outbuildings. All worked tirelessly to make the estate work. Most vegetables and fruits and livestock would be raised by the estate to feed this small army of servants. The main difference between the Nepveus and the Juneaus was a matter of means.

At the time, the Nepveus lived in a largely agrarian world with over a thousand acres of land. The land would generate income and provide a reasonably lavish life. The Nepveus could do virtually nothing and still maintain the chateau and a lovely townhouse in Angers and Paris for the winter. Furthermore, they would pay the servants literally pennies a day, plus room and board. This life, a vestige of a feudal society, seems to have suited all parties well. The owners lived a comfortable, large life while the servants had work for life, a place to live, occasionally education for their children, health care as such and a real sense of where they fit in the world. I will not glorify the servants' life. It must have been brutish and hard at times. But each and every man, woman and child had a place in the community, in the universe. It was simpler and more unjust at the same time.

We didn't have a thousand acres, but that little Guard's House was working well for us. We had booked, in this our first full year, about 15 weeks. Grand total for all our efforts: 7,000 euros (£4,800) or so. Better than nothing. But in the scheme of things, close to nothing. Our guests seemed to be pleased. No complaints. Just the comings and goings of happy holidaymakers enjoying their few weeks in the sun.

As the summer wound down, Hercule continued his crafty work schedule and I failed to correct him. The boys took a few weekends away from the chateau and met an occasional girl along the way. When the team was gone, the chateau was quiet and lovely too. I continued to work alongside them when time permitted. Some days I thought of myself as a latter-day Levin from Tolstoy's *Anna Karenina*. Like Tolstoy, Levin, one of my favourite characters in all literature, would work in the fields with the peasants in a romantic, honest attempt to get back to basics, to feel and smell and work the land. As we worked in the hot midday sun, I often thought of one particular passage:

In the very heat of the day the mowing did not seem such hard work to him. The perspiration with which he was drenched cooled him, while the sun, that burned his back, his head, and his arms, bare to the elbow, gave a vigour and dogged energy to his labour; and more and more often now came those moments of unconsciousness, when it was possible not to think of what one was doing. The scythe cut of itself. These were happy moments... as though by magic, without thinking of it, the work turned out regular and well-finished of itself. These were the most blissful moments.

Indeed, these were the most blissful moments. I can't honestly say that we were ever really unconscious of what we had undertaken, but there were times when all was right with us and the chateau. The work never seemed to end but on some days, this was fine with us. Most of the work with the boys focused on the outside of the chateau: shifting what seemed like tons of stones from long-abandoned projects; trimming hedges; mowing the lawn; rearranging the hundred or so doors and shutters in the outbuildings; and other things that made the property seem more manageable. Inside the house, we knocked down walls that were not part of the original structure, scraped more wallpaper in a seemingly endless task to find the plaster, and moved furniture from one end of the house to other trying to find the right fit for each room. At times the tasks were mundane and tedious. Then there were moments when everything seemed to come together and we witnessed the appearance of progress. From time to time, after a long day's work, we looked back and said yes, this was a good day.

One day, I happened upon Hercule at the end of his ritualistic French lunch.

'Hercule, do you have a moment?'

'Sure, what's going on?' So, this was it. The hard decision. Bud and I had argued about Hercule's status on the property. As we received more *devis*, we realised the mountain of costs and work ahead of us. Hercule did play a part in ordering the property and the boys had carried out his plans well, but we simply couldn't afford him... or his ways.

'I wanted to let you know we are thankful for all your hard work and advice. But as things move along, our costs and our worries are mounting. I have to give you notice. We will help in any way we can, with recommendations. But I have to give you your two weeks'.'

Hercule turned red. 'What do you mean? We had an agreement.'

'We did. And we agreed to three months. We are now in the fourth month. Like I said, we will pay you for the coming weeks while you sort out a new situation.' So painful.

'Why don't you stagger the work so you won't have as many expenses. Do some rooms now, wait on others. Open with fewer rooms.'

I was a bit taken aback at Hercule's advice. I felt awkward receiving business insight from our gardener. He wasn't entirely wrong. But then again, this was about more than money. It was about Hercule's self-realised retirement, long lunches and love of whisky.

'We've thought about that,' I managed. 'But we are pushing ahead with the original plan to open in the coming spring with seven rooms. It's the only way we can make it.'

'I can't believe you bought this chateau with no money,' he added. If only he knew how little money we had. This would be something we encountered in the coming months – every workman and visitor and supplier and friend would take one look at the castle and assume we were very wealthy people. It is not an illogical assumption, but in our case, entirely false.

'I'm sorry to say, we are already very tight. I hope you understand. And again, thank you for all your hard work.'

I had never fired anyone in my life and didn't like the smell of it. It appears I would make a terrible CEO or lord of the manor. Hercule was our first casualty. He took it well, though. He slunk off to his room to lick his wounds. I slunk off likewise to Bud and related the story. She was pleased. I felt a little depressed.

The next day, Didier turned up, with his *devis*. Bud and I quickly seated ourselves with the man himself in the library. We braced ourselves for the worst. In the time since his visit, we had gathered *devis* from a few other painters. The verdict was poor: one came in at 57,000 euros (£40,000), the second failed to turn in an estimate and the third was a respectable 37,000 euros (£26,000). Just painting, mind you. We had received another estimate for all the exterior windows: 12,000 euros (£8,300). That seemed fair. This would include sanding, recaulking, fixing broken panes and three coats of paint. We had no idea what things should or would cost, but this seemed, on an instinctual level, to make sense. That's all we had; instinct.

'This is the best price I can do,' Didier began as he pulled a sheaf of papers from a thick brown envelope. 'And I can begin in September, maybe late August.'

We greedily took the papers and awaited our fate. Bud's eyes lit up. She handed me the document. I searched almost frantically for the grand total.

'We will have to make some adjustments but this is pretty accurate. Maybe there are things I forget but this is good.'

I was almost shaking, with relief. 25,000 euros (£17,000) with an estimate of six months. Brilliant. Bud and I had to restrain ourselves from embracing him and begging him to move in with us.

'This looks fair,' I stammered. Bud and Didier spoke haltingly of what exactly the *devis* included. It was fairly comprehensive: one servants' staircase, 11 rooms, including large bedrooms and bathrooms, and two long first-floor corridors. We figured there was about 6,000 square feet in the *devis* and it would take him six months. The chateau would be ready just in time for next season. We were fit to burst with joy.

Being novices, we failed to negotiate or talk him down. The fees made sense and we were happy to book him. We signed straight away and paid one-third up front. Mocques the plumber would be coming later in the autumn. Everything was finally falling into place.

There was one last bit of business. Even though I had quit my job in New York earlier in the year, my company continued to pay me for accrued holidays and other such things through the early summer. With this bit of documentation and ersatz income, I met with our local bank manager to request a remortgage with an additional 50,000 euros (£34,000) for *travaux*, or works. We could already surmise that with the incoming *devis*, the cost of Hercule and the boys, bundled with another full year before we were off the ground, we would need this extra money. One year into the project and we were already running out. The loan went through at a lower interest rate than we had been paying. Our new mortgage: 2,500 euros (£1,700) a month, the same amount we had been paying but with a much needed 50 grand in the bank. For 25 years. Not bad for a chateau, but a painful burden with little or no income for the next year.

By late August of our first full summer at the chateau, Andrew and Richard had gone back to Ireland. Hercule packed his things quietly and discreetly while John and Tom remained for the last weeks of their school holiday. As the summer faded and the guests dwindled to a few late holidaying souls, John's sixteenth birthday arrived without notice.

'We were wondering if you wanted to go into town for a drink. It's John's birthday today,' Tom said.

'Sure, let me check with Bud and make sure she's OK. You know, it's always good to get planning permission for a night out,' I said.

The chateau was in good order and Bud thought it would be a nice idea for me to go out with the boys. Around seven that evening, the boys put on their best jeans and clean, beloved sports shirts showing off the latest line from Kilkenny's hurlers. They spent time pomading their black mops of hair, and then after dinner we piled into the old red van and started off to Angers, our nearest large town of around 300,000 people.

Conversation was modestly stilted on the road but we all anticipated a nice, relaxing night out with a few cold beers. In half an hour, we arrived in the centre of Angers and parked the dying truck near the hub of bar activity. In no time, we located an Irish bar along the *'rue piétonne'* and sat out the front. The evening was warm but pleasant and loads of students seemed to be enjoying a cold one and watching one another keenly.

After about three pints of Guinness, the conversation picked up.

'You can't ever tell Marion about this but there was one time we were in the bar near Ballacolla back home. John was eyeing up some lad's girl. Now this lad was a thick-necked, strong little fecker...' The stories spun out quickly and passionately as John and Tom told me of their adventures with girls and fights and drink and all the things young men do in the countryside of Ireland. Most of the stories began with the admonition: don't tell Marion. Marion was Bud's good friend from home and mother of these two strapping young men. I assured the boys that everything at the table would remain between us. Pub confidentiality prevents me from relating the full details of the adventures of Tom and John. Let us just say that the conversation was lively and violent and ribald. My adolescence was never so active or risky.

Soon I was telling stories of documentaries I had shot on dogfighting and Ultimate Fighting, the human equivalent of cockfighting where two brutal, inhumanly fit and strong men fight with no gloves and few rules save no eye-gouging, pulling hair, biting or groin kicks. The lads knew the 'sport' well and revelled in the details of faraway battles. A few more pints and we were eager for another bar.

We drifted off down the street as the boys enjoyed the sight of French university girls smoking and laughing and holding forth on the square. We landed at a nearby bar and positioned ourselves out the front for optimal viewing. The boys chatted quickly and started in – with a full helping of Irish charm – on the girls at the table next to us. All was proceeding as planned on this their last night out. John, well intoxicated at this point, took it upon himself to sidle up to the bar for a closer inspection of the girls inside. Tom and I held the fort out the front and enjoyed a perfect summer evening. By 10.30, the sun still hovered low on the horizon, as we sipped and chatted and recounted the summer's events, surrounded by the medieval Norman buildings.

Our calm reverie was suddenly broken by a loud fracas several tables away. Tom and I turned quickly to investigate the source of commotion. Two men, Moroccans, had pushed a couple up against a wall. They were yelling and gesticulating madly. Suddenly, one of the aggressors slapped the man hard across the face while the second aggressor grabbed the woman's arm, restraining her from helping the luckless man. Another man, seemingly part of the gang, stood watch in the middle of the street, gazing at his partners and looking up and down nervously. We took this all in within seconds. John continued his excursion in the bar chatting with unknown denizens and enjoying his Guinness.

Tom and I automatically stood up, sensing danger and overly ready for a little action. All that chatter of bar fights and Ultimate Fighting and vigorous talking shite made us hypersensitive to an impending opportunity. Tom was obviously fight-ready. I felt fit and relatively strong after a summer working and lifting with the boys. But the truth was, I had not been in a fight since my last year in secondary school. That one turned out OK for me but was over within minutes. My normal capacity to reason was inhibited by the source of most fights: beer. As we stood up, we glanced warily at one another filled simultaneously with repulsion and excitement.

Be careful what you ask for. Just as we stood up, rather blatantly, the three bad guys caught sight of us. The lookout man started over and stood directly in front of me while the woman-handler stood directly in front of Tom. The worst one, the hitter, decided to finish up business with his victim. The men started to yell and flail their arms. I couldn't understand much of what they were saying. I presume it involved well-worn phrases like 'This is none of your business, sit down', 'Do you want some of this?' and other pre-scuffle warnings and beratings.

Out of the blue, Tom's guy squatted down and kicked him just below the knee. Without hesitation, I leaned back, balled my fist and threw my entire 190 pounds behind a punch that connected with a loud crunch against my foe's mouth. He fell into a heap as Tom began his well-rehearsed work on an unsuspecting kicker. Out of the corner of my eye I saw only the last second of a punch coming from my left side, before I felt it hit right above my eye and I reeled backward. I think it was the original aggressor. As I stumbled back, I could see Tom standing over his charge, knee thrust down into the poor thing's chest, Tom wailing away as his victim tried to cover his face.

I immediately grabbed my puncher's shirt, pulled him in close and opened up a flurry of punches directly into his surprised face. The first guy I had hit struggled to his feet, bleeding from his mouth. At that moment, John finally copped on and came running out of the bar. As soon as he reached the middle of the street, the bloody-mouthed fella stood up and cold clocked him. John fell in a bundle on the paved stones. By this time, Tom's guy was rolling around on the ground nursing his wounds. My partner and I had managed our way across the street into an alley. I continued punching him and holding his shirt as John's assailant rushed to the melee. This one began reaching over his associate's shoulder, landing the odd punch while I worked away. For one brief moment, I looked down and saw my torn shirt and drops of blood on my front.

Then, with a fierce yell, Tom ran at full speed from our right and hit the original puncher with his full force and weight. I worked my guy to the ground and stood on him proudly. After Tom's final victim spun into a wall and plopped on the ground, Tom yelled, 'Don't fuck with the Irish!'

At this point, four or five *gendarmes* arrived on foot and broke up the fight. It wasn't clear right away who was at fault. The cops arriving on the scene could only have seen one big melee. But this being France, home of liberty, equality and fraternity, the *gendarmes* roughed up the darker of us, the Moroccans, slapped plastic restrainers on their wrists and hauled them off to the police station. We stood, hearts beating, shirts torn, blood dripping, trying to explain to the cops exactly what happened. The barman and several customers rushed to our aid and quickly relayed the night's events. Soon the cops left. We sat down.

The barman came up to us, 'You have all done what we could not do. Thank you so much. You will drink on me for the rest of the night.' Our fellow café denizens came over one at a time to shake hands and thank us. John and Tom's girls moved to our table as they recounted the unfolding of John's birthday night out on the town. We settled down and told the story over and over again, filling in details, embellishing and setting the record straight. Adrenalin continued to course through our veins as we relived the best and worst of what we had done.

After telling the story for the thirtieth time, we climbed into the van and started home. We told the story to one another several more times and arrived at the chateau. We walked into the kitchen and made Brie and ham sandwiches and told the story again.

Suddenly, Bud walked in. 'I can hear everything you're saying. It's two a.m. and you guys woke up Blue. Sam, what are you doing?' She was mad now, yelling. 'I'm almost nine months pregnant, you are a father and thirty-four years old and you're fighting like an animal in the streets of Angers. What were you thinking? And look, you tore your shirt. This is ridiculous.'

Of course, Bud was right. Infantile. Adolescent even. Who did I think I was, Hemingway?

'How could you put yourself in danger like that? They could have had knives or Lord knows what.'

It was true. It was totally irresponsible but I was still secretly a little proud. The boys stood quietly as Bud

165

rightfully reprimanded us. I could see them stifling giggles as Bud's indignant harangue continued.

The next day I was sore and somewhat bruised. We were all hungover, and quietly recounted the fight amongst ourselves as I drove Tom and John to the train station.

I pulled up and we unloaded the boys' bags. We shook hands. I thanked them for their summer's hard work. We promised to keep in touch.

Tom added as they passed into the train station, 'Oh, and Sam, please don't tell Marion.' I nodded in assent and opened the truck door. Driving back to the chateau, I felt a tinge of regret and thought ruefully, I am no Levin.

CHAPTER TEN

Wild Boar and Vegans

'What's that noise?' No answer.

Bud was sleeping soundly. Seven in the morning and for half an hour there had been a persistent, annoying buzz in the distance. Blue had been up most of the night crying in a fit of baby discomfort. Now this.

Rolling out of bed, I pulled on my trousers and shirt. I stumbled around looking for my shoes and finally went downstairs into the kitchen. I burst out the back door, grabbing a thick, long stick along the way, before launching into the woods determined to find out who or what was disturbing my precious sleep. As I walked deeper into the woods, the buzzing, whining sound of a chainsaw became more apparent, punctuated by the revving and idling of a tractor. After about five minutes, I came to the edge of the woods where I saw a blonde curly-haired farmer working

167

away on a large, fallen tree. I watched for a few minutes so I could understand exactly what was going on. It seems the tractor was pulling a very large tree off our property and into the neighbouring field while the farmer worked his busy-bee way through branches and vines. I looked to the right, then to the left, and could see major, major work going on.

There in the distance sat a sprawling earth mover with a huge digging bucket clawing away at a small hill that separated my land from the farmer's. We knew when we bought the chateau that Monsieur Cocteau was an aggressive farmer, chipping and angling and pushing his way centimetre by centimetre into Bonchamps's grounds. So the former owner told us. Evidently, he had taken to cutting branches and uprooting trees that dared to hang over the property line, without permission. I'd ignored the warnings.

Cocteau had ripped out bushes and trees and an entire kilometre of hedges in the hope of gaining a few extra centimetres on which to plant his corn. It seems he had been very busy on previous days when we weren't paying attention.

Furious, I spat out, '*Bonjour*. What are you doing?'

Cocteau walked over and offered his hand. I shook it impatiently and asked again, 'What are you doing? I'm the new owner of Bonchamps.'

'We are removing the *talus* [small hill-ditch]. It will make room for new crops and it is messy.'

'And this tree? I think it is mine. Why are you taking it?'

'Oh, well, it was dead. I was removing it for you.'

I think the technical word for Cocteau is 'cheeky'. I was furious. Yet I stifled my outbursts for two reasons – one, I did not know the exact legal situation of the *talus* (whether it belonged to me or him) and two, I had some vague sense that one should, generally speaking, get along with the neighbours. Something inside me said well, of course, he was right to clean up his patch and make room for more crops. The tree, still cheeky. Theft, really. But with thousands of trees around the *parc*, I was willing to overlook it.

'I see you cut some branches and trees here. I want to be clear. I don't want you to touch anything on the property without speaking with me first. We can work something out. Just let me know.'

'No problem,' Cocteau said with a slight grin on his weathered, red face. Yet he appeared surprisingly young. Perhaps it was the eyes or his short-cropped hair. Or maybe it was his stance, a bit insolent and insecure.

For the rest of the day, Cocteau continued his destructive handiwork. Every time I heard the noisy saw or caught an earful of the tractor tugging and straining, it made my blood boil. The *talus* had served as a nice buffer between his crops and the beginnings of our woods. I could see how the weeds and nettles and briars would bother a guy trying to plant and harvest crops. But as they say, good fences make good neighbours; and when lacking a fence, a *talus* is second best.

The former owner, Monsieur Pernod, had actually warned me about the Cocteaus and the surrounding farmers. At the closing of the sale, after giving the advice about doing everything myself, he had archly whispered in my ear at the closing, 'Watch the *paysans*, or peasants. There is a saying in France: "If you give a *paysan* a hand, he will take an arm". Beware.'

At the time, I found this offensive. First of all, I was a peasant, really. My ancestors had been poor immigrants and I just might, at any moment, have at least one uncle in jail. Also, considering myself an open-minded liberal and wanting to embrace French country ways, I refused to think of these hard-working, salt-of-the-earth farmers as peasants. And this coming from Monsieur Pernod, who as far as I could surmise, reminded me of my Louisiana country cousins.

The more I talked about my experience with our few acquaintances in town, however, the more I realised that *paysans* were revered in France. You might even call yourself a *paysan* and be proud of it. Pernod's slight was not meant as a slight but as what it was: a warning against crafty country people.

The farmer-*paysan* calls forth loads of passion in France, all over Europe for that matter. Forty years ago, 20 per cent of the population in France still had ties to farming and an agrarian life. But, like most Western industrialised nations, this number has dwindled as people, after the war, moved to the cities seeking jobs and a way out of country life. Today, the hardy few in farming account for roughly 3.5 per cent of the population. And agribusiness is consolidated into the hands of fewer and fewer mega-corporations, not unlike the UK and the States. Some reports tell us more than 30,000 farms in France disappear each year.

Perhaps it is for this reason the rare farmer is held in such high esteem. This romanticised notion is akin to the American cowboy, a myth only tenuously related to the reality. Most French view the farmer as the custodian or caretaker of the land. This little deceptive confection is wrapped neatly in the firm belief that most French, even if they've been living in the big cities for decades, have ties to the rural parts of France. There's much to gain from this delusion. France receives more than nine billion euros a year in subsidies, over 40 per cent of the EU's total agricultural budget. As we struggled to get the B&B up and running, this simple fact coupled with my noble neighbours' surreptitious activities started to bother me. No one offered me sizeable subsidies to start a business that could, just possibly, employ people… in rural France, no less.

Over the coming months, I saw Cocteau tear up trees, level ditches and dykes and bury streams, and wreak general, all-round havoc on the environment outside of town and around Bonchamps.

And as Cocteau nipped and tucked his way into our property and stole trees, the Pasteurs, who had so kindly offered home-made wine and foie gras those many months ago, continued to draw water from our pond to water their crops. They had reminded me of their rights. But when I looked closer, the deed of sale said the Pasteurs had the right to draw water from the pond 'in times of drought'. This *arrangement* was in force just up until the local town provided water service to their farm. The town had been sending water the Pasteurs' way since the mid-eighties, yet they continued to draw both in times of drought and in times of plentiful rainfall. 'Lend a *paysan* a hand…'

The Pasteurs' use of our water wouldn't have been a problem if they hadn't nearly drained it that first summer. They had rigged a small, powerful pump with a long hose that extended several yards into the pond. With this makeshift contraption, they would draw water, send it to another pump on their property and irrigate their corn and wheat crops. Given the dryness and the heat of recent years, it was simply too much for our little pond. Week after week, the water's edge receded. The process did produce one benefit: as the water drew back, a lovely mosaic of paved stones revealed itself. That was a nice effect, except that the pond was home to a beautiful and diverse ecology which included frogs, birds, fish, herons, *ragondins* and the thousand other living things that make up a country pond. And a low pond made the property look less attractive, depleted, despite a new-found stone border. For Bud, this aesthetic consideration was the least of her worries. She wasn't so concerned about the unkempt look of the place. She cared only for the animals and their livelihood.

The *ragondins* were a particular source of conflict between us and the Pasteurs. We loved them, but our farmer neighbours, and all other French country farmers, hated them. I knew the *ragondin* from Louisiana where we call them 'nutria'. They are cat-sized and vaguely beaver-like with long teeth, furry bodies but a tail like a rat. I suppose they are rodents, but they were our rodents. The Pasteurs had declared war on these fast-reproducing characters. They said the *ragondins* dug out the sides of the pond, carried diseases and deserved to be killed. Chevalier Pasteur used to catch them, on his side of the pond, and shoot them each morning. We confronted Chevalier, whose name means 'knight' in French. I'm not quite sure if knights used their formidable fighting skills to kill *ragondins*. He said he enjoyed it and had a right to shoot them because they were wild animals and belonged to no one. As long as our furry friends clambered onto his side, Chevalier could do has he pleased. If I'm not mistaken, Chevalier called this 'hunting'. The fact that he would generally shoot the poor things as they wriggled in one of his home-made traps did not deter him from viewing this as a sporting game. The tension with the farmers mounted. We were beginning to feel besieged on all sides.

***

One night, Bud and I managed to go out to eat. This was rare since we'd had Blue. The restaurant was a lovely, intimate *auberge* on the banks of the River Mayenne about 20 minutes north of the chateau, with stone and wood beams and old tiled floors and a divine menu. All local produce, all local wines – thanks to the farmers, of course. This was the flip side of the equation. The French are obviously passionate and proud of their *menus gastronomiques*, and rightfully so. Eating out for Bud in France was always a problem. I would start by saying: 'She is a vegetarian.' Then there would be a look of bemusement followed by bewilderment, followed by that whiff of Gallic disgust. Then came the begrudged plate of chips and a plain, lonely green salad. Bud often jokes about her second-class status in France, her lack of true personhood. Part of being a human in France is to eat and enjoy meat. Why live, after all, if you aren't here to eat everything that moves, save dogs and cats? But Bud, for many years at this point, had not eaten anything with eyes or parents. She wasn't a proselytiser. You could eat as you wished. She just couldn't do it.

We had heard good things about this restaurant, however. Bud was sure they could conjure up something nice from the garden, if not the woods. She started off with a creamy asparagus soup which hit the spot. We polished off our starters and drank wine while we waited for the main course.

Mine arrived first. Rare, almost bleating lamb with rosemary and fig jus surrounded by the most beautiful millefeuille pastries with local mushrooms, sautéed green beans and a small mound of potatoes coated in Brie. Bud's plate followed. A large white, gleaming bowl of boiled vegetables.

This in the land of culinary paradise. Bud looked down. 'They really must believe that just because I'm a vegetarian I don't really want to eat. I must be on a diet.'

Bud called the server over.

'Do you see my husband's plate? There are wonderful things all around the meat. Potatoes and green beans and mushrooms. Please give me that. A lot of that. This here is, well, it's rabbit food.'

'But, madam, you ordered from the 'coin minceur', the diet part of the menu. We thought you do not want to eat.'

When Bud had placed her tentative order she failed to notice that the veggies were all tucked into the Siberia of the menu. Unfortunately, there were no other choices. You could have meat with small sides of veggies or boiled mush.

So it was confirmed. As a vegetarian, you have no rights, you are not a citizen and you should be given boiled food. The waiter quickly brought out a lovely plate of just what I had, *sans* meat. It all boils down to a cultural misunderstanding. The one thing Bud had conceded when we moved was her veganism. To pass up the cheese in France really would be criminal. The French give a little, Bud gives, we are all happy.

The next morning another wake-up call. Too early, too loud. I struggled out of a deep, sweet sleep to the sounds of yelping dogs. It wasn't the first time, but it certainly was the loudest. I stumbled out of bed and, like a fireman on call, wiggled into my clothes and set off downstairs. I limped into the hallway and was met by Didier, our painter. He was struggling with some bit of sanding machinery and offered me an eager '*Bonjour*'.

'There are hunters in your woods,' he said helpfully.

'I'm going to meet them. Thank you.' Then I noticed something. There had been some niggling little thing about Didier that didn't quite sit well with me. We loved Didier. He was a perfectionist and a great, great artisan. But as I shot downstairs, hair sticking up and sleep still in my eyes, I saw them. Didier's tiny feet. That was it. A brief thought crashed through my head. Those are the smallest shoes I had ever seen. They were fit only to be hung from a car's rear-view mirror. That's what had been bothering me from the first time I'd met him.

I entered the kitchen and bolted out the door. The sounds of barking dogs echoed through the woods. There must be a dozen or so. This was the latest trick. The farmers knew they couldn't hunt on our property so they would send the dogs into the woods to flush out the deer. In this case, they were looking for wild boar, or so I had heard at the *boulangerie* the day before. It seemed there was a herd of ravenous maneating boar carousing the countryside looking for children. Or corn, at least.

I ran here and there in the woods trying to catch a dog or two. Two little fellas had wandered into a disused chicken coop so I bolted the door and locked them in. My only success. The dogs kept coming and I had no chance of catching them. At the edge of the woods, I could see hunters perched like birds of prey just waiting for some scared *chevreuil*, or small deer, to come bolting out. By the time I made my way to the edge of the woods and approached the hunters, they had all loaded up, jumped into their small utility vans and sped off to other, more promising destinations.

I went back to the kitchen. By this time, Bud was awake and making tea.

'I don't want them in the woods,' she said. 'One of us should go talk to them.'

'Bud, we can't fight them on every corner. We can't stop the dogs coming in the woods. They will just say they got away from the hunt.'

'I will go talk to them, then.'

'I'll come with you.'

We loaded into the van, Bud about to pop with baby number two, Blue sleepy-headed but up for the ride. I jumped in and we sped down our dirt road to the top of the property. There sat Chevalier, gun in hand, surrounded by three or four like-minded farmers.

'What's going on?' I asked angrily.

'We are hunting the boar. The mother and her babies have destroyed our crops and we have a right to hunt them.'

'You are not allowed to hunt on our property.'

'We are not on your property,' Chevalier said. He was right. They were just at the edge. Waiting. Chevalier peered at us through his thick glasses, sweat dripping from his grey curly head, rubber boots and torn shorts completing the picture.

Bud stepped in, 'Chevalier, I am a vegetarian, I don't eat meat. I don't want any hunting around or on the property. Please respect this.'

At this point, Chevalier translated for his comrades in arms. One older man stepped forward. He wore a thick beard, an enormous belly, chock-full of boar sausage, I presumed. Suddenly he started yelling and pointing in Bud's face. I couldn't believe my eyes; here was a man that we didn't know trying to intimidate my pregnant wife by screaming. Just months after my rumble in the streets of Angers, I felt confident of my own potential to intimidate.

I stepped in front of this audacious assailant, pointed in his face, yelling. In English.

'You get the fuck off my property,' I yelled repeatedly, emphasising each syllable with a clarity that transcended language. I grabbed the man's gun and held it firmly to the side, thinking, *that gun better be made of chocolate because I'm going to make you eat it*. I thought maybe this wouldn't translate so well, so I kept it to myself.

Chevalier quickly stepped in. 'That's enough, that's enough. We will back away. Jean-Paul, call your dogs.'

The old man fired a parting volley, 'You should go back to your country. We don't want you here. We have the right to hunt.' This last phrase he repeated many times as he wandered off.

'This is my country and I will stay here as long as I like,' I ventured.

The troops eased away and set up shop in a neighbouring field. Hard feelings all around.

'Sam, you didn't have to be so aggressive. I was handling it fine.'

'No one, and I mean no one, is going to yell at my wife and try to intimidate her.'

'You're right, but you could have been calmer. We need to live with these people.' Bud was more amused than scared or annoyed. It did bother her deeply that people were killing living things but she wasn't entirely comfortable with confrontation – at least not the way I went about it. She did have a point. Better to negotiate than bully.

In a sense, it was true. What right did I have to come to the French countryside and tell these farmers what to do? They had gained the right to hunt through a hard-fought and vicious battle over the centuries. There was a time when tenant farmers needed the chateau owner's permission to kill their own chickens; nothing would be killed without the say-so of the *seigneur*, or lord. The kings of France had long hoarded the sacred right of the hunt. Hunting on private property was punishable by death up until the turn of the last century.

In the last presidential election, the Chasse, Pêche, Nature, Traditions party (party for hunting, fishing, nature and traditions) had garnered close to four per cent of the vote while sending a good few representatives to the European Parliament in the past few years. This was a profound issue and I could feel and understand their anger. Here we were, 'rich' Americans buying up their patrimony and then demanding they obey our rules. This after a thousand years of battle to win the right to live off the land and do as they please.

All this was further complicated by my own brief career as a hunter. I used to go out with my father into the swamps of Louisiana. We only managed to knock down a few ducks here and there. My brief hunting life ended one day when I was 15 and shot a squirrel in the woods with a small Beretta .410 shotgun. He squirmed violently on the forest floor. I moved closer and saw a long black mark along the spot where his genitals used to be. It made me sick and from then on, I only went to the woods and the swamps to eat and drink beer with the men.

★★★

The next morning came again much too quickly. Groggy and feeling hungover without the benefit of having drunk anything the night before, I was aroused from a deep sleep by a persistent clanging. I rubbed my eyes, looked at the clock on my nightstand and thought this had to stop. I couldn't take another premature wake-up call. I quickly realised the clanging was coming from a bell at the back of the house. The bell, mounted about five metres up the stone wall outside the kitchen, was loud. Bud and I had surmised it was the bell used to call the workers and servants for dinner or to do chores from the far corners of the estate. It was our only 'doorbell' and someone was rigorously tugging the rusted metal chain.

I stumbled downstairs and flung open the door. Two men were leaning casually against a small utility truck. One looked vaguely familiar.

'*Bonjour, je suis Monsieur Cocteau. Et voici mon fils.*' I am Mr Cocteau, he said, and, pointing to the younger one, 'he is my son.'

The younger man was the tree thief. The older man was identical to his son; stocky, with bandy legs, glasses from the sixties, a white T-shirt and long, green rubber boots. He continued in French, fast and heavily accented. I should know an accent since mine could cut wood.

'We need to talk. Do you remember yesterday?' He peered up at me with raised eyebrows and a slight smirk. He seemed to be enjoying this. But I could tell he was not happy. I had some remote recollection of yesterday... I ate, pulled weeds... of course, the wild boar incident.

'That was my brother you met,' he said. Oops. 'Do you see that chainsaw in the back of my car? I could cut your sign down this morning.' Cocteau was referring to the panels we had posted at the end of the lane: '*Château du Bonchamps, Chambre d'hôtes et Gîites, Mariages et Seminaires*'. The signs sat on the lonely country road and no one but the locals would ever see them. But we were happy to install these small symbols of our new business.

'Why do you want to do that?' I asked, not quite sure what was happening.

'You cannot yell at my brother when he is trying to hunt boar. We are trying to protect our crops. These beasts create great destruction on the land. It costs us money.' The son glanced at the ground with reddened cheeks, seemingly not really wanting to take part in this exercise of male dominance.

I tried to force my brain to work. This wasn't good. Opting for the path of least resistance, I asked them to sit at the teak table just outside the kitchen so we could talk.

'First, let me make you some coffee.'

'*Oui, s'il vous plaît.*'

I padded inside, ground the coffee, poured it into a large, glass French press and waited for the water to boil. I didn't know what to do, but hospitality seemed the best approach. I poured the coffee, stepped out of the kitchen and sat with the Cocteau men.

'So, please tell me what is going on?'

'You see, we must kill the boar to save the corn and the wheat. They reproduce and destroy many things. It costs money.'

'Yes, you said that. I understand. But my wife does not want animals to be killed here.'

'*Pourquoi?*'

'She is an animal lover and a vegetarian.' The Cocteaus laughed. What an absurd concept!

'That's OK, my daughter-in-law is a vegetarian too and we laugh and tease her about it. But we respect this.' This was unexpected, to say the least.

'Then you can see the problem she has with hunting.'

'Yes, but it is our right. And we are trying to live with the land and protect our things. And the mayor has allowed us to hunt. But, of course, we need permission to hunt on your property.'

'I understand. I could say it is not possible to hunt here. But if you tell me in advance, maybe we can work something out. But honestly, we are afraid for the children when there is shooting. And we will have guests here who will be unsafe.'

'What sort of business are you running?' This was a welcome change of tone.

'Let me show you.' I then took these hardy farmers into the chateau and gave them the finest, most extensive tour to date. They walked around the house, eyes wide and very curious. They told me they knew the house but had never been inside, despite living less than a kilometre away for 40 years.

We ended up in the library, shelves lined with old books, a massive oak-carved mantelpiece. They were impressed. My goal was to impress but also to show them all the rooms we had to rent out while we lived in just a small part, modestly, not unlike them; workers, just trying to make a living, like them.

I think they got the point. They smiled and talked briefly about their families. They told me they moved to the region four decades ago but still felt like outsiders. They said they knew how hard it was for 'blow-ins' like us. Considered an outsider after so long? My, we had a long road ahead of us.

We wrapped up with the normal courtesies and well-wishings. We hadn't really resolved the outstanding issue, but good feelings presided. I think they simply wanted a little respect. Don't we all?

As I escorted them to their truck, Monsieur Cocteau stopped abruptly. He turned quickly and a big, self-satisfied smile spread across his face. He pointed into the distance. There, as sure as we were standing there, were a family of wild boar trotting around the apple orchard which we could just see through the trees. There was one immensely large bristle-backed, long-tusked male accompanied by his slightly smaller mate rooting around with three little ones nipping at their heels. I couldn't believe my bad luck. Bud and I had often wondered why the orchard looked as if a bulldozer had dug up large patches of grass and mud. Here was the answer. Hungry, destructive boar.

'See. You should know they do the same thing to our crops. And think of ten or twenty doing the same thing. This is why we kill them,' Cocteau said, delivering his final argument. For him, the matter was settled. As they drove off down the road, I could see the father patting his son on the shoulder and tilting his head back in uproarious laughter. 'We showed him,' he might have been saying.

I could certainly see their point. Here some American and his Irish wife sought to overthrow their hard-won rights. Of course, we owned our property and had the right to deny hunting and incursions. We wanted to protect Blue, and ourselves, from stray bullets and overeager hunters. I couldn't come to an answer, a peace, with this question. Like many things, life is complicated and unclear. But I left our meeting resolved to tread more lightly, to respect the farmers and their rigorous lives. It was all foreign to us. And so were we to them. This, I promised myself, I would try hard not to forget.

CHAPTER ELEVEN

Autumn Sonata

We were lurching into autumn, and the long, pretty summer days were starting to shorten. One by one, the sundry workmen we had cobbled together from seemingly infinite phone calls placed with the help of the Pages Jaunes, or Yellow Pages, started to appear like mushrooms after a vigorous rain. Didier was fully engaged, winding his way from bedroom to bedroom. The oak exterior windows were in poor shape, so Ludovic began his journey – sanding, stripping, resealing and painting (three times over) 156 windows. And our carpenter, Gilles, was set to begin. Gilles had come recommended to us by Didier, with the warning that Gilles was in fact *marginal*. What this meant, I wasn't sure. I assumed it meant something like the English 'outside the mainstream'. As a rule, we liked marginal people, feeling sometimes that we too didn't quite fit into the conventional run of things.

185

The autumn days were crisp, brilliantly clear and bracing. A very pleasant time to be in the Loire Valley. The leaves started their little sojourn into dormancy and near death, the pond swelled with a few days of rain and a certain quiet melancholy descended on the property as everyone readied themselves for winter. All the worker bees from the summer, the boys and Hercule, were gone now. It was just us and the French gang. We waiting for the new baby and the artisans toiling gently, quietly, imperceptibly away in the bowels and heights of the castle.

The time was nearing. We would, in a matter of days, embark on a journey – the birth of our second child. Our first birth experience was a near idyll at a stand-alone birth centre in the middle of Manhattan. The birth centre was staffed exclusively by midwives and all medical intervention was viewed with suspicion. There were no pain medicines, no monitors, no doctor meddling. Just a midwife, a woman, her husband and a baby. And a nice large tub filled with warm water for the comfort of the mother. Blue was born in water and rested with her mum in complete peace, free from the wandering hands and fussy intrusions of more traditional hospitals. This, our second baby, would be born in France. The French had different ideas about birth and motherhood.

Well-meaning neighbours and friends had directed us to a private clinic in Angers. We were told the care was more meticulous, more specialised, more personal. And the baby would be delivered by a doctor, not a midwife. Bud and I have a natural distaste for and distrust of doctors and much prefer the experienced, not-so-medical hands of a woman artisan whose métier it is to deliver babies. If we had thought clearly about the implication of doctor 'care', we probably would have opted for the public hospital where midwives do all the heavy lifting unless, of course, there is a serious problem. But we were a little anxious about having a baby in a foreign land with a language not our own. So we opted for caution and went the private route.

Roughly a week before the big due date, we met with the doctor to lay a firm birth-plan, as they say in the business of having babies. We drove our beaten-up red truck into the big city and arrived at our appointment a little early.

All the normal things unfolded with the midwife: blood pressure, heart rate, pee in a cup.

Then the doctor came in and Bud laid out her plan.

'I do not want an epidural and I want free movement during labour. And if the baby tears me when he comes out, do not cut, let it tear. I want the least possible intervention.'

'This is not the way here. We will intervene as we see fit. Are you sure you do not want a painkiller?'

'Absolutely not. It passes from me into the baby and can have effects. Inability to breastfeed, lethargy, and so on.'

'It is nothing for baby. Everyone here takes the pain medicine.'

'I am not everyone. Please respect my wishes.'

'It is your body. But if the baby goes over the date, we will have to induce.'

'Everything will be fine,' Bud reassured her.

Despite the odd expressions and occasional grimaces of the doctor as Bud laid down the law, we had found the medical system in France exceptional. We no longer had insurance from the States and we weren't quite in the system in France. At this point, we had not properly registered the business and had not been paying into the social system. We would have to pay for the birth out of our own pockets. So far, this had not posed a problem. Bud had undergone some of her obligatory doctor's visits with a couple of sonograms, each one amounting to 39 euros, whereas in the States, the same procedure would run into the hundreds if not thousands of dollars. And the care was prompt; no long waits, agreeable and attentive staff. As Americans, we had long heard of the ills and horrors of socialised medicine (man goes in for appendectomy, comes out without one leg... that sort of thing). Not in France, it seemed. We hoped for the best.

By the end of September, Bud was overdue. We had learned from Blue's birth that being late was no cause for concern. A few days, a week, the kind midwives at our New York haven showed no signs of concern or haste. Let the baby come as she will. France was different.

When Bud was a day late, we received an urgent call from the clinic. We chose not to answer the phone and to ride out the panic. The message left urged us to sprint to the hospital for immediate and much needed care. We were able to ignore the urgent pleadings of our doctor because we had faith in the simple fact that more than 80 per cent of all births are normal with no complications. We had no reason to believe things were complicated. So why intervene?

In fact, we weren't quite sure whether she was a day or a week late. Depends on who you asked or what calendar you consulted. The French usually counted 38 weeks while Yanks liked to think more in terms of 40 weeks. It's all very inexact in any case. The next day, we decided to go in. Just to say hello. And assure the doctor that *we* had everything under control.

'You are late and I am very concerned,' the doctor began.

'It is actually not clear when my exact due date is. I think we have time,' Bud responded.

'I do not like this. I want to induce you,' the doctor said.

Bud stood her ground. 'We do not think it is a good idea. Once you begin on this path of intervention, it leads to more intervention and problems. We truly believe this.'

The doctor was displeased. 'This is not the way things are done in France. I say what is appropriate. We must induce you.'

'We will not do this and there is no argument. It is bad for the baby.'

'Then you will sign a document saying you forego my recommendation.'

'No problem.'

'May I examine you?'

'Of course.'

The doctor made the examination, then said, 'You are partially dilated so it appears things are moving along. But if this continues for another day we will have to take immediate and invasive action.'

'We will see. And then make a decision.' No budging Bud on this point. I simply watched as Bud took things into her own intuitive hands.

Strangely, later in the evening as we were having a nibble in the kitchen, Bud felt those familiar pangs that let us know, without a doubt, she was going into labour.

'Sam, I think it's beginning. I swear she induced this somehow. During the exam, I think she might have rubbed some gel down there to speed things along.'

'I'm sure it will be all right. You can handle it.'

Easy for me to say. We set our little plan in order, taking a long walk in the woods and making sure our overnight bags were ready. I began videotaping here and there, for posterity. Things were proceeding nicely. I was checking my watch, timing the contractions, both their length and the interval between each, like a good husband. I thought quietly to myself, what happened to the days when the father could pop off to the pub, sip nobly from a pint and wait for the whole thing to wrap up?

Everything was going smoothly. Then it struck me like a bolt of lightning.

'Bud, what are we going to do about Blue? Is she coming with us?' We had debated whether or not Blue would attend the birthing. In the end, we thought it might be a little too traumatic for two-year-old Blue to see her mother in such pain.

'Good point. Call Véronique. You talked to her before about this, hopefully she's ready.'

Véronique was a friend and sometime house-cleaner from the village. I had mentioned to her the impending birth and our half-baked plan which included phoning her at the last minute, possibly bringing her own three children to the chateau, and asking her to sleep on the sofa while Blue played in the television room. When I first spoke to her about tending Blue in our absence, she simply responded, '*Mais elle est sauvage, non?*' But, she is wild, no? I wasn't surprised by her observation. We had found in our short time in France that the French were rather more strict with their children than we tended to be. Other people had noted the animal nature of our only daughter. We liked to think she was simply carefree and expressive.

'Véronique?'

'*Oui.*'

'It's Sam. Bud is going into labour. Are you available to come over now? We need someone to watch Blue this evening.'

'It is no problem, but my husband goes to work at five tomorrow morning. Can you be back by then?'

'Yes, we should be done by then.'

It is clear we are not the best planners. Luckily, Véronique was free. She came by at 8.30 and wrangled with Blue as Bud felt the surge approaching. By 10.30 that evening, Bud's contractions were coming fast and furious. We loaded up the van, said our goodbyes and started down the road as Blue yelled at the top of her lungs.

The trip was not easy. Riding in the van was like sitting in a tractor on a very bumpy road. The road was perfect all the 30 minutes to the hospital, there were just no shock absorbers. We arrived at the hospital, where everything was closed up tight. I approached the side entrance and found a sign which told me to 'appuyez ici' or 'press here' for emergencies. So I did as ordered and heard a voice greet me over the intercom.

'My wife is in labour. We are here to have the baby,' I said.

'Please come in.'

We entered the dark hallway and made our way dutifully to the third floor. We stepped out of the lift into the main waiting area. A midwife appeared from the shadows and led us to a room. Bud stopped suddenly with another contraction, unable to move, paralysed with the weight of the impending explosion.

We hurried with our things to a clean, private room where I made ready our few belongings. The next contraction was nearing as Bud doubled over and let out a tremendous groan, a bellow really. Another midwife rushed in to give aid. Bud moaned loudly again and the midwife frantically started shushing her. I couldn't believe how frenetically she was trying to quieten Bud. Appalled and angered, I said, 'You need to leave this room immediately.'

Bud reprimanded me, 'Sam, please don't fight with the midwife. It's OK.'

'I can't believe she's "shushing" you. They're so damn discreet here, they don't want you to act like a normal woman and let out the pain.' The French are a very *discret* people. It is always imprudent to make a scene, whether at a restaurant, grocery store, or anywhere in public. Generally, this is a wonderful, valuable quality. Not here, though, not now. I think it was odd for the midwife at this clinic to hear a scream. Our doctor had told us most, if not all, French women have *péridurales*, or epidurals. But that wasn't Bud's chosen path.

'It's OK. Relax,' she managed through pants and grunts.

Personally, I would have an epidural for teeth cleaning. Bud was different. She wanted it *au naturel*, real and full of all the good and bad feelings associated with childbirth. God bless her.

Sometime after midnight, the doctor arrived. If she was happy, she didn't show it. She was all business. She led Bud into the birthing room. I should say 'operating room', for it was all bright lights and clinical alienation. The doctor instructed Bud to lie on her back, the worst possible position in which to give birth as there's no gravity. Bud tried in vain as the 'transition' began. Apparently, this is the most painful time as the baby actually 'engages' and moves down the birth canal. Ouch. The doctor peered down there. The baby was head down but his face was turned the wrong way. Not good.

Bud's labour stalled at this point, while the doctor and her dutiful midwives were busy fiddling with the stirrups. Again, the worst possible thing for a labouring woman but convenient certainly for the doctor.

'Stop messing with those things!' Bud bellowed. She was at the point of no return. She heaved herself over on all fours and began the final, primal push.

The doctor leaned back and petulantly threw up her hands, then folded her arms.

'If you are like this, I can do nothing to help you,' she complained. Astonishing, a hissy fit in the middle of a birth. I was speechless. Who says the French are difficult?

Bud continued her hard work and just as the head appeared, she turned over and assumed the 'proper' position for our sulky doctor. With a tremendous effort and a concentrated energy found possibly only in nuclear reactors, Bud forced the little fellow out. And so Grim was born. He immediately breastfed and began the journey into the rest of his life.

Bud passed out on the birth–bed-slash-operating-table and I fell asleep uncomfortably on a nearby chair. The doctor was long gone by the time we drifted off. I set my alarm for 4.30 a.m. so that I could begin the trip back to the chateau and Véronique could see her husband off to work.

I returned with Blue shortly after 6 a.m.

'Sam, I have to get out of here. They were waking me up all morning to make sure I was sleeping.'

'Are you sure you want to go? They say you have five days in the hospital minimum.'

'Yes, let's go. Let's talk to the doctor when she comes in and get out of here.'

By mid morning, the doctor's rounds landed her in our room. She was a bit stiff and cold with us as, I'm sure, images of Bud's rebellion flashed in her mind.

'We would like to leave today if that's OK.'

'You cannot leave. You just had the baby. I cannot give you permission to leave.'

I am never good when told what to do. Neither is Bud.

'Well, we're leaving. It's more restful and better for the baby to be at home.'

'You must sign yourself out and sign a statement saying it is against medical advice.'

'No problem, just show me the paper.' We signed yet another piece of paper.

'And I will not continue to have Mrs Juneau as a patient.'

That was a new one. We had never been fired as patients before. Fair enough. I suppose there comes a time in a doctor's life where the burden is greater than the reward. We signed all the documents and headed downstairs to pay. I entered the payment office warily, as I couldn't imagine what the cost would be. As the accounts woman began printing up our bill, Bud and I looked at one another, our eyes searching for a sign of hope, a sign that it wouldn't crush us. The same thing for Blue had run into the $6,000 (£3,200) range all paid for by insurance, but this time we had no safety net. The bill took an awfully long time to print and contained many pages. When she was done, I extended a shaking hand. 1,021 euros (£700). Brilliant. This was a break we really needed, and briefly reaffirmed our love of France.

We returned home without incident and Bud took to bed with the lovely, strapping Grim. I can't really give you a good reason for his name. Upon hearing the new name, some of our family and friends predicted bullying and a childhood of misery for the poor thing. My mum simply said 'Oh,' when I told her. And again, 'Oh, Sam.' As in, 'Oh, Sam, how could you do that to your offspring?' I had met a lad once years back in a pub in New York. He was Swedish and quite tall with long, black hair, a sharp nose and a prominent jaw and broad forehead. My friend knew him and introduced us casually. He said, 'Sam, this is Grim.' The name sort of shocked me. I thought it was unforgettable and unique. After I told Bud about my meeting later that evening, we both agreed it was one of the most striking names we had ever heard. Now, here was Grim. Under stiff resistance from the in-laws, we comforted ourselves with our choice by noting the name means 'daring or bold' in Old Norse.

I served her breakfast in bed for the next few weeks as we settled in to the new room we had prepared. Didier, the painter, had warned us that he was making good progress and that we needed to move the family bed. We chose a lovely large room down the hall. The room had eighteenth-century wood panelling on the walls which neatly hid vast oak cabinets. There was a later period marble fireplace with a sweet, grand *trumeau* with intricate neoclassical carvings of nymphs playing among swirls and gold trim. The floor was composed of *tomettes*, or terracotta tiles. Perhaps cold in the winter but pleasing to the eye. This would be our new nest for the long winter ahead.

We had bought a Louis XVI silk-covered bed at a local antiques show. This would be our bed which we'd share with hungry Grim. Blue would sleep in a perfect wrought iron single bed that we found in the attic. There weren't many treasures like this in the house when we bought it, and we found this particularly pleasing. We had decided to name all of our rooms after trees on the property – the Chestnut Room, the Oak Room, Sycamore and Sequoia Rooms. This we called the Cedar Room in honour of the massive 250-year-old Lebanese cedar planted behind the chateau and in clear view from the windows of this room, with a nine-metre trunk and sprawling branches extending skyward.

Like many deciduous trees, the cedar had the peculiar habit of shedding branches every so often. The top of the giant was littered with broken bits and pieces and tended to create a shabby yet grand appearance. Like most things at Bonchamps, the imperfect decay of the tree accented nicely the house's faded elegance and irregular beauty. This specific tree had the added virtue of serving as a lookout for the two rather noisy owls that lived in the rear tower of the house. I had met one, in the library on that eventful night a couple of springs prior.

Every evening, just at sundown, the owls perched on the large stone oculus that led into the tower above the attic. With a screech and a dramatic flurry of feathers and impressive wingspan, the owls would fly out to the cedar, a sort of scouting spot for the night's hunting. They were just white and brown barn owls, nothing fancy or overly colourful, but they were our owls. The fact that they left tons of waste and undigested small animal parts in the tower bothered us not one bit. We felt privileged to have them as guests. Or perhaps we were their guests. In any case, they offered a glimpse of wildness, a little spectacle to punctuate the cool evenings that now descended upon us as we stumbled into October.

Every day I would make my rounds of the house and the property in general to monitor the work and make sure our merry band of artisans were happy and plugging away. One morning I stopped in on Didier as he pried loose bits of worn plaster from the ceiling.

'This is very fragile. Old. I will try to repair but you really need a plasterer here.'

'Do what you can and if we need someone else, I will get them.'

'I am not really comfortable doing this work and it's not budgeted. But I can do some things for now.'

'Please do. And let me know what your additional costs are.'

I realised the only way we could survive on our small pot of money was to guard costs and milk the artisans. Sounds ruthless, but it was the only way we could make it to the next summer, our first full planned season. I had offered to pay Didier for his extra labour but I was sure his costs would be far less than a skilled, registered plasterer.

I chatted briefly with Didier about the upcoming sardine festival in nearby Cheffes. It seemed odd to me that a town so far inland would have a sardine festival. Didier assured me it was a grand event with thousands of people, cheap wine and good food. Perfect. He noted too, casually and with gusto, that the end of every sardine festival climaxed with dancing girls from Paris. Nude dancing girls. A must-see if ever there was one.

I left the room with Blue and started down the hall. Just behind me, I heard a crackling sound, then a rumble, and finally a tremendous, house-shaking crash. I picked up Blue and rushed back to Didier. There on the floor, in a heap of dust, wood laths, plaster and assorted rubble, lay small

Didier with a bewildered look on his face. And there, sure enough, his little feet poked out of the debris, pointing up to the hole in the ceiling.

'What happened?' I cried.

Didier wiped the dust from his eyes and peered out from his plaster tomb as a cloud of dust billowed down the hall and out the windows in the corridor.

'I was pulling loose some plaster here in the ceiling. I think the weight of old plaster and some rotten wood laths made the ceiling fall in. *Quel bordel!*'

I looked up and saw a gaping hole in the ceiling that took up the better part of the room.

'I am so sorry,' I said. I felt guilty that I had pushed poor little Didier beyond his skill level into near disaster.

I leaned down and started to clear the debris away from our shocked painter as he picked himself up and dusted himself off. Blue began to cry. Needless to say, after this, Didier was less willing to take on other jobs not in his métier. We decided to leave the hairline cracks in most ceilings and perform minor cosmetic surgery on the long-failing plaster. Luckily, the actual structure of the walls and their large stones were in decent shape. I asked Didier if he thought there were other unstable ceilings in his path. Didier shrugged, not seemingly concerned, and said, '*On verra.*' We will see.

I told Bud about the most recent catastrophe. For the time being, she was preoccupied, caught up in the bliss of new motherhood, caring for our new baby and breastfeeding 17 hours a day. Bud was good in this state and nothing unnerved her. Progress was being made, the men were showing up and working diligently and meticulously. All was good in the chateau, although the money was dwindling faster than we had hoped. This problem was something I dealt with, for the moment, courtesy of that old, trusty friend denial. We would have to address the problem at some point, but not now. Even if we did open for business in the coming summer, it would take a good deal of time to actually make some money. I wasn't sure what to do about this nettlesome problem.

As the autumn began to show the first hints of a colder, darker time, Ludovic, the exterior window painter, showed up every day with rarely a peep. I became used to bringing him coffee on the colder days as he continued his thankless task.

'How do you continue day in, day out when you have so many windows to do?'

'I don't think about the other windows, just the one I'm working on,' he said, resigned and surprisingly content.

Ludovic was in his late twenties, it seemed, with dark hair and dark eyes and a slightly sad aspect. He was hearty and seemed to take the work in his stride. Every window received the same care: sanding, filling in broken and rotted parts, replacing broken panes, resealing panes (all 24 of each window), painting and repainting as he passed from one monumental window to the next. He had the capacity to endure with this, what seemed to me, most tedious and arduous task… the same thing, over and over again, without apparent end. We would see him from time to time at the local pub/pizzeria when we would venture there for takeaway. He was usually nursing a beer with a buddy, chatting amiably.

He had his calling, a decent though modest salary, he took long lunches, the state took care of all his basic needs. And when he worked, he worked at his pace, answering to himself and satisfying his need to do a job well. This was the first time I realised the profound and fundamental difference between who he was – a man happy with being – and the never-ending aching and ambition of American life. I'm not saying all the French are content with little and I'm not saying all Americans are hungrily scoffing at the trough of greed. It's just that Ludovic came to symbolise for me the 'less is more' attitude. A way of sustaining oneself without the constant, niggling longing for more, more, more. I don't want to romanticise the lack of ambition of a young man in the French countryside. But there is almost certainly something there, something real that says the best you can have is what you currently have. It leaves one less unsatisfied. Didier seemed to share the same contentment with his lot.

The following day, we had a brief spell of warm weather, odd in late October. I asked Ludovic to join me and Gilles, the carpenter, for a drink during lunch. Gilles had been showing up sporadically, willy-nilly, like the cliché about Mediterranean workers told us he would. We didn't mind because he was a very kind and sweet man. He wore thick glasses and had a gangly body and a distracted, almost mournful, solitary way about him. We would talk often, when he did show up, about the work, about the French countryside, politics and whatever else helped us wind our way through the day. All the time, he would cut and plane cabinets, kitchen storage units and surrounds for the bathtubs.

The sun was shining, so we sat out the back around an old wrought iron table and took a little rosé with a lunch of baguettes and dried ham alongside a few hunks of tomme Pyrénées cheese.

'I will not be here next week,' Gilles bashfully stated.

'OK, what's going on? We need to finish the surrounds and get the cabinets in order.' I felt panic creeping in.

'Well, I have a problem. It is not your problem, but mine. You see, you know now the rivers are rising and they are full?'

'Yes?' I did not know quite where he was going with this. But my affection for him made me curious of his path here.

'Near my house, the river is particularly high. It is flooding our back garden. It is *inondable*. It is all I could afford because I do not work all the time.' *Inondable.* Liable to flooding.

'I'm sorry to hear that. What do you normally do when this happens? Do you have to move for the flood season?'

'Yes, sometimes I go to stay with my mother, whose house does not flood. It is hard on the kids too.'

I did not know that he had children. Five, as it turned out.

He continued, 'And this year, my wife walked into the river.'

'It's a bit cold to swim this time of year,' I replied innocently.

'No, she wanted to end her life. I had to save her from the current in the river.'

Almost speechless, I managed, 'I am terribly sorry.'

'It is not uncommon for her. She has her black periods. For the past few years, she has tried this. It is not easy.'

It all made sense now. Who of us would not be *marginal* with a burden like this?

'Of course, take the time you need and let me know later when you can return.'

'I will.'

What is there to say, really? Our endeavour, the work, the mounting money worries, the stress of the birth, were all things chosen by us. Here Gilles was faced with a real difficulty, a tragedy of nature not of his choosing, an affliction that struck a good man and his children and his sick wife.

It became time, within the week, for Gilles to leave. He would go and not return. The puny sufferings we had so eagerly chosen faded into their rightful place of insignificance alongside this man placed in our home, quite possibly, to show us the goodness and bounty of our lives.

CHAPTER TWELVE

Tempest

We didn't really know where the tempest came from. It just blew up one night from nowhere. Crisp, jovial autumn had turned into its meaner, brooding older brother winter. Just like that. The house was colder inside than outside. The puny space heaters and 1950s radiators spluttered away trying to throw a little warmth into the vast hollow spaces of the chateau. We made do some days by turning on the hob full blast and using a good three months' butane *gaz* in one morning's coffee and baguette break. Then it came.

Our beloved workmen had been busily scraping, tapping, scrubbing, sanding, painting, plastering and plumbing away for a good few months now. On the odd day, I would lend my unlearned and woefully unskilled hand to knock down or pull out or place the odd bit here and there. Bud and

I continued our examination of the outbuildings finding bits and pieces. The Irish lads had organised the hundred-something nineteenth-century oak doors laying in good repair in the stables. They managed to store them in an empty attic by stacking them neatly against the walls and separating them by size and colour. This treasure trove included all the doors that were removed from the chateau in order to make way for the new hollow-core pine doors chosen by the former owners of the institution. As we poked around, we found lovely stone tiles, octagonal in shape and sandy coloured, a fairly common pattern from the eighteenth century; and pinkish-white square marble slabs, lovely for bathrooms: both remnants of renovations past, thankfully left for us to be recycled in the chasm of this home's endless improvements.

Of course, our real desire was to find treasure, something of such inestimable value, something so precious that magically all of our money worries would evaporate and we could restore the house to its one-time shining glory. Sadly, it was not to be. But if you needed a thresher or an old washing machine, a porcelain heater, handsome horse stalls, terracotta tiles, intricately carved wrought iron window guards or broken pieces of handmade porcelain tiles, Bonchamps was the place to find them. Bud in her infinite frugality would find a use for all these sundries.

Most of our days were spent rooting around in the outbuildings and talking to the artisans, making hundreds of small decisions that, hopefully, would turn into a harmonious whole. We spent other days shopping for furniture in *brocantes*, or thrift shops, less expensive antique shops and *vide-greniers*, or car boot sales. There were always worthy and interesting items to be had, for good prices too. We planned on six bedrooms to start the bed and breakfast. Two of the bedrooms were suites and really had two bedrooms each. So that was ten rooms to furnish, plus the dining room, library and our private salon. Generally, we stayed close to authentic, mostly nineteenth-century reproductions of older pieces while putting together a nice collection of new mattresses, towels, linens, bathmats and all the minutiae needed to create a comfortable stay for our hoped-for clients.

Bud continued to breastfeed Blue part-time, while Grim grew inordinately from mother alone. Some days, and some days all day, she had two tiny creatures lashed to two swollen breasts. Our stated and intended goal, to spend as much time with our children in their tender years, was being achieved. Some days, we weren't quite sure we would ever meet our deadlines and plans for restoring the house. But the children were benefiting, so we told ourselves, from the constant care and endless preening of two attentive, if not harried, parents. While Bud fed the babies, I helped cook, clean and tidy the house like a good little househusband.

Ludovic continued what I considered to be the most tedious job known to man – painting all the windows on the property. He would come rain or shine, in good health and bad, with sander, paintbrush, bucket and odd panes of glass, weatherstripping and putty. I would wander out from time to time and marvel at his perseverance. I truly believed the sheer size and drudgery of the job would crush a lesser man.

Didier, meanwhile, was working his way through the house, painting and mixing colours, scraping and repainting. Mocques the plumber would come in too, install a bathroom here and there and leave. We would not see him for weeks, then all of a sudden, he appeared, his lined, smiling face a wonderful sight as the house was slowly but surely rehabilitated. He fitted and positioned and refined first one, then two, and then five bathrooms, all perfect, in our minds, for our future guests.

In early December, the air was cold, the ground damp, the wild boar were busy digging up large swathes in the apple orchard, and we shivered and felt physically miserable. Emotionally, we were quite happy with the progress. We had managed to pick and choose enough furniture to fill at least three-quarters of the rooms. The work was roughly 60 per cent done – at least the work we had planned on doing. If you looked at the overall project and included refinishing the facade, repairing the stone decorative elements, replacing the roof and heating systems and cleaning up the outbuildings, we were at three per cent. That was a generous estimate, too.

The day began as most other days began. The kids roused themselves from deep sleep, we followed, performed our daily 'toilette' and trundled downstairs for coffee and croissants. But this day, massive clouds could be seen on the horizon, the most enormous bank of blackness we had ever seen. All the artisans showed up, quite early, to begin their labours of love and necessity.

'There will be a big storm tonight. So I will leave early,' Didier said as I crossed him in the hall.

'Will it be so bad you have to leave early?' I asked.

'There was a storm in ninety-eight that killed thousands of trees, winds very high. This might be such a storm.'

I had heard of this storm. It had struck with devastating force, wiping out forests and roofs and gargantuan swathes of vegetation across France. Versailles had lost thousands of old-growth trees that are just today being replaced. Our own little forest still revealed dozens of massive fallen trees. Now Didier had said there might be another. As the day advanced, the clouds closed in like forces of evil amassing for a shocking assault on our little community. By late afternoon, we were enveloped in thick blackness as the sun began its slide down behind the pond.

The workmen scurried home early as agreed amid many '*bon courage*', hoping to install themselves in their cosy lairs to ride out the storm. By 7 p.m., all was still and eerily quiet. The trees did not move and the cats took refuge in the million hiding places around the property. When we turned into bed around 10 p.m., it was still quiet. We drifted off to sleep slightly disconcerted by the deafening silence.

I shot out of bed at Lord knows what time like a cartoon character, practically hitting my head on the three-metre ceiling. The noise, louder than anything I'd ever heard, issued from the heavens and exploded just outside the house. It also woke Bud. Amazingly, the children slept soundly. We darted through the bathroom and into the adjoining room which faced out the front of the house overlooking the pond. The room was for the kids but since they slept with us, it served as a dressing area and toy dumping ground. We stumbled over the remnants of a busy child's day and searched for the lights but there was no electricity. We neared the window as lightning illuminated the inside of the room through thick oak shutters. It shone like spotlights with the brilliance of tiny suns.

I opened the double window with a turn of the lead lever. The window flew open and banged ominously against the wall. Glass flew across the room as a massive gust encircled our dazed figures. But I wanted to see more, to feel the power of the wind, so I pushed open the shutters. The three gargantuan, ancient sycamores next to the pond were swaying in the deluge like drunken sailors. And then another crash so loud we both ducked down instinctively. We rose slowly and peered out the window.

Just over the pond, a hundred or so yards from our window, long, thick lightning bolts danced before our eyes. It was as if Poseidon and Zeus were having one final battle, exchanging thrusts and parries with their lightning bolts, performing for two cowering mortals. The bolts zigged and zagged and darted and flew and spun and struck left and right, up and down. I had seen the Northern Lights in Alaska and other phenomenal natural phenomena such as splendid, massive cloud banks and the spewing of giant volcanoes on my travels. But this – this was exceptional. We must have seen a couple of hundred lightning bolts in those endless minutes.

The tempest pursued itself well into the night as we trotted back to bed and tried to make sense of the most spectacular show we had ever witnessed. Nature had reared its head to remind us of our place in the universe.

The next morning was not so titillating. Depressing, in fact. Amidst all of the crackling and noise and fireworks, we might not have heard another crash inside the building. It was my habit to explore the chateau after any storm to look for damage. With trepidation, I made my way to the second floor and started my survey. About halfway through, I entered a small sitting room, formerly for the servants. Pine floors, nice mouldings and a small, discreet marble fireplace where the *domestiques* would lounge after a hard day's work. There I found a large chunk of plaster splattered dramatically on the floor. I could see up into the attic, and beyond that, sky. We had had small leaks and minor irritations here before, but this was significantly more than minor. Also, the water had poured, apparently, in a nice steady stream into the room and down through the ceiling below. Of course, this was a room Didier had just finished painting.

I finished my rounds by moving to the third floor tower attic. There too sky, beautiful sky, and water and damp everywhere, but no visible leaks though into the room below. The roof was composed of 400 square metres of black slate hammered with small nails into laths of wood. No insulation, no lining, nothing to protect it from outside except for these thin, feeble slivers of stone.

With our money dwindling into the hands of good workmen and eager antique sellers, we made the call. For the time being, we could only see fit to patch the holes. I arranged with a local artisan roofer to replace the many missing slates on the main house and outbuildings. That was another two or three thousand euros we would never see again. There went another few beds and linens and half an armoire, or maybe a nice sofa, in one night of nature's apocalyptic temper tantrum. This strain led to a small tempest of our own, a heated debate about the viability of our project.

One day, all the roiling tensions came to a head. We were sitting in the music room in front of a massive open fire. The children were napping upstairs. Lately, I had been impatient with Bud and the kids, short with the workmen and generally grumpy. It was at points like this I needed my wife to step in and settle the anxiety beast.

'Sam, we need to talk,' Bud said firmly. 'I know the pressure of getting this going has been causing some problems. But you have to remember, we are not that far from opening. Just think of what we've done. There's not much left to do. And what else are we going to do, give up now? We haven't even really started the real work, the B&B. You've got to relax a little about the money.'

'I know you're right. But I must say you were right from the beginning. It's too big. There's too much to do. It seems that for every step we take forward, we take a step or two backward. And this is just to get the doors open for the first season, which will be slow in any case.' I was calm and it felt good to acknowledge the rightness of Bud's misgivings on that first visit to the property.

Bud proceeded patiently. 'We really don't have a choice. It would be impossible to sell this thing. It's really a white elephant. I can understand why no one was willing to take it on.'

There it was. The truth. Even if we wanted to bail out, to seek higher ground, we were tied to the monster house. I couldn't see any way we could unload the burden, despite our persistent improvements. Who in their right mind would take on such a project with so much left to do? I felt like a trapped animal, not knowing which way to turn. Unlike Sartre's *Huis Clos*, hell wasn't other people. Hell was a lack of possibility, a dearth of options.

'You're right. The only question is how long will we have to pay for this mistake?' We both laughed. Somehow, the tension was lessened as we acknowledged our fate. We had made a choice and now we were bearing the consequences. There was no way but forward. Stick to the plan and try to make it work. Something would come through to help us over this last mental hurdle.

Later that day, we took a short trip with the children to the Château de Brissac. This was one of the grande dames of the Loire Valley. I had picked up a brochure at the *boulangerie* and discovered that each year, Brissac and its Duc and Duchesse opened its doors for a Christmas fair. After an hour of driving, we arrived at the gates of the 'tallest chateau in France', or so the publicity said. The house was massive, built on medieval ramparts and substantially renovated in the fifteenth and sixteenth centuries. Spread out on the impeccable lawns, under sequoias and Lebanese cedars like our own, artisans and craftspeople had set up booths.

Inside, the little bazaar continued as wonderfully creative people offered handmade ornaments, smoked eel, delicious cakes and hand-painted pottery for sale. We made our way around the labyrinthine halls into splendid Renaissance galleries and massive rooms. As we meandered, I noted that the floor tiles and wood panelling and ceiling decorations were not so different from our own. Brissac was more splendid and more authentic than our own chateau. But Bud and I enjoyed examining the similarities and truly felt a certain pride, a contentment in being part of the select fraternity of *châtelains*.

As we were making our way down the main staircase, a white stone confection of carved heads and wild animals, we bumped into a handsome, tall family coming out of a hidden passageway just to the right of the staircase. They were all sporting new ski clothes and carrying skis and poles and mittens and bags. This seemed odd until, as we followed them down the stairs, the manager of the chateau greeted them and introduced them to a group of tourists. As I heard the words '*Duc et Duchesse de Brissac et leurs enfants*', I was overcome by a sense of camaraderie and deep relief. Even the nobility had to share space with strangers and charge admission and open their private lives in some small way to strangers. In a very real sense, the lord and lady of the manor were in the exact same position as us. Owners of an unwieldy and demanding chateau forced by penury and necessity to open their lives to the scrutiny and roving eyes of people outside the family. We hadn't really dealt extensively with the intrusions of outsiders but it was nice to know that even the privileged, the nobles, might share some of our financial woes. Why else would they let people into their house?

Bud and I drove back to our piece of paradise talking about the similarities of the two houses and sharing thoughts on the difficulties that all estate owners must bear. Constant renovations, incessant lack of funds and a persistent need to always come up with ways to keep the mission underway.

This small insight into the Brissac world gave us a new sense of perspective. In spite of the ups and downs of chateau ownership, we, like the Duc and Duchesse, were truly blessed to share our lives with a part of living history. It was things like this, the occasional readjustment of attitude, the sometime realisation of our good fortune, that gave us sustenance to continue something that was too big, too grand for physical, mental and financial resources. Our moods were at times determined by the weather and the stubborn implacability of the estate. But my, was the chateau lovely in that storm.

CHAPTER THIRTEEN

Open for Business, Almost

Our first months of the new year were frenzied. We were pushing the workmen like sweaty, tired horses to get everything finished. Our money problems continued even though, now, seven months after I had made an agreement with the bank, our new loan was coming through. The extra 50,000 euros we extracted from our new loan would just cover the remainder of the work and a bit more furniture; a small plaster to help us make it through to the beginning of summer. After that, we would have to rely on the business. Such as it was. That is to say, non-existent.

As our kindly French count down the road had pointed out, we were off the beaten path. There were roughly half a dozen magnificent Loire Valley chateaux within 30 minutes of the house. But the big ones, the ones people really came to see, were 45 minutes to an hour and a half away, more towards

Tours. We were closer to Angers, a lovely town and former seat of the Plantagenet dynasty. There were medieval buildings and nice squares, a grand fortress, a famous tapestry and calm, shop-lined pedestrian avenues. But it wasn't near enough to the most visited Loire Valley chateaux of Chambord, Blois, Chenonceau and Azay-le-Rideau. We were hamstrung from the beginning, and we knew it. In our more defensive moments, we would argue, 'Who wouldn't want to stay in a vast seventeenth-century chateau in the French countryside?' But the answer was clear: anyone who wanted to be near the famous sites in the region.

Because I was such a poor artisan, I would have to show my worth in the marketing of the chateau. I set about sorting out *annonces*, or publicity, on the best French- and UK-based accommodation websites I could find and afford. Guidebooks, I knew in spite of my ignorance, would take more time. You had to contact the book publishers, set up appointments, wait for the writers and editors to pen their glowing thoughts about the house and then, after all that, wait for the publication of the travel guide, usually a year later. We had to get a quick start on the Internet and make our way from there.

In late February, as the last rooms were being put to bed and the last bathrooms being plumbed and spiffied, I received a call.

'*Allô?*' I answered.

'Yes, *bonjour*, do you speak English?' the caller enquired.

'Yes.' I was never sure if it was good or bad to reveal my identity as an American. Some people, after all, wanted a true French experience complete with French aristocrats.

'I'm calling from California and am interested in renting your Guard's House this summer. I have some work in Le Mans.'

After my experience with the Guard's House the previous summer, I vowed to be more honest with the guests and lay out the pros and cons of a stay *chez nous*.

'That's great. But I must tell you, Le Mans is about fifty minutes away. It's mostly autoroute with a good four- or five-lane motorway but it is a sizeable commute.'

'That's fine,' he said. 'I like to drive and your place seems really beautiful.'

'How long were you thinking of staying?'

'Eight weeks. Is it available?'

I stifled a gasp and pushed forward. This was too good to be true. Early in the year and we already had a good part of the summer booked, potentially.

'Yes, it's early still and the house is available.'

It wasn't a ton of money, about 4,800 euros (£3,300), but it was a start.

'OK. Well, I'll talk to my wife and have her call you. She has some questions.'

'No problem. Please let us know. I do have requests for the house, though no solid bookings yet.'

'Will do.'

I ran to find Bud. We spoke excitedly about our prospects for the summer. The work would be done soon and we were all optimism and hope. Funny how one small signal, the slightest interest in our little project, could throw us from pessimism and worry into delirium. Despite outward appearances, however, there was something inside both of us, call it perhaps a fear of success, that slightly dampened our enthusiasm. We felt, as with most things, if it seemed too good to be true, it probably was. Like a chateau for less than half a million euros. Like eight weeks' rent out of nowhere.

Our free time was scarce in the run-up to spring. We ran here and there gathering final fittings, pieces of furniture, utensils and linens while consulting and debating with the workmen. On the odd days when we had little to do – more specifically, on the odd days when we could do nothing because stores were closed and all Frenchmen disappeared into the somnolence of frequent holidays and Sundays – we would travel around the Loire visiting chateaux and eating out. It was one of the reasons we moved to Europe and in particular France.

On such days we would load up the rickety old van with the kids and their belongings and head off for a picnic and a visit. Even in the waning days of winter, we found sunny days and a mild climate. We discovered turrets and castellations and towers and rivers and small, old villages. The variety and depth of French patrimony was more astounding than I had imagined. It was days like these that made me thankful for our choice. On these days, we would slip into the gentle flow and profound beauty of our chosen land. The worries of renovations and money and heating would fall away like leaves from a tree. The fact that there were some million leaves lying around the property from a long winter hardly dampened our spirits. There would be time to rake them up as there would be time to bend our energies to the work ahead.

It has been said that what I lack in good sense I make up for in pragmatism. I suppose buying the beast was not entirely pragmatic. In any case, the new year also brought talk of a new American venture. Amidst much sabre-rattling, rhetoric and bombast, it seemed that my country would again launch into something big – this time the invasion of Iraq.

The French papers were filled with denunciations and critiques of American imperialism and calls for patience. I knew my countrymen well; there would be no such nonsense. The French pointed out the hubris of Mr Bush and his cohorts, the need for the son to rectify the father's failures, America's love and thirst for oil, America's unreflective support of Israel, Bush's desire to be seen as a man of action after the tragedy of 9/11. Deep down, I felt sympathy with these arguments as American animosity towards the French grew and metastasised into a nasty little monster. This led to not a few arguments and heated exchanges with my friends and family back at home. In the end, though, put bluntly, this was a good opportunity to support my family financially. I wished the big event of the year could have been the Olympics or the World Cup but alas, it was a war. And wars need journalists.

With a quick check, for the thousandth time, of our bank account, I made a call to my old employer, NBC, in London. I figured they would need a hand if and when the fighting, or should I say bombing, began.

I chatted with the London deputy bureau chief, Suzette. She thought there would be a need for extra hands on deck. We agreed on a price per week and it was quickly settled.

NBC would fly me to London, put me up in a hotel for the duration of my stay and pay me. Ideal. This seemed to come just at the right time – right before the summer onslaught (didn't we wish) and towards the end of renovations. Bud was hesitant knowing she would be stuck in the chateau by herself with two screaming kids (sometimes quiet, but mostly screaming), but we needed the money.

It was by no means lost on me, the hypocrisy and desperation that led me back to my employer. This, the same employer that I had just left a year ago. Not a bad lesson for a stubborn man.

NBC's commitment was for two months, possibly more. Just before the start of the war, I took the Eurostar to London. I arrived at the offices in Hammersmith and felt happy to work again. Sure, we had been working on the house but it wasn't the same as being part of something larger, getting paid and having pressing deadlines and office protocols. I realised people sat in tight, grey cubicles dreaming of the life we had made for ourselves. Despite the glories and challenges of our short time in France, I had occasionally felt the isolation and boredom of the French countryside. Often I would sit and reflect on what it would be like to work in a proper, conventional job. This schizophrenia – contempt for the working, commercial world and a desire to be a part of it – defined a part of my experience at the chateau.

The office was soon busy and correspondents and producers were being sent here and there, spur of the moment and in a mad rush. Twice I went to Brussels to cover the European Union as they dilly-dallied on whether or not to put their lot in with the Yanks or not. Like the journalists who covered these massive institutions, the elected and non-elective leaders of the EU Executive Council and Parliament sat around, smoked, drank coffee and debated what they might or might not do. Then called it a day. Not bad work if you can get it. It suited me fine.

Expense accounts, decent dinners not prepared by myself, new places and people to see – it was very exciting. But as the long chain of gossip and rumour wound its way to my lowly freelance self, I started to remember why exactly I had left corporate America – the whimsical and urgent decisions, or non-decisions, on how to cover this or that, the contradictory instructions from New York, the manpower issues, the long hours. It seemed like no one was ever happy. Plenty of griping and moaning.

In that first month, the war was going so 'damned well', according to the Americans, that there was talk of a small expansion and veiled threats towards Iraq's neighbour, Syria. The Syrian border was posing a problem for the US – arms shipments, refugees and terrorists were pouring through the porous line separating Syria and Iraq.

Suzette approached me one day. 'Sam, we need you to go to Syria. Bush is making noises and we want to report on it.'

This put a slight crimp in my cosy little London–Brussels–France tour of duty. But I was excited by the prospect of going so I called Bud. We spoke about the work on the house, the comings and goings of the kids. Then I hit her with it.

'Bud, they want me to go to Syria.'

'Isn't that near Iraq?'

'Actually, it's next door. But I think things are calm there for the moment.'

'Oh, Sam, I don't know. It sounds dangerous.'

'Well, there's danger pay associated and it might be a nice trip.'

'I don't care about the money. It's most important you get back here in one piece. London is one thing, but Syria? Can you promise me you'll be OK?'

'Not really, but I'm pretty sure it will be safe.'

Just then, Grim started yelling and Bud was forced to offer one parting comment.

'I have to go Sam. It's so hard here being alone. But you do what you think is best. And for Christ's sake, don't get hurt.' I knew Bud was lonely. So was I. Because we had bitten off more than we could chew, we had no other choice but to soldier on.

With that tepid endorsement, I told NBC yes. The trip to Syria was thankfully uneventful. One day into the trip and the story was dead. President Bush had declared the Syrians to be reasonably cooperative. Tough luck for us. The journey did afford me the opportunity, however, to shop for furnishings for our bed and breakfast.

One morning into the second week of this brilliant, unplanned holiday, I went to the souk in search of rugs. I walked along cobbled streets, eating my lamb schwarma and searching for a not-too-intimidating rug shop. I rounded a corner and found my place.

I spoke in English and told the owner I was looking for rugs. He invited me in and sat for half an hour chatting and drinking tea. Very French, these Syrians. Transactions would only be oiled by sufficient social interaction.

The owner, a tall, handsome man with light eyes and a perfectly groomed moustache, ordered his minions to bring rugs. So they came by the dozens. Every so often I would say yes and these would be put aside. I haggled over each and every rug and in the end haggled some more. I ended up buying 17 rugs for the equivalent of 2,000 euros, or £1,400. When I had bought rugs in France, a single four-by-three-metre rug was at least the same price and sometimes much more. The owner ordered a worker bee off to buy me two large suitcases and we carefully packed the goods away.

'Are you sure I can get these out of the country with no problem? Are there any tariffs or special forms I need?' I enquired after I'd paid my money.

'Everything will be fine, my friend. May I drive you to your hotel?'

Before my departure, I visited our fixer, a man named Thabet. He was a Syrian who knew how to get things done. We chatted idly about the trip and thanked one another for pleasant company. I mentioned in passing that I had bought a load of rugs and I planned to furnish my bed and breakfast with them.

He looked startled.

'Are they old rugs?' he asked.

'Yes, mostly, I think sixty to a hundred years old.'

'Oh, no. You can't take these out of the country. There is a law about exporting antiques from Syria. There will be great fines and possible prison time.'

I begged him for a solution. We sat for coffee and mulled over my predicament. The rug store owner had seemed so nice. Thabet's face brightened after about 30 minutes and three cups of the strongest coffee on earth.

'I will send my man, Mohammed, with you. He will take you to Lebanon and you can fly out of there. But you may have to bribe the border guards.'

Not quite the solution I was expecting. The idea of bribery and border guards and Syrian prison sent shivers up my spine. We worked out the plan in detail. I would leave the next day. That night I spoke to Bud and told her of my rug adventure, omitting only the fact that I had to cross into Lebanon with contraband.

The next morning, a van showed up with Mohammed driving and a journalist colleague in tow. We packed the truck full of equipment, placing the rug bags on the bottom according to Mohammed's instructions. He thought the border guards might be too lazy to unload all of the equipment.

It was only a few pleasant hours to the border. Finally, we arrived at a standard looking border crossing complete with broken-down cars and long lines of people passing to and fro, declaring and not declaring, arguing and being waved through depending on the whim of the guards.

Mohammed told us to wait in the car. He asked for 150 euros, just in case. I could feel cold beads of sweat popping up on my forehead. What was I thinking? Was a well-appointed chateau worth this stress? I was losing my nerve.

We grabbed a grilled chicken sandwich from a nearby stand while Mohammed chatted and drank coffee with the border guards. After about two hours, Mohammed came towards the van.

'The major will come to inspect the van. Remain calm and be polite.'

My hands started to shake. If ever I would lose control of my bodily functions, now might be it. Mohammed entered the border office and came back leading the major to our van.

'Hello. How are you today?' he greeted us with a sly smile.

'We are very good. Hot day, isn't it?' What else could I say? Possibly, 'Please, sir, I don't want to go to prison – take the rugs, please!'

The major was a portly man with a heavy beard and moustache. He was trailed by a young man with a machine gun and a dopey smile. His top four buttons were open on his uniform and one shirt-tail dangled sloppily in front of his large belly. He stood with us outside the van and enquired about our visit.

I told him it was lovely and I would like to bring my family back. This was true but did sound a little sycophantic. We spoke for a long time, the major testing his English and making jokes about America. We shared cigarettes and stood in the noonday sun.

After about 45 minutes, he shook our hands and wished us a good trip. We were through. The price: 150 bucks and much figurative and literal sweating. The next day I flew from Beirut to Paris with 17 rugs. Another problem solved.

CHAPTER FOURTEEN

Debut

I was gone almost two months, with a short visit home in the middle. Within days of my return to France, all hell was breaking loose. Bud had gone through a tough time alone with the two kids, workmen and enquiries. Scarcely a booking in sight, but plenty of calls.

'You know that family that wants to book for eight weeks this summer?' Bud started, as soon as I'd set foot through the door. 'The wife has called me no fewer than fifteen times. She wants to know if we have a pool, where the nearest grocery store is, do we have bikes... on and on and on. You really have to call her.' That was fine. Bud and I had split the duties – her primary responsibility was the children and the house and mine was the business. Or lack of it.

'OK, OK, I just got back. I will call her.'

'Also, Mocques wants to talk to you about the last two bathrooms. I told him to go ahead and start. He wants to put a third hot water heater on the second floor to feed the two bedrooms in the middle of the house.'

'Sounds good. What's the problem?'

'Well, he's already started chipping out the exterior back wall and is going to dig a trench the length of the house to join up with the septic tank. It will take a lot of work and time. He needs your help.'

I scurried around the back of the house where Mocques was working away with hammer and chisel. He was gouging a huge hole into the back wall of the house and carving his way down from the first floor to ground level. No sledgehammer, just his simple tools and two bare hands. Debris and rocks and the guts of the wall lay strewn for yards around the terrace. We spoke about what needed to be done. It was decided I would hire a *pelleteuse*, a digger, to run the trench 30 metres to a large pipe which would then join up to the septic tank. I felt confident in my skills as a digger. How hard could it be? I gazed up at the deep crevice. How in the world would we ever fill that in?

I made the trip to a large hardware services store in Angers and arranged the delivery of the digger at 60 euros for the day.

The next morning the digger showed up. I mounted the little yellow bull and played with the controls as Mocques smiled at my shenanigans. He was covered in dust and small stones. Pieces of rock nestled in his eyebrows and his hair was now entirely white with dust.

Mocques instructed me as if I were a child. I would start by the main pipe and work my way backwards to his holes in the middle. The trench must form a *pente*, or slope, from the bathroom drainage pipes to the big connector pipe.

I started off well, digging my hole precisely and neatly laying the refuse to the side for future removal. Mocques interjected here and there, corrected my line, made sure I was digging deep enough. By midday, I broke for lunch. Mocques went home for a quick break with his family.

Bud and I sat at the wooden table just behind the kitchen and soaked up the noonday sun. As usual, we satisfied ourselves with juicy tomatoes, olive oil and a local goats' cheese with a few glasses of wine.

'I think these Guard's House people might be a nightmare. It makes me wonder if all of our guests are going to be so demanding,' Bud commented.

'I'm just grateful we have a good solid booking like that.'

'How are the B&B bookings?'

'Same as last week. One week in June booked by that German couple and some Spaniards at the end of the summer. That's it for now. But we needn't worry. It's only late April.' On the road around the world, I had kept close track of all enquiries and correspondence via the Internet.

We worked out that we needed about 500 nights at an average of 125 euros (£86) per night plus 15 weeks in the Guard's House to break even. That totalled about 70,000 euros (£48,000) for the year. This would cover most of the heating, house insurance, linens, basically almost all the costs of running the estate, but did not include our food and new shoes from time to time for the babies. So far, we had eight weeks booked in the Guard's House and barely 14 nights in the chateau. The season was fast approaching.

I returned to my ditch-digging duties shortly after lunch. Mocques came back and gently, though persistently, guided my meanderings. At one point, I grew a little tired of his input. Jesus, I could dig a hole. Stop bothering me, I complained, but more gently. The trench grew in length and I pulled even with Mocques.

'Look,' I said. 'I am an expert plumber and a very famous digger.' He laughed and continued chipping away.

I repositioned the digger for a last few digs, just to clean things up and make the pipe laying easier. Feeling good about my accomplishment, I dramatically raised the large claw higher than needed be, with my tiny controls in hand, and swooped the thing down into the dirt. Mocques watched. A few seconds later, the dirt started to move and pulsate. This grew stronger until a pool started to form in my beloved trench. If only it were dark and I had struck oil! Instead, water poured out of what appeared to be a black pipe. Of course, how could I not puncture the water main! Mocques laughed heartily, certainly aware of my bravado. He calmly jumped down, surveyed the damage and trotted away to cut off the water supply. The water stopped just as he came back and patted me on the shoulder.

'*Ça va, ça va*. It happens to the best of us,' I think he said.

I spoke to Susan, our soon-to-arrive Guard's House guest, for, I think, the thirteenth time just one week before she arrived, family in tow. Each time she called, there was panic in her voice. Inevitably, it was some minor question involving logistics and facilities. I wondered if all the clients we lured to our lair would be so high-maintenance. Never mind, I told myself, it was great to have this booking and I should be happy. Alongside her eight weeks, we picked up another five primarily from Brits and a few Irish. Not bad. The Guard's house was now in better condition after a fresh coat of paint and a new carpet and the estate looked reasonably good. I had spent hundreds of hours mowing and preening the lawn. I had it down now to almost a fine science. Fifteen hours a week to mow just the bare minimum. Another two to three hours trimming and pruning. It wasn't precisely how I had envisioned my life at the manor but it was satisfying to see the result at the end.

It was time to assess and take stock of our work. In the past year we and our artisans had installed nine bathrooms; painted 20 rooms and the main 40-metre great hall; sanded, rejoined and painted (three times) 156 windows; cleaned out most of the outbuildings; repainted and furnished the four-bedroom Guard's House, furnished four double rooms and two suites, a dining room, library and salon; *and* we'd had our second child. Not a bad year's work. We were ready. Now, where were the bookings? We had one night or two scattered in different weeks throughout the summer with the Germans and Spaniards making bookends in mid June and late August respectively. Luckily, I had made some decent money with my work during the war, but it was nowhere near enough.

A CHATEAU OF ONE'S OWN

Susan arrived with her husband and three children in early June. She told us she wanted her family to spend a few nights in the chateau before they implanted themselves in the Guard's House, so this was arranged. I greeted them heartily, shaking hands all round. Susan was short, round and smiley with long blonde hair and adorned in a massive sheet that draped itself loosely across her body. Tim was a strapping guy, well over six feet, possibly 17, 18 stone. Shortly into the conversation, Tim asked me the best way to get around, the fastest route to Le Mans. He revealed they only had one car for the entire summer and that Susan would be stuck at the house for eight long weeks. I hinted that this might be a bad idea. Sure, it was beautiful, but kids needed to be entertained and taken away to see the sights. There were things to do: climb trees, walk in the woods, fish in the pond. In the end, though, today's children always need a bit more stimulation than country life has to offer. But he insisted it would all be fine. I then gave them a quick tour of the house and showed them their suite. They seemed delighted. I told them breakfast would be served between eight and ten. There didn't seem to be any problems and they headed off to have dinner in our nearby village.

The next morning I got up at seven so I could head off to the *boulangerie* and collect pastries and bread for breakfast. Bud and I had decided to stick with the French continental breakfast: croissants, pain au chocolat, baguettes, freshly squeezed orange juice, fruit, yogurt and cheese. A choice of coffee in a French press or an assortment of teas, hot chocolate for the younger ones. And we decided to be generous about the portions. We had always detested a stingy breakfast. We still remembered, six years on, the bed and breakfast in Vermont where the owner measured out cups of coffee to guests while eyeing every portion taken.

I dressed quickly, excited at the prospect of serving our first guests of the season. It was late May, the sun streamed through our oversized windows, Bud and the babies slept soundly. I used the back servants' stairs to reach our oversized, industrial kitchen. As I walked through the door, I was met by a round, puffy-eyed creature rooting around in our refrigerator. It was horrifying.

'Susan!' I stammered.

'Oh, hi Sam. I was just putting some bottles in your fridge for the youngest. I hope that's OK.'

'Uh… sure. Let me help you.' I couldn't believe there was someone in my kitchen. Would all our guests come and go into our private area so blithely?

After our shocking encounter, breakfast went very well. Everyone was pleased and our guests ate hungrily and abundantly. Thank goodness we had decided to be generous.

Later that day, the German couple arrived, neatly dressed with fashionable glasses in a sporty new Audi. They seemed reserved and a bit hesitant. I showed them in and tried to give them space and time to take in the house. They were astounded by the size and generosity of their suite and loved the bathroom. Over the next week, they came and went quietly, eating long breakfasts in the dining room and reading in the library. It was precisely this type of person we longed to court. Professional with disposable income, quiet and smart and interested in relaxation and nature. Really, that was all we had to offer. And our Germans were perfect.

Susan, Tim and their kids were well installed in the outbuildings, safely restrained from early morning encounters with a befuddled owner. Several times each day, Susan would wander down to the chateau looking for this and that. It appeared what she really wanted was companionship. We tend to be fairly generous people but are very, very guarded, stingy even, about our personal time and space. Susan would come in and out of the kitchen at will. It was our first dilemma with a guest, and I honestly did not know what to do. How could I possibly tell her, without being too blunt, not to come into our space? I failed miserably and we simply endured her visits. Soon, they became less frequent as we greeted her with tight-lipped responses.

The summer was long and hot. For weeks on end, the temperature soared to over 40 degrees as we, and our poor guests, suffered in silence. All over France, the country was gripped in a devastating heatwave as thousands of the elderly died, neglected and abandoned by holidaying French families. Poor Susan was stuck in the Guard's House with three young children, no car, no air conditioning, no pool and a husband working long hours far away. We took pity and opened ourselves to her a bit more but remained guarded after the previous invasions. With the duties of the house, the occasional guest and our own two children, we simply did not have the energy to nurture this tortured woman.

DEBUT

Things cooled down by late August. The next day, Susan and her family would finally depart, and be relieved of the heat and solitude. Spirits were high as we all shared a bottle of wine at the front of the chateau, overlooking the pond as the sun set. At around 10.30, we turned in for the night. It was cool and the sky was illuminated by a billion points of light and a bright moon that shone like a spotlight on the back of the chateau casting long shadows to the front of the house, showering towers and weathervanes and the deep valleys and peaks of the roof.

'Sam, I think I hear a voice. Wake up!'

Groggily, I roused from a deep sleep. I could hear it too. It was coming from outside.

'Sam, come quick,' the voice came again. 'We need help. Susan's having an attack!' I stumbled over to the window and looked down. There was Tim, yelling for all he was worth.

'Susan was stung by something and she's having an attack.'

I looked at Bud.

'I can't fucking believe this. Their last night and she has an attack. We will never be rid of her! I'll check it out.'

I put on my trousers and ran downstairs. Tim and I ran to the Guard's House. All the lights were on. I looked through the window and saw Susan laid stiffly on a chair, panting, red and obviously in distress.

'What happened?'

'We were upstairs putting the kids to bed and something huge – a hornet I think – came out of the ceiling and stung Susan on the neck.'

The children were crying. Susan was in bad shape, hair dishevelled, large curtain cast over her quivering body, sweat pouring from her forehead. She looked like she was in labour except for the large welt where her neck met her shoulder.

'Sam, I think you should call the emergency guys,' Tim said, his voice full of panic.

Sounded like a good idea. I ran downstairs and called the emergency medics.

'*Bonjour*, we are in Juvardeil and I have a guest here who is having an attack. She is shaking. Can you send someone?'

'*Oui, monsieur, où êtes-vous exactement?*'

I gave directions and the operator asked more questions. Was she on medication? I asked Tim. Yes, Valium. Well, that explained a lot. Was she numb? Yes. Was she red? Yes.

Within minutes, the *pompiers*, or firefighters, along with emergency response units arrived at the front of the chateau.

'Hold tight. I'm going to bring them here,' I reassured Susan.

'OK, but hurry!'

I covered the distance from the outbuildings to the main house quickly and waved two trucks and an ambulance in our direction. The paramedics swarmed like bees when they pulled up to the Guard's House. They gave Susan a cold compress and measured her heartbeat and took her blood pressure.

I interpreted as best I could as they fired questions at an ailing patient. In the flurry of diagnosis she admitted she was taking Prozac, an antidepressant. Roughly ten guys stood in the small dining room of the guest house and examined Susan. I could see out of the corner of my eye two fellas chuckling quietly in the corner.

A woman doctor made her way in and examined Susan.

'Tell her she just has a bite. Possibly a hornet. It will go away,' the doctor said, calmly with barely concealed contempt. My heart was pounding but I settled down when I could see the team found Susan's predicament humorous. The doctor asked if Susan was normally allergic to bee and hornet stings. If she was, this could in fact be deadly without an Adrenalin injection. No, Susan replied as she settled down, content, it seemed, with all the attention.

'It's more than a bite. And why are they laughing? This is serious!' Tim almost yelled.

'I think it will be OK. She says that hornets are very nasty and it was good to call for help.'

I lied. I didn't want them to feel like complete idiots. The emergency team was thorough. They injected Susan with a small jab, Adrenalin from what I could gather, and then after ten minutes started to load up. I sat with our beloved guests for about half an hour more to make sure all was fine.

I trudged back to the main house and explained to Bud what had happened. A better man would have been compassionate but I was actually quite angry at all the hysterics. I felt that Susan, ignored and rebuffed for most of the summer, was making one last desperate cry for help, for attention she so longed for. You denied me all summer, I *will* make you pay attention to me!

'Bud, will all of our guests be so difficult? I don't know if I can take the intrusion, the constant little crises that might arise. And now this.'

'It's OK. It's been a long year, but things have run smoothly generally. I know we talked about making friends and acquaintances with our guests, like Frank and Rosemarie at Roundwood. But we don't serve dinner and we aren't them. We like our peace and quiet. We don't want to engage too much. That's just the way we are. If we accept that, and the guests don't expect too much more, we will be fine.'

Bud was right. How could we have misread ourselves so? Hoteliers were a true breed; running a hotel was a real métier, a vocation to provide service and attentiveness. We were, quite possibly, the opposite of this. What had we gotten ourselves into? I was overreacting. It was just one guest, one family out of a couple of dozen. Time to get some sleep.

A couple of days later, our last guests of the season arrived. These were the Spaniards, from Madrid: two couples with six children between them. They would have the B&B part of the chateau to themselves and we could wind down from a long, overheated summer. They arrived with jamón de serrano, Manchego cheese, olives and delicacies from Spain and asked us to join them for dinner. I found half a dozen or so bottles of Loire Valley wine, mostly red, and we all sat out the back of the chateau. We laughed and talked and joked and shared good food. They were delightful people.

Over their two-week stay, they came and went and occasionally dropped in, discreetly and non-invasively, to say hello and ask for advice on places to visit. Their children filled the halls of Bonchamps with yells and joy and running and laughter. Blue played with the older and the younger of the Spanish gang. It was much as we had envisioned our life in the chateau, in France. It was what we wanted and hoped it would be. They were perfectly self-sufficient yet open and interesting. They were delighted to have the run of the house (except for our private wing which they never violated).

On the afternoon of their departure, I sat in my office and reviewed the summer. We'd filled 13 weeks in the Guard's House (eight of those painful) and 83 nights B&B, making a grand total of 16,000 euros (£11,000). Needless to say, this was a far cry from what we needed. I reviewed our bank account online... 4,500 euros. That was it. No credit, not in France and no other resources. Our property tax bill, the *taxe foncière* and *taxe d'habitation* had arrived: 2,400 euros. We had burned through the bank loan, eaten up my healthy income from the Iraq war and used our meagre earnings from the summer just to maintain the house, in fact just part of the house.

I looked ahead to a long winter. As I discovered from talking to other B&B owners in the area, the season was painfully short running from late May to early September. That meant we had three or four months each year to make 70,000 euros. Seemingly impossible. It was clear I would have to go to New York to work. I would tell Bud later. For now, I sat back in my wooden chair, smoked my pipe and gazed out the window at our trees, standing like silent sentries, and whispered, 'What have we done?'

CHAPTER FIFTEEN

Lords and Lordlets

At last, a night out. As with all parents and people who work for a living, there had been precious little time for ourselves. Just as the summer wound down, we received a call from Helene de Richelieu, who was putting together a dinner at *her* chateau. It had been some time since we visited her husband, François. That jaw-dropping encounter those many months ago had set the tone for our tenure at Bonchamps. No matter how much denial or perseverance we were able to muster, sometimes in equal parts, there always lay just beneath the surface doubt about our venture, thanks to Monsieur le Comte François de Richelieu.

We always these days referred to de Richelieu as 'Fontaines', the name of his chateau. Unlike us, *arrivistes*, Fontaines inherited his pile from a long line of aristocrats in Anjou.

He took over the house in the early 1980s and had since polished and renovated and moulded the thing into one of the finest private chateaux in France. But there was a catch: the count and his baroness wife operated a B&B just like we commoners did. It was painful, I'm sure.

We had been in sporadic contact with the Fontaines, mainly by phone. They, and their circle, seemed very curious to know how we were faring. Our purchase of the chateau had provided a short-term, revocable ticket to the inner sanctum of Anjou's aristocracy. We saw this as a perk of our adventure, and were happy to accept the dinner invitation.

We arranged a babysitter, dressed casually so as not to show how truly impressed we actually were, selected a nice bottle of champagne from our vast wine cave of three bottles and headed off for dinner.

We arrived at the entrance of Fontaines' *grand parc anglais* and turned cautiously in. The lawn spread out like a vast green savannah, perfectly manicured, dotted with small benches and arrangements of hedges. We pulled up to the front the house. Unlike the crumbling cornices and dilapidated facade of our monster, Fontaines was without fault. Wisteria clung to simple wood trellises, windows were painted bone white, tuffeau and cornices sculpted as if new.

On the front lawn, we could see a group of people sitting, chatting and gesturing, enjoying a quiet preprandial cocktail in front of the ornamental pond while the sun drifted down behind the nearby hill. We parked our 1987 Mercedes to the side of the chateau. We had finally replaced the old red van with this modest and mostly reliable purchase. Not exactly luxurious, but sufficient for our needs.

We approached François and offered our gift. He greeted us warmly. We exchanged *bises* all round as Fontaines introduced us to the other guests. There were about six couples in all, comfortably wearing their well-used summer wardrobe, linens and whites and nicely fitting cotton shirts. The ladies were lovely and elegant and the men handsome and assured.

We met Jake and Eleanor, a polite and engaging English couple. Their story came quickly after the first introductions. They had left England some years ago for a worldwide voyage on the high seas with two young sons. Somehow, they landed at Fontaines and installed themselves in the *orangerie*. They ended up living there for five or six years, at a reduced rent while François renovated the place. Recently, they had bought a fourteenth-century manor house with a moat not far from us. They both had wonderfully posh accents that rolled out of their mouths as if they were constantly making important and interesting points. I can take or leave a fancy accent but it can add to the sophistication of a late summer meal.

With a modest buzz of excitement, we all trundled into the great hall. I was struck again by the opulence and taste of Fontaines' country home. Fine furniture in Louis XIV and Louis XV style, the real things, not like our nineteenth-century knock-offs. During a conversation about house insurance, Fontaines had once told me the furnishings in the house were worth roughly four times the house itself. It was a delight to be surrounded by beauty.

We dallied in the hall and shortly entered the Fontaines' private area which consisted of an entire wing complete with salon, kitchen and dining room. We entered a vast room with oak panelling and fat, sumptuous drapes fitted around massive windows like Renaissance bishops. A fire was roaring in the monumental stone fireplace just behind the large oak table. I was excited about the meal as Fontaines had arranged for chefs from the famed Cordon Bleu school in Paris to work at the chateau in the summer. It was part of his marketing plan but also had the benefit of providing him and his family and friends with meals fit for kings.

Wine was poured, a contradictorily dry and fruity Sancerre as we were all seated around the table. I was put next to Eleanor and Helene, the mistress of the house. Eleanor was full of questions and intent interest. Our conversation was filled with observations of living in France. I tended to express my frustration with French ways while she corrected my misapprehensions by beginning each sentence with 'Here in France, we...' More French than the French, it seemed.

Bud was placed between François, the count himself, and Jake. I could see her struggling with the French as the two men spoke of meaty, businesslike things and Bud looked on. Jake suggested English and Bud relaxed into the meal. The wine came freely and generously. I knew I liked Helene when she tapped her glass on the table for a refill. It shattered under the weight of her imperious touch and we all laughed heartily.

The first course was simple and neat – fresh greens with a light vinaigrette, Roquefort cheese, walnuts and foie gras.

We rested and the chatter became livelier. We then feasted on rare steak, green beans sautéed in olive oil and garlic with creamy, rich, buttery, tomme Pyrénées-laden potatoes. Bud worked away on her vegetarian fare and seemed content. I could see through the kitchen the masterpieces that awaited our sated mouths – Cointreau soufflés that formed small, perfect clouds on top of large ceramic bowls. This was the life of a *châtelain*.

Large wooden boards of pungent and colourful cheeses were passed around before the dessert. Bud said no, thank you, there was animal product in the cheese, and she would pass. Fontaines looked up.

'Brigid, why do you not eat cheese? You are not hurting the animals. The cheese does not have parents or eyes. You are not killing it.'

'Because there is animal rennet in it. They use the lining of animal intestine to help solidify the cheese.' Bud tended to stay away from the mouldy, strong cheeses which always contained this ingredient. She did enjoy lighter, white cheeses, like goats' and some sheep's milk that tended to be rennet-free.

This caused much consternation and chatter around the table, finally a hot debate. François had never heard of such of thing. He chastised Bud lightly.

'This is crazy. How can you not eat cheese in France? It is hardly a life worth living without cheese, not to mention meat.'

As Fontaines launched into Bud, the others smiled and peered at one another behind large, full wine glasses.

'And all these cats. I detest cats. When we were young, we would go out into the outbuildings and shoot wild cats. It was great fun.' He roared.

Bud was not amused. The others looked on, aware, I presumed, of this ritual, this testing that might or might not have been François' after-dinner game.

'You are a big man to kill cats. That takes a lot of courage,' Bud replied calmly, acidly.

He laughed. 'You are a vegetarian but by the look of it, you do not suffer from your diet,' François said, looking Bud up and down. Bud smiled uncomfortably. François, saw her becoming upset and backed off.

'I respect your decision but I simply cannot understand it. More wine,' he bellowed.

Soufflés went all around and we punctured our little treats with the tines of our forks with mouth-watering anticipation. Soon afterward, we retired to the main salon in the other wing of the house.

'This is a lovely room. Just stunning,' I observed.

'Yes, indeed, do you see that painting there?' Jake pointed out a small tableau of the Ascension of Christ surrounded by Mary and a few apostles on Calvary. 'It is a Raphael. In the family for generations.' I was astounded. We had furnished our house with pictures cut out from art books and glued to wood planks and varnished. We even had a few Raphael prints in the house. This was indeed a different world.

We lounged on fine embroidered sofas and drank cognac. François was feeling mischievous again.

'So, how is the business? Difficult, no?'

'Well, our summer was OK but we made nowhere near enough. And you?'

'We had a bad summer,' he confided. 'Since the 9/11 attacks in America, people are travelling less, scared. We are down almost forty per cent since before the terrorism. But it's not just Americans, it's everyone. It is a hard time. And like I told you before, you will have almost no French guests.' François became animated. He was on a roll now, and warming up to his favourite subject.

'In any given year, France is the fifth largest economy in the world, just after the United States, Japan, Germany and now China. France is always richer than the UK with the same population.' The old rivalry never dies. 'And yes, France does produce some of the finest things on the planet in fashion, food, design, wine. We even produce aeroplanes, steel and an immense harvest each year. But, France is an impoverished nation. The entire country is without a *sou*.'

As François lectured, I thought of something I had recently read. George Bush had gibed that the word for 'entrepreneur' does not exist in France. I'm sure one of his dutiful lackeys wrote this cute quip, but it hit the mark. In our short time in France, we came to feel and see the innate conservativeness of the people. No one seemed to speculate, no one invested and home ownership was painfully low. In the UK, United States, Ireland and a handful of other Anglo-modern capitalist democracies, home ownership is tied intimately to what it means to truly make it. It is the sign that you have arrived.

For my money, there is no better way to build wealth than to buy property. There is no equal way for an average, working man or woman to get ahead, to change their lives, to better their lot. The vast majority of French are excluded from this 'dream', They either choose to exclude themselves or are forced to subsist on meagre salaries, burdened further by hefty taxes and a gargantuan bureaucracy.

François continued.

'The banks are terrible here. Up until recently, bank loans were always fifteen years with twenty per cent down and no more than two times the lead wage-earner's salary. Impossible. Can you imagine the weight that places on a new buyer? The French government in its grand *paternalisme* has declared, by law, you cannot have more than forty per cent debt, although this is changing gradually.' It seemed things were changing a bit. We had a 25-year loan, though the bank had been reluctant.

'And home equity loans are unheard of in France. Can you imagine an America or Ireland or England without home-equity loans?' It was true. This is arguably the lifeblood of a consumerist economy.

I nudged into his soliloquy. 'The capitalist *dream* you find in the US and Britain is almost certainly a myth. The person who comes from nothing, pulls him- or herself up by the bootstraps and builds an empire *does* exist. Statistically, though, where you are born is most likely where you'll end up when you die. But, and this is very important, not necessarily. In France, almost without exception, it seems to me, where you are born *is* exactly where you will die, socially and economically.'

'That is why it is good to be born at the top, *non*?' He smiled.

The full weight of these realisations had been crashing down on us in the past months. The tiny resources and cheapness of the French kept coming up like a bad rash. French people would call us and insist on paying 30 or 40 euros (£20–£28) for a night. I never failed to point out that there was a camping site not far from the chateau.

One cannot run a business in a country where the local people do not or cannot support you. Thus the chateau had sat, unloved and unbought for years, as fear, conservative natures and lack of resources crushed the possibility of big dreams.

I was warming up too. 'Well, your criticisms may be true but part of the reason we appreciate France and enjoy your markets, the country life and the non-consumerism is the very thing that keeps the people impoverished. It is a simpler life, a life found in Britain or the US possibly forty or fifty years ago. Effort and risk are not appreciated but if you have to work, why not work thirty-five hours a week and take five or ten weeks' holiday? There are no iPods, no one drives a Hummer and no one has two hundred channels of television with nothing to watch. Everyone takes two-hour lunches, a universal ritual observed by every human in France. These are good things, *non*?'

'Yes, yes,' he said impatiently. 'But for us this is bad. Holidays here are simple with more than eighty per cent of French families staying with family on holiday. The rest go camping. Unfortunately for us, none of them stay in country chateaux at a hundred euros a night. France is a very good place to retire but not to run a business like ours.'

I could see that we were ignoring the rest of our lively party. We edged closer to the larger group. Bud was engaged with Helene talking about fabrics and hiring good help to clean our large houses.

I sat quietly and ruminated on the count's ruminations. The constraints and barriers to self-improvement in a more traditional, paternalistic culture are burdensome. Some days, over the summer, usually after some tussle with the infamous French bureaucracy, I had longed for the capitalist dream, the freedom to earn and spend and advance economically. Some days I felt like a committed, card-carrying libertarian. Life is not always black and white, as I would want it to be. Clearly, 'freedom' is not all about escape.

The night wore on and people began to leave. We didn't want to be the last out so we said our *au revoirs*.

As I was leaving, François pulled me aside.

'You should think of doing weddings and renting out the whole chateau. To foreigners. It could be good for you instead of continuing the *chambres d'hôtes*.'

I wasn't sure if François was trying to get rid of the competition or simply offering sound advice, but I feared he was right. This might be a good route.

'You should go talk to the La Fayes. They have a chateau near here and they have been doing weddings.'

We spoke excitedly and tiredly of our vigorous evening as I drove slowly down winding roads. I shared our conversation with Bud and brought up the idea of weddings.

'What do you think? Do you think he is right?' Bud ventured.

'I'm afraid so. Plus, you know, we're almost out of money again. I think I'm going to have to go and work in New York.' This was a bomb. Bud blanched.

'I've been thinking that. You know how hard it is here alone. I don't know how much longer I can take this. But I know you have to go. I just can't talk about it now. Can we talk about it tomorrow? In any case, let's go visit the La Fayes and see what they are like.'

We returned home to our own behemoth, tucked in the babies and kissed them goodnight. We snuck into the other bedroom and made love, ever so briefly forgetting the worries and fears of our new life as the lingerings of a delightful evening faded away.

The next day I did a quick search on the Internet and found out a little about the La Fayes. They were actually the de Coutures, Régis and Nicole. But it made sense to call them by their house name. By all appearances, they seemed embarked on a similar project to our own: three rooms to let and weddings made to measure.

We piled into the car and drove for 15 minutes in the direction of Fontaines until we came to a large brown sign, 'Château de la Faye'. We manoeuvred our way onto their entrance road and passed dozens of towering sycamores lining the way. In the distance we could see a handsome house, in the sixteenth-century chateau style with machiolations and towers and a small, older chapel sitting in front amidst well-maintained French hedges and flowers speckled everywhere in an explosion of colour.

We came to what appeared to be a side entrance. There were cars parked willy-nilly and a large catering van out the back. We got out and knocked on an open door. We waited briefly and decided to enter and climb a small wooden staircase capped with a heavily carved wood ceiling with coats of arms painted every few inches. I saw a door to the left slightly open and knocked again.

'*Oui?*' came a fatigued voice. We entered a large room lined with large shelves and filled with tattered, ancient books of all shapes and sizes. The furniture was worn but elegant. The walls were filled with old photographs and an old tea service sat on a lovely oak table in the middle of the room. There in the corner sat a figure hunched over a small table folding napkins.

'*Bonjour*, we are the Juneaus. We bought the chateau in Juvardeil, Château du Bonchamps. We were nearby and wanted to stop and say hello. But I see you are very busy.'

A sixty-something woman dressed fastidiously and with a kind, open face approached us and offered her hand. I recognised her as Nicole, the lady of the manor, from her website picture.

'It is so nice to meet you. Please come in. Yes, we are busy, we have a wedding today. There's so much to do but we wanted to meet you. We heard some Americans bought Bonchamps.'

Just then, her husband slipped into the room wearing thick rubber boots, a Barbour-type jacket and a torn, plaid shirt. His hair was sticking straight up as if he'd been recently shocked.

'Régis, these are the owners of Bonchamps. They came to say hello.'

He smiled briefly and flashed us a wild-eyed look.

'Yes, yes, I know this house. My parents used to eat there and I spent much time at the house as a child. It is so nice to meet you. My, you have a lot of work to do there! It was a mess.'

Nicole offered us coffee; we declined in light of their current engagement. But she insisted so we settled in for a short stay and told them about our various renovations. Régis gave us a tour of the salons. Tables and china and flowers were set magically in three adjoining rooms with massive Renaissance-style sculpted fireplaces, fine parquet floors and slightly tattered, handsome *toile de Jouy* on the walls.

'This is our last wedding. We hate them because we have to live in a small room for two days, there are people everywhere, the smell of the caterers' food, hysterical brides. It is too much,' Régis told us.

'We are too old for this,' Nicole explained. 'It is so little money for so much effort. And we have to do all the cleaning afterwards, or it's not worth the money.'

'How many weddings did you have this year?'

'This is our fifteenth.'

'How much do you charge?'

Nicole spoke evenly. 'About 1,500 euros for the day. The people will not pay any more than this. Plus they take some rooms sometimes, and pay extra. Your chateau would be perfect for weddings with the great big hall and the salons. You should take our business. We do not want to do this any more, at our age. We will send you our enquiries.'

'We were thinking about it but we did not want to hurt what you were doing.'

'Please, please do it. We are definitely finished. It is no life, really.'

Bud and I looked at one another, not sure whether to be happy about this new business idea or frightened to death.

Régis looked at me. 'How is the tannery by your chateau? It is a beautiful house, but the smell sometimes. I remember it from the 1950s, as a child.'

'It's not so bad. Some days we smell it, most days it's nothing.'

He smiled, not really believing me. 'Listen, you should go walk around the gardens with the children before you leave. Everything is almost ready for the autumn. And you must come back for the pumpkin fete we have every year.'

We said goodbye and made a tour of the grounds as the guests arrived outside. We peeked in the chapel with its hull-shaped wooden roof and colourful frescos clinging just barely to the thick stone walls. We walked past a large pond, just like our own, and entered their walled garden after passing by loads of brick and stone outbuildings. The garden was a little paradise, even now in September. Orange pumpkins and a hundred varieties of squash with a dozen colours, blues and whites and reds and yellows, sprouted and hung and dangled every which way. Standing guard to the side was a massive sequoia tree like our own. There was a little plaque nailed hastily to the trunk: 'This is the largest measured tree in Anjou. Measuring nine metres in girth.' I would have to see about that. I made a mental note to measure ours.

So that was it. We had the La Fayes' *imprimatur* to take over the weddings. No fear of hurting their struggling business. This opened up all new avenues for us. Sure, it would be hard, but we could survive for a day or two as people took over the house. We made all sorts of plans about inserting a little kitchen on the second floor for the times when the caterers took over our kitchen. And if we did 15 weddings a year, that would come to an extra 20,000 euros (£13,800) annually (minus lost B&B revenue during those times, of course). This could help and we were excited. We would expand our business, diversify, just like real people with a real business. Bed and breakfast, self-catering and weddings. There was hope at last after a meagre and sometimes dispiriting first summer.

But first, I would have to leave home, again. Abandoning my family. Whatever we had embarked on, this was not what we had hoped for. The whole point of the damned idea was to spend more time together, not less. Here I was, like some migrant worker caught in the vagaries of an impoverished country, forced to leave, to scrape together a living, drifting in and out of family life based on economic need. Come to think of it, this is what my French and Bud's Irish forebears had done for centuries.

CHAPTER SIXTEEN

Necessities

It was decided that I would leave soon and seek work in our old stomping grounds. But first, the harvest. Bud and I delayed and debated and contemplated and finally decided to pick our apples. It was difficult to do anything with two children much less climb trees and carry apples and load crates. The poor things were falling quickly. We thought it would be nice to serve apple juice to our much-desired guests, and it might be fun too.

We dug around in the outbuildings gathering old wooden boxes and fruit crates from times long past. We bundled the kids up into the van and made our way to the west side of our property. There, lined in semi-even lines, were 20 unhealthy looking apple trees bearing small misshapen apples of yellow, red and green. Across the pebble road which ran through the middle of our property was a line also of handsome, splayed pear trees, pinned obediently like little crucifixes against the broad, high stone wall of our garden. We decided to mix the two into a fancy Bonchamps blend – more out of necessity as the apples were sickly this year.

I ran around like an eager fool shaking trees and tossing apples and swinging Blue and Grim in wide circles as they laughed madly and we filled crate after crate. Bud worked more diligently with less fanfare and achieved more with less work. The children, with their small, cherubic bodies rolled on the damp, cool grass and nibbled every so often the juicy flesh of our modest harvest. They laughed and fell and got up again, delighted with this new game. Peals of laughter filled the air and echoed off the tall, dark woods just beyond. Hours later, Bud and I grew tired of our new profession and decided to call it quits, the decision made easier by the fact that hundreds of tiny, biting spiders loved to call the apple tree home. I lugged out an old set of weighing scales made of wood and iron and we measured our take. Two hundred kilos. Not bad.

We loaded our treasure into the old red van and drove to a local cooperative for pressing and pasteurising and bottling. Late in the evening, we drove back to the house, fiercely proud of our new-found farming skills. One hundred and fifty-seven bottles filled with golden brown liquid and fresh, tiny pieces of apple. We sat in the kitchen sampling the vintage and drinking long, satisfying glasses as Blue and Grim slept soundly on the cats' bed. Of all the possible places they could sleep in the house, they inevitably chose this untidy resting place. All was right in the Juneau household, at least for a day.

Ten days later, I landed in New York without a job or a place to live. I had managed to line up some interviews through old contacts in the business, but nothing was certain. It was a risk but I figured there was always work in New York. And what else could I do? We had no choice.

My best lead was a show about Hollywood and crime on a network called Court TV. The station was devoted exclusively to trials and the law and the live programming of infamous and tawdry cases. I had a couple of buddies working on the show *Hollywood At Large* and the supervising producer was an old colleague of mine from when I made documentaries.

I arrived in New York a little sad but very excited to be back for the first time since we'd abandoned ship. I took a taxi and as we drove across the Fifty-ninth Street Bridge straight into the heart of Manhattan, I was once again astounded at the breadth and height and grandeur of the city. The contrast with our homely little country town with its neat, routine ways and small row houses made me feel like a Lilliputian.

I went straight to the Court TV headquarters from the airport and was met by my friend Steve with a hearty handshake and a full smile. Steve and I had worked together on the old documentary show and had had loads of laughs. He was in his late forties but had a childish, devilish passion that always got me going. He had been an on-air presenter for years and was now toiling away behind the camera as a writer and producer. It was good to see him.

We had coffee and talked about the old days as I waited to meet the executive producer, a woman named Judy Bishop. After a few minutes, her secretary called me into her office.

'Hi, very nice to meet you. I'm Sam Juneau.'

'Good to see you. I've heard a lot about you. Sit down, please.'

Judy was a well-put-together woman of a certain age with blondish-brown hair, a fashionable black wool skirt and knee-high leather boots. We chatted briefly about the flight and the friends I had working with her.

'So, Sam, one of the producers told me you have a chateau in France. Why on earth are you here looking for freelance work?'

'It's a long story, but basically I need the money. It's that simple. We've started a B&B and now we are running out of money and I'm here to throw myself at the mercy of New York TV once again.'

I had planned to be honest about my desperate situation without really appearing too desperate. I showed her our website with pictures of the chateau and she was speechless. She eyed me curiously and briefly asked me about my other work experience, but I could tell she was familiar with me from speaking to my friends.

'So, when can you start? Does tomorrow morning suit you?'

'Perfect. I'll be here at nine. What's the rate?'

'How's two thousand a week?'

'It's a deal.'

It was that easy, thankfully. We were very needy at this point and I was grateful my gamble to fly to the States paid off so quickly. The pay was decent and the work seemed exciting.

I called Bud with the good news just as she was settling into bed.

'Bud, I got a job today on Court TV. It's two grand a week so we can breathe easier for the time being.'

'That's great, Sam. But today we ran out of gas for the heaters and it's freezing here. They're coming in two days to fill the tanks up but it'll be about two or three grand.'

Great. One and a half weeks of work just for the gas. And that gas would last us about two months, maybe two and a half. Thankfully, we only used the gas in the winter. I might have to stay a little longer than anticipated.

Now for a place to stay. I had a few options but all were short-term, mainly friends here and there. For the first week, I could stay with David, a friend from my college days who lived alone in Greenwich Village. My other immediate option was another friend, John Paul, who lived on a large estate about an hour north of the city.

After my triumphant interview, due entirely to the goodwill of friends, I headed downtown to David's and got out of the cab a few blocks early to enjoy the walk. I was on sensory overload after so much country life and isolation and the profound preoccupations of running my own estate. The shapes and sizes and faces and thousands and millions of particular and unique bodies darting everywhere at once filled me with exhilaration and excitement. The shops and the consumers and the goods and the plenty and the bounty and the large SUVs and fierce, hornet-like taxis swerving the streets wore me down in about 30 minutes. I found my way to David's art deco building, contacted the concierge, worked my way through his many locks and passed out on the sofa.

A few hours later, at around 7.30, David came in the door. It was New York after all – how could he possibly be home at five like a good French worker? In fact, he told me later, 7.30 was average, and a bit on the early side. We went to dinner and caught up on all the news. I slept fitfully, my dreams filled with images of the day and at least one thrilling, somewhat terrifying pursuit dream.

The next morning, I headed off on the subway to my new job. It felt good to be back in the mix. I couldn't say how long that feeling would last, but for now I was energised, delighted to be part of the working world, delighted to earn a few bob and support my starving family. Well, not quite starving. It's hard to get sympathy from anyone when you live in a chateau in the French countryside.

I quickly inserted myself into the job and took my fair share of ribbing. The kids on the staff called me 'count', prompted by my dear friend Steve. It didn't take long before I was back to my old self. Steve and I worked hard and did good work while bantering and playing and acting like eight-year-old boys. We told jokes and made fake farts and made fun of people and complained about the way things were run and ate almost everyday at a true New York diner just across the street. After the rich, beautiful country fare of France, I was beyond myself with joy to be eating hamburgers and fried chicken and waffles every day. I thought I had died and gone to heaven. That's one thing about being an expat – the longing, the lack of familiar tastes and sounds does wear on you over time. In France, everything was different, from sirens to TV to food to the weather to the pace of life. The old and familiar fit me like a well-worn coat.

Over the next few months, I worked on all sorts of salacious and fun stories. I interviewed Bianca Jagger about the lawsuit she had launched against her landlord over some mould in her apartment. New York made you crazy in that way. Scarce resources, small dark spaces, and astronomical prices all lead, eventually, to the day when you will sue someone. She was very sweet, another woman of a certain age but sexy and lively nonetheless. Just before the piece aired, she would call me and leave messages at work making sure I didn't forget about this and that fact or these and those grievances. She would always begin with, 'Saaaam, darling, I need so much to talk to you…' Then she would dig into the minutiae of the risks of black mould. It became a running joke in the office and most people then called me 'count' or 'Saaaam'.

Then, all hell broke loose. It seemed Michael Jackson, the King of Pop, the best-selling performer in the history of the universe had allegedly made a transgression, against a young, dying Hispanic boy. This story came down the pipeline like a whirlwind and hit us like a ton of bricks. Diane Dimond, an experienced and tenacious reporter, then working solo, had gotten exclusive access to the raid on Neverland Ranch, north of Los Angeles. It was announced breathlessly that she would be working for the network and our show on this and other stories.

The day the news broke we scrambled like chickens with our heads cut off to edit and piece together Diane's footage and reports from the great, sordid event. We crashed and put a rather lengthy and balanced package together in a matter of hours and made air that night. The next day, Diane showed up at our offices.

She walked into the room after we were all seated. She was striking, youngish and very well maintained with perfect anchor person hair, a wide, white toothy smile and good skin. She greeted all of us and settled down to business.

The following days were consumed with a repackaged rehashing of the infamous allegations. We worked long hours and in the madness, I realised I had overstayed my welcome at David's in the Village by several weeks. So, at the end of this insane week, I packed my one little bag with three changes of clothing and headed off on the train, like a good little commuter, to Bedford, an hour north of New York and the home of my friend John Paul. It felt odd walking through Grand Central Station, one of thousands rushing to make the train, coats and briefcases and hair and legs dashing and careening across the concourse. JP met me at the train station an hour later and we drove five minutes to his house where I promptly passed out on the sofa. Too much activity for my country self, too many stimuli.

The next day I awoke to a brilliant blue sky and the warmth of a cosy bed. I had spent the night in the guest house with JP. His father owned the property and came out from the city on weekends. Bedford had the convenience of a good commuter community while feeling and looking like a small New England town set in the remote countryside. The area was home to the rich and famous, people like Donald Trump, Susan Sarandon, Martha Stewart and a bevy of movers and shakers in the New York area.

We drank coffee in the morning and went up to the main house around one. I greeted JP's father, a robust, businesslike man who talked fast and accepted no bullshit, and his wife, a lovely French woman originally from near Toulouse. Immediately she and I hit it off as we both pondered the beauty and greatness of France while pooh-poohing the crude and unsophisticated ways of America. Here I was, working in the most tawdry, consumer-driven sector of American culture, the apex of all that was crude and base and unreflective in the US, and I was talking about the depravity of the nation that gave me the opportunity to buy a chateau and now enabled me to support my poor family. Absurd.

We sat down for a formal lunch, filled with wine and four courses and after-dinner drinks followed by a long conversation in front of the fire, all served up by pleasant and well-treated servants. Shortly after we had had our fill of gossip and entertaining, I called Bud.

I thought it might be nice to share such a pleasant, soul-affirming experience with my beloved. But the picture on the other side of the Atlantic was not so festive. I was seeing old friends, running around New York, working on an exciting story and feasting like a spoiled Renaissance cardinal at a fine country estate. I was indeed lonely for Bud and Blue and Grim but consoled myself with a few treats here and there. Bud wasn't having it. Nor should she.

'It's not fair. It's freezing here, I have to take care of the kids by myself and I saw a rat the size of a dog trotting down the stairs last night.'

We spoke at length and determined that, even though I had only been gone a month, I could not, should not leave her with the running of our property. We would have to come up with something to change our situation.

I couldn't help it. I repeated, by the grace and generosity of my kind hosts, the same spectacle on Sunday – food, wine, dessert, more drinks. On Monday, I rose from my weekend-induced daze and trundled off to the train to make my commute to midtown Manhattan. I boarded with hundreds of my fellow 'Man in the Gray Flannel Suit' comrades and arrived early at the office. Instead of working on the television show, I searched all morning for wedding and marriage websites and set about advertising on as many as I could find. I found a particularly good guide that had both an Internet and guidebook companion that focused exclusively on the centre and north-west of France.

I was determined to be with my family. Certainly, my welcome back to New York was splendid. But I couldn't help thinking over and over, the life we were living now was a long way from our stated and intended goal. In fact, it was the exact opposite. I also booked a flight home in two weeks so I could spend at least a few days at home before I returned to continue my getting and spending and working in the Big Apple. My final personal call of the morning was to the only rat-catcher listed in Anjou. I set up an appointment at the chateau with Bud and turned my mind to the work at hand.

That afternoon, we had another meeting with Diane and the troops. Just before the meeting, Judy, the executive producer, called me into her office.

'Sam, I have an assignment for you. I want you to go with Diane to Los Angeles to cover the preliminary hearings of the Jackson trial. You'll be out there from the end of this week probably for a week. She's tough and aggressive and will need your help. Are you up for it?'

'Sounds great,' I replied, unbelieving of my good fortune. I had been to LA before on stories and liked it there – the sun and the sense of possibility. But this also solved a more pressing problem: I could stay on the road in a hotel at company expense and not impose too desperately on my friends.

Diane and I met at the airport. She was flying first class and I was in the back with the peasants. Somehow – perhaps the check-in woman recognised her – Diane arranged an upgrade so we could both sit up front and discuss business. This was a far cry from the goats and chickens I had flown with on my way over from France on my budget flight. I liked the way she did business.

We arrived in LA and hired a baby-blue Jaguar with a sunroof. It was sunny, and 78 degrees. We left the airport and started out towards the Beverly Hills Hotel, the site of a secret crisis meeting being held by Jackson's financial advisers. Diane had somehow convinced the powers that be it was necessary to stay at this hotel so we could scour the lobby, look for scoops and interviews and possibly get the inside track on the inner workings of the Jackson camp.

We checked as the fanciest cars pulled up loaded with their well-heeled passengers. We spent the afternoon making calls, setting up interviews and trying to stir up information on the secret meeting. Shortly after dinner, we retired to the bar with our cameraman Peter and a few other newsies from various networks. We chatted excitedly about the purported meeting as Sylvester Stallone, all five–foot-nothing of him, sidled up to the bar with a young cutie. James Caan sat in a dark corner with another twenty-nothing hottie. He recognised Diane from television and asked her to join them for a drink. Diane waved me over and we chatted with Sonny Corleone for a few minutes. He seemed like a nice man but I couldn't help searching his hairline like a mildly deranged child trying to count the number of hairplugs in his famously enhanced pate.

The next days were filled with interviews, past and present Jackson accusers, attorneys, minor celebs and experts of every sort and colour. A week into the trip, we made our way to Santa Barbara to stage our next set of interviews before the big court hearing just north of there. Santa Barbara is quite simply one of the most beautiful spots on earth. It is a place where the spectacular Santa Ynez Mountains crash like silent titans into the rough and splendid waters of the Pacific

Ocean. The weather is perfect, sunny and 80 degrees most times of the year; the people are friendly; there is no disease and no poverty and the streets are clean. This is entirely untrue yet it seemed to be the case as I installed myself in a large suite boasting a vast balcony with clear views to the horizon of the roaring sea. I would keep this one to myself for now. It was just too much. Fortunately, for the sake of my conscience, we only stayed there for three days.

Our stay in paradise was nearing its end and my flight was set to leave from New York on Friday. On Wednesday, I got nervous as the hard-driving, never tiring Diane kept turning up old contacts and new voices for our pieces. Late that evening, I timidly told Diane my situation – I had to go back to France for a few days, it was a life-or-death situation. As a mother and grandmother (hard to believe), she was understanding and insisted we start back at the earliest possible time. We called our travel people and booked the earliest flight for Friday morning. If we hopped on that, I could just make my evening flight to Paris. Five hours from LA to New York, two hours at the airport and then seven hours overnight to France. It had to be done.

Midday Saturday, I arrived at the train station in Angers from Paris. Bud was there in our heaving, partly rusted 17-year-old Mercedes with two beaming faces sitting in the back peering out the window. I jumped into the car and burst into tears. I hugged and kissed my dear little family as if it had been years since I'd seen them. Such is the life of the emigrant coming back to the homestead after scraping together a living in a foreign land.

Later that night, we all nestled into bed, our one large bed, cranked up the ailing heating system and drifted off to sleep, four little birds in the nest. Just after sweet sleep's comforting touch, I heard a yelp.

'Ouchhh! Dammit!'

I leaned over as quickly as I could in my post-flight stupor and flipped on the light.

Just then, I saw the back end of something hairy and a long, spindly pink tail slip into the bathroom.

'What happened?' I yelled.

'That rat just bit me,' Bud replied calmly.

I was home at last.

CHAPTER SEVENTEEN

Clouds Gathering

After weeks relying on the kindness of friends and strangers, sleeping on sofas, crashing at country estates and living in four-star luxury on the road, I had found my way home for Christmas. The time had passed so quickly I had trouble getting my bearings back at the chateau. The mood in the house was not particularly festive but we were all grateful to be together after our time apart.

In the quagmire of my Michael Jackson duties, I had managed to field a couple of dozen requests for wedding visits. One, made by a young French count, was particularly urgent as he and his fiancée intended to marry in two months' time on Valentine's Day. On my first day back at the house, I groggily greeted the young hopefuls who had visited to look around the place for their wedding venue. The count was average height with dark hair, dark eyes and a barely hidden snarl. I didn't quite know why he was so displeased but his countenance did not match his easy-going speech. His beloved was tall and willowy with black hair and long elegant fingers.

We seated ourselves in the large, warm wood-panelled library. I made coffee and sat with the two babes (they couldn't have been more than early twenties) and we chatted of little things concerning Anjou – the weather, the upcoming festivals, the happenings in Angers. I gave them a tour of the house and some of the grounds. They seemed excited and decided to book. The rate was a modest 1,200 euros (£830) for use of the chateau for the day. I told them they could stay free of charge on their wedding night, as the honoured couple, and the other rooms would range from 74 to 94 euros, breakfast included. They didn't want to commit to the rooms so we signed an informal agreement and parted ways.

I wasn't entirely happy with the price. I had recently seen *Gosford Park* on DVD. I looked up the house on the Internet, featured so stunningly in the film. Wrotham Park, a mid eighteenth century Palladian villa with a vast park, offered wedding receptions for eight hours only at a cool £4,000. I must be honest, Bonchamps did not have the perfection and quality of this English masterpiece. But my resentment grew as I pondered the market for weddings in France. I had done my research and I knew the prices – the prices people were willing to pay. For our first year, we decided on 1,200 euros. The upper end for a stately chateau in the central west of France was 1,800 euros (£1,200), still one-third the tariff of an equivalent English country house. But we made our decision and wanted to build up business and get referrals later on down the road. I mused, why couldn't we live in a country where people made real money and weren't afraid to spend it? The answer, sadly, was we never could have afforded such grandeur if the market were more competitive, more aggressive. Such was our lot. Still, a thousand or so in February, plus rooms, wasn't a bad start.

I met with about half a dozen other couples over the holidays. I could only wait for their responses as I trudged back to New York after only a week at home. Bud would have to take care of the arrangements for February's wedding. At the end of January, I received a call.

'Sam, we have a major problem. You know that gigantic Lebanese cedar right next to the house? With the huge branches? The one where the kids always play?'

'Yes?'

'It fell down in a storm yesterday. It's blocking part of the road and is splayed out all over the parking area, the field where you want the guests to park for the wedding.'

'Any other good news?'

'Oh, the gas bill came. Nineteen hundred euros.'

I quickly got on the Web and looked up as many arborists as I could find in our little region. Call after call, the verdict was the same – at least 1,000 euros, sometimes up to 3,000… oh, and we can't do it until late April. The cost would swallow any profit we hoped to gain from the wedding. Bud called in a few friends from the town and nobody could even contemplate taking the monster on. Months, they all said. I left it at that, hoping for some minor miracle.

But not all was lost. Since Christmas, we had pulled five more weddings and bookings were up nicely since our first summer. We even had a full house for Easter for several days. So, our season was starting in early April now, not late June like last year. The Guard's House, the dutiful money-maker, was filling up nicely too.

Another spot of good news came from Bud's sister Mary. Over the months of my long American sentence, Mary was able to make repeated and dutiful trips to help care for the children and provide Bud with company. Somehow, she had arranged with her job to take a leave of absence. She was the eldest of Bud's nine siblings and had fallen madly in love with Blue and Grim. She seemed to have an endless capacity to care for and play with the tireless, sometimes relentless babies. Her visits and selfless generosity helped keep Bud sane during that long dark winter.

Five days before the wedding, I landed myself back at the chateau, ready to take care of business. As Bud drove us up the long dirt road to the house, there, lo and behold, were no fewer than 13 neat and perfectly straight stacks of wood, cut and sorted, good to bad, ready for carting off and burning.

'Bud! What happened? Who did that?'

'Who do you think? Jehan-Claude. He's been here since the tree fell. Day and night, when he's not working, cutting the thing up.' Bud smiled. She'd been keeping this from me as a surprise.

Dear, dear Jehan-Claude. Shortly before we bought the chateau, he and his wife had made the short move to the end of our long road where they took up residence in a small stone farmhouse. We had called on the man several times over the past year and a half to fix drains, repair the old, beaten-up washing machine, sort out minor electrical problems and rake leaves. JC was our saviour.

Relieved and profoundly thankful, I began raking and mowing and sweeping, vigorously and vainly trying to get the grounds into some semblance of order. Bud took over the cleaning and laundering of the linens with Patricia, a local woman who had worked for the association for Down's syndrome adults back in the 1990s. She was smart and efficient with strong, thick arms and the work ethic of a tireless plough horse.

Over the next 72 hours, tables, chairs, flowers and decorations arrived, always accompanied by the sweet, happy smiling faces of the bride and groom. The caterers piled into the kitchen in the late morning of the day of the wedding and began their intricate work. My nerves were taut as I feared for the success of the big day... would there be enough parking, would the guests like the house, would the happy couple be pleased?

The wedding began in earnest around six in the evening. The caterers were on their marks, music was floating gently on a mild sunny day and the wine and cocktails began to flow. Bud and I and the babies retired to our '*appartements*' just above the kitchen, watched videos and peered, all of us, out the window as a pageant of guests arrived with grins and looks of awe in their gleeful eyes. The only bit of news to dampen an otherwise stellar debut was the fact that not one of the 150 guests took a room for the night. I had set a generous price, the price of a crack house in the East End of London, 74 euros, *with breakfast*, and not a soul booked a room.

Around three in the morning, things started to settle down and the music finally stopped playing. Luckily, Blue and Grim slept right through and I made the final rounds to make sure all was in order. The caterers had cleaned up, nothing appeared to be broken, drunken couples staggered out the door and people took long, lingering sips of champagne as the party was finally at an end.

The next morning, I was up at seven with Patricia to do a final clean up and serve breakfast to our newly wedded guests, our only guests, Monsieur et Madame le Comte. They rose and appeared at around noon. I poured coffee for them. They were quiet and utterly depleted after the night's revelry. They seemed pleased as they worked on croissants and fresh apple juice.

'*Ça va?*' I ventured.

'*Oui*, it was a wonderful day. *Génial. Étonnant.*'

'And the guests, were they happy?'

'Everyone loved the house,' the bride said. 'Just one thing, though. You really have to lower your room prices, because you won't have any guests if the rooms are so expensive.'

I thought my head would explode. Seventy-four euros per room (94 for a suite that slept five) and you're telling me I have to lower my prices? Do you realise the cost of maintaining the property, the cost of heat just for one day for your wedding? On the verge of losing it, I smiled.

'Thank you so much for the advice. I will keep that in mind. I'm delighted you had a lovely day.'

I couldn't bear to think Fontaines was right. It killed me. How could you make a living in the service industry when the local people, your neighbours and new-found countrymen, would not spare a *sou* to spend a night, one godforsaken night, in a chateau after a splendid wedding?

My night-time bedside friend Balzac wrote, 'Finance, like time, devours its own children.' This niggling reality, the truth about our prospects, had begun its feast.

CHAPTER EIGHTEEN

L'Espoir

Insanity: doing the same thing over and over again and expecting different results. With this nugget of wisdom tucked firmly in our hatbands, we ploughed ahead. I struggled back at the chateau for a month and a half after that first wedding and then continued my vagrant and transitory existence in New York, made a few more trips out to California and made enough money to keep the ship afloat until the summer season began. I had been in the big, bad city for five months total with time off back at the castle for good behaviour. It felt good to bring in some dough, but fundamentally the situation was untenable. This summer was make or break.

By late May, we had nine weddings lined up for the year with more requests for the next year. I got smart after that first experience and made renting of the chateau contingent on booking all the rooms. This helped a little and most people conceded. This brought income from half of our wedding receptions to about 2,000 euros with the others languishing in the 1,200 euro mark. Our bookings for bed and breakfast in the chateau were up to about 180 nights with 14 weeks in the Guard's House, plus the weddings. Not terrible, but not yet sufficient.

We busied ourselves with all the duties of spring cleaning. The chateau looked good, the trees and flowers were blooming, the bees were active. So we joined in and quickly made another baby shortly after my return, a lonely sailor back from the high seas looking to reclaim his wife and his life.

In the late afternoon one warm, sunny day, Bud called me over to the house as I mowed our unruly lawn. This minor chore consumed no fewer than fifteen hours a week and became alternately a time of solace and annoyance.

'I was cleaning up the Oak Suite and I saw a couple of dozen bees climbing the walls. Maybe you should take a look.'

We went up to the second floor together to see what our new friends were doing. I leaned down and opened up a retractable metal chimney cover that sat just inside the fireplace. This was a simple covering to prevent draughts from coming down the chimney. We heard an enormous roar, the buzz of thousands of little bodies moving and shaking and doing their springtime thing. I peered carefully up the chimney and spotted a grotesquely large hive wedged into the brick walls of this long disused shaft.

L'ESPOIR

I called Jehan-Claude on the phone and he suggested I call the *pompiers*, or fire brigade. I quickly set up an appointment. I tried to insist in my pidgin French that they needed to come that day or early the day after as we had guests the next night.

Bright and early the next day, the *pompiers* showed up, including some of the same lads who had investigated the infamous hornet sting incident. They arrived with a massive crane and set to work scurrying on the roof and down the chimney with ropes and ladders and various contraptions. The visit caused all sorts of excitement for the children. Blue ran around the red beast of a fire engine while Grim crawled behind, the two of them like intoxicated banshees, screaming and climbing on steps, pulling on cords and hoses, delighted.

An hour later the job was done. I thanked the men and considered it well worth the 40 euros, the standard fee for beekeeping duties. Later that afternoon, an elderly couple arrived in a red convertible sports car. They had booked two nights in the Oak Suite, a mini-honeymoon, the two of them on second and third marriages (so the affable man had told me down the telephone from Wales). I greeted them and gave the quick tour of the library and dining room while enquiring as to whether or not they desired dinner that night in our little village. As we arrived at the door to their suite, it struck me that I hadn't reinvestigated the room since the firemen had exterminated the bees. I flung open the door hastily, stepped in first and searched the room frantically. Clean.

No sign of bees. Relieved, I bid them good day and let them get down to urgent business.

Patricia and I served them breakfast the next morning and they disappeared. They seemed pleased and full of energy. Late that night as Bud and I watched the BBC's *Pride and Prejudice* for what seemed like the fortieth time, I heard a knock on the door.

'I'm terribly sorry to bother you, but we have a little problem in our room. Can you come take a look?'

'Of course.'

I followed the spry gentleman up to the room. His mood was good – which I assumed was due either to the euphoric success of his mini-honeymoon or to the fact that the problem was not particularly major. As he led me into the room, I heard a slight chuckle. His new, freshly bathed wife sat on a small sofa reading a book. He walked over in front of the fireplace and just stood there.

There, on the floor, sat a slow-moving golden stream with a pleasant, familiar scent.

'We were sitting here reading.' Sure, you were reading, I thought. 'And all of a sudden we heard an enormous crash. I looked around for the source of the noise and as I poked around the fireplace, this river of honey came seeping out.'

I was mortified. 'I am so sorry. I thought we had taken care of this. What an alarming thing to happen. I can move you, immediately,' I stammered, and tried to be as solicitous as I could muster. They insisted on staying and assured me they were delighted with the accommodation.

They seemed embarrassed by my attentions. They frowned at one another and looked me over. A long moment passed and nothing was said.

Finally, 'We've had a perfect stay and you've been so hospitable. But we have one favour to ask.'

'Anything.'

'Can we stay in this room another night? I know we didn't book it for this evening, but we would love to grab an extra day.'

'Of course. It would be our pleasure.'

'And please don't charge us for the room service we've had here tonight.'

We all laughed heartily and I left them to their business. So it had been with most of our guests. In general, so far, they had been a good, unique group of open and adventurous people who thought a few days or a week in the French countryside with good books and lovely trees and pleasant walks might be a good way to unwind and 'escape into authentic French country living'. Or so our publicity said. And as people came and went, it proved true.

In the thick of the summer, our friends Dennis and Marion came – that Marion, who was the mother of the famous Irish brawlers of Angers, the boys who had come two summers ago to work the property. Dennis and Marion came as friends and worked like dogs, helping us hold up the fragile venture. Their only need was bed and food, their only desire seemingly to work in the sun. One night they were sitting out the back of the chateau, drinking wine late into the evening. Bud and I had gone to bed. At around 11 o'clock I heard a tap at my door.

'Sam, it's Marion. There's a guest down here who needs something. He's pretty angry. Can you come?'

I peeked out the window and saw the stout Englishman who had arrived that afternoon with his wife and two grown children, standing belligerently on the driveway with folded arms. I put on my clothes and went downstairs to face whatever music our revered guest was playing.

'Good evening. What can I do? Is everything all right?'

'No. Everything is not all right. We are in the Poplar Room and there is a group of Americans above us making all sorts of noise. We cannot sleep. I just travelled overnight on the ferry, arrived in this morning and drove five hours to get here. Where, by great misfortune, I was seated next to this same family at dinner at your local restaurant and was forced to watch while they acted like complete animals.'

I could believe every word he was saying. The Americans were a loud, flashy set of mother, grandmother and three grown, hipster kids from Miami. They wore thick leather belts and gold jewellery draped over thick leather skin, toughened from too much sun, finished off with gobs of make-up and teased up hair. Since their arrival they had been incredibly high-maintenance, demanding directions repeatedly (Americans are the worst at driving and understanding European roads) and hairdryers and extra pillows and special breakfasts and long chats about property and money. Despite this, they weren't bad people, just boisterous. I had actually enjoyed some of our discussions and got a good laugh out of their antics.

But I knew what he said was most certainly true.

'OK, well, come with me. I will sort out the problem. I can talk to them.'

'Wait a second,' he commanded. 'What sort of place are you running here that you don't even know what is going on in your own house? Tell me.' As I headed off to solve the problem he grabbed my arm. I had no inclination to stand here and talk more. But he was very insistent.

'Well, Mr Portsmouth, as you can see the house is very large and I can't possibly hear or know what's happening in the other wing unless, of course, you come and tell me, as you've done. Now I'm going to do something about it.'

'That's not acceptable,' he said, now purple with rage.

I was growing angry also. But I remained calm. He proceeded to catalogue their transgressions: loud radio playing (and we didn't have radios in the rooms), bouncing on the beds, yelling.

'Would you like me to give you another room?' I thought this was a generous suggestion. Actually, offering him another room, a larger suite, was a good deal more work for me and Bud.

'What?' he practically yelled. 'They are the ones misbehaving and we have to move. I can't believe you suggested that.'

'OK, OK. Relax. Let me go talk to them. I'm sure we can work it out.'

'No. You wait. I'm not finished.'

That was the final straw. When I have a problem, my first inclination is to deal with it head on. This man wanted to talk and lecture and hold forth on the shortcomings of the establishment. It felt as if he was unloading a year's worth of work frustrations in this one conversation. His all-too-brief holiday amidst long hours chained to the desk would serve as an opportunity to release all the built-up tension.

'No, sir. You are finished.' I spoke firmly and menacingly. 'You will command me to do nothing. I am the lord of this goddamn manor and we will solve this problem the way I see fit. You can either come with me and sort this out or stay here and stew.'

This proved too much for Willy Loman. He leaned into me and spoke quickly and furiously. 'I will not be treated like this. I am here to rest and I am very tired, exhausted. All I want to do is sleep.' At this point, he was shaking, red-faced and sputtering.

I said, 'You better back off immediately.'

Just as things were about to reach a crisis point, Dennis walked calmly over to our potential melee. Dennis was a policeman in Ireland so he knew his way around a brawl in the making. I felt comforted by the fact that he was a mountain of a man with impossibly broad shoulders, a thick neck and legs like tree trunks. He listened quietly, towering over both of us. Dennis had been sitting out the back drinking wine for a good long time by this point. Suddenly out of the depths of his being, he roared, 'Enough!' The sound he emitted shook us to the core. My dear guest turned white. I thought he was going to faint. It was the loudest noise I had ever heard issue from a mortal's mouth.

At that moment, having heard the ruckus, Bud poked her head out the window.

'Sam, it's OK. Just go take care of it. They shouldn't be moved and the Americans should be quiet.'

Bud's calm, sweet Irish voice quickly served to settle everyone so we could get on with the important business of restoring peace and quiet to the chateau. The effect of that astounding bellow seemed to smooth the tensions. I thought quietly to myself that a little humour, a calm head and a loud yell might just be what's needed in international diplomacy.

I walked up to the second floor, knocked quietly. The mother answered. I said, 'I'm sorry to bother you but we have a little problem. The fella downstairs is very upset.' I looked around the room and saw our wannabe rock stars lounging around, throwing a beach ball, while the youngest laid into a very good air guitar. I asked them to turn off the radio that they'd brought with them, stop jumping on the beds and quiet down. The mother smiled at me and said, 'No problem. I'm so sorry. I don't know what to do with these kids.'

And that was that.

The next morning I went out of my way to serve our English friends first. I was attentive and asked them how they'd slept. The couple were sheepish and had looks of consternation on their faces. Before the awkwardness could continue, I spoke up. 'You'll be happy to know I'm implementing a new no-American rule at the chateau.'

I didn't know how this would go down. I laughed first and thankfully they joined in, happy to have that little unpleasantness behind us.

Two weeks later, we were preparing for our seventh wedding. Six down, three to go. These days always upset me. It was early August and the strain of running the B&B

was beginning to wear us out. This was a big one: close to 200 people, definitely the upper limit of our capacity… for both the chateau and our tired selves.

The difficult times were the weddings: the grind of helping set up, accommodating caterers who moved like invading forces into our lives for a day, sometimes two, music until 3.30 a.m., loud departing drunken revellers, anxiety over the health and safety of the chateau, claustrophobia from being locked up in our set of rooms with two squirming and sometimes tangling children, all the worries that come from accepting (normally) 100–150 living beings into your house. It was unnatural to have to share your space, even though the space was quite large, with total strangers. It had seemed easy when we began. How hard could it be to clean a few rooms, serve a nice breakfast, with home-made apple-pear juice, no less, to greet guests and take their money? The simple answer: extraordinarily hard. *Caveat emptor*.

This was one of the weddings for which I had not enforced my 'all rooms' rule but, in spite of that, all the rooms were booked by guests of the wedding. Our first guests, a couple in their mid to late forties, arrived at 1 p.m., roughly three hours ahead of time. They were a well-dressed couple down from Paris for the day. I greeted them and showed them to the second floor. They had booked our cheapest, smallest room at 74 euros but it did have a lovely view of the pond and the setting sun and was most comfortable.

I showed them their accommodation. Immediately, the husband spoke up.

'Is there no key?'

'No, we do not have keys for the rooms. If you have something valuable, I am happy to keep it safe for you during the wedding.'

'This is terrible. I cannot believe there are no keys. I must have a key.'

'It's not been a problem to this point. But there is no key for your room.'

He said thank you and closed the door with a huff. Ten minutes later, I heard a sharp knock at our salon door. I was in the middle of showing the chef where all his accoutrements could go.

I answered. It was Monsieur Picky .

'*Oui?*'

'There is dirt in our room. It must be cleaned.'

'It should be in good order, but I will send Patricia up to inspect it.'

Patricia went up to the room and returned five minutes later looking rather confused.

'The room was clean. He pointed out a very small water ring on one of the radiators and a dead bug behind one of the curtains. Other than that, it was very *propre*.'

The man came down five minutes later with devilish determination.

'Sir, this is not acceptable. You must come and see the room.'

'Let's go,' I offered hopefully.

I entered the room after my cherished client where he proceeded to point out tiny specks of dust, the accused water ring (a stain from the nineteenth century, I surmised) and another fly behind the door. He insisted I bend over to observe his proud find.

'And we must have a key.'

He then demanded I lean down to inspect a bit of dust on the skirting boards. At this, I stood tall and said, 'Sir, that is enough. Patricia has cleaned this room and we are not going to continue this dance any longer. If you would like another room, I can move you next door. It is larger and I believe, by chance, there is a key.'

'Very well. Yes, please do that.'

I showed him the room and walked away, certain that I had no reservation in this one room. I had previously thought all the rooms were booked, but when I referred to the diary, no one was pencilled in.

I presumed the matter was settled until about 30 minutes into the pre-dinner cocktail party, when a tall, tanned, elegant French woman approached me in the kitchen and asked me to show her to her room. Assuming everyone had already checked in, I scurried over to my reservation book and scanned the pages. There she was, written in near-insane scribble at the bottom of the page under a group of cancellations, booked into the room I had just relocated Monsieur and Madame Picky to.

'I'm terribly sorry. I've put someone in that room, but I have another room across the hall with a double bed that's available.'

'I'm sorry but that won't do. The room is for me, my husband and our daughter. We need the extra bed of the room we booked.'

We all padded upstairs to the double-booked room where I found Monsieur Picky lounging on the bed, perfectly content with a big smile on his sharp face.

'I am terribly sorry about this. I realise I said you could have this room but I've made a mistake. These people here have three people and they need this room.'

'This is outrageous!' he exclaimed.

'Yes, I've made a mistake. For your trouble you can stay with no charge.'

'But there isn't a key for the other room.'

Madame Tall and Tanned stood in the hall observing this humiliating ritual.

'I've told you about the keys. We do not have keys. It is pure chance that this room has got one.'

'I cannot accept this.'

The summer had worn my now erratic and generally unstable self. A more mature, suave and professional hotelier would have made things work in the gentlest possible way. Instead, I persisted, 'I am the lord of this manor and I have decided there are no keys. You can stay in the other room at no cost, with one condition: you must never come to this property again.'

Tall and Tanned laughed out loud at this crude American comment. She seemed to be enjoying the tussle.

Monsieur and Madame Picky gathered their things and left the chateau. I'm not quite sure if they ever attended the wedding or not. Perhaps, I thought, the hospitality business was not my calling.

Around 11 that night, Bud, the children and I turned in. I planned to get to sleep early and make my rounds to check on the house at 3 a.m., and again at 7 a.m. in order to prepare for breakfast.

But at 11.30, I heard a loud banging on our door.

'Mr Juneau. Please come quickly. The groom needs to see you immediately. There has been an accident.'

I jumped out of bed, struggled into my clothes and shot out the door.

I entered the great hall where a long line of tables had been spread majestically down the whole length of the room. The party had stopped and there was a gathering in the middle of the hall.

I hastened over and there, to my horror and astonishment, sat a round little man with a napkin draped over his head thickly stained with dark red.

'What happened?' I said as I rushed to his side.

'It is nothing really. I was playing with your shutters, just there, by the window. I should not have opened it. When I did, a large metal bar fell down from just inside the window casing and hit me in the head.'

Astonished, I managed, 'Can I call the paramedics for you?'

'It has already been done. I'm terribly sorry for the trouble.'

'Please, let me get you something.'

'No, no, *tout va bien*. Please don't worry yourself.'

I sat with the kind man and thought, if this had been another country, possibly my own, a country where people sought money wherever it was available, a man in his position – sitting in a chateau, just injured by a metal bar that had broken off from our window – might be saying, 'This is an outrage. I will sue you for everything you own. I will own you.' For the first time in a long time, I was grateful to be where the mercenary aspects of life were less pronounced.

Eight minutes later, the paramedics and *pompiers* arrived. Among their happy, bemused faces, I recognised many of my old buddies from the infamous bee and hornet episodes. They tended to the jolly guest, bundled him up and shipped him off to the hospital for a few stitches.

Exhausted, I reassured the groom, expressed my apologies and returned to our room.

'What happened?' Bud queried.

'One of the guests was poking around with the shutters and a metal bar fell on his head. He needs a few stitches so he's gone to hospital. I think he's OK.'

'I think it's time to find another line of work.'

Perhaps. But for the time being our choices were limited. We would continue doing what we had been doing all along and expecting a different outcome: namely, running a B&B, gîte and wedding venue day in, day out, fielding catastrophes like inept amateurs, all the while hoping for peace and quiet and contentment.

As we neared the end of the summer, we soaked up the relief of our modest success like a potent tonic. The final figures were coming in: 383 nights in the B&B, 14 weeks in the Guard's House, nine weddings. Income for the year through to September: 57,000 euros (£39,000). Not disastrous considering it was a first *real* year with advertising and time to get the word out. With the money from America, we could just about support the house and its many, clamouring needs. Obviously, this was a gross amount, not including the endless '*redevances*', or payments, to the French government, particularly heinous for a small business in its first years. In the end, we had not a cent to spare from our upkeep, the seeming infinity of bits and pieces and necessities needed to maintain and nourish an active family of four, soon to be five. Not to mention the cost of maintaining twenty-odd cats – it seems strays were more than happy to join our original fifteen.

Our last guests of the season arrived on a late afternoon in mid September. I could hear the smooth purr of a car cruising up the lane to the front of the house. In a black, sleek, late-model Audi sat two distinguished and cool customers.

I laid my pruning sheers down and welcomed them. Johan and Monique were Dutch-speaking Belgians from Antwerp. He had thick greyish dark hair, a perfectly pressed white cotton shirt and handsome, casual loafers. Monique was tall and slim with a modern haircut and thin, refined features and full lips. They were lively, spoke perfect English and we made a connection immediately. They were thrilled with their room, the Chestnut Room on the ground floor. It was vast and nicely appointed with a bathroom the size of most hotel rooms in Europe. They planned to stay for two nights. We arranged a time for breakfast and they set off for the evening.

The next morning I began the breakfast service. They appeared to be well rested and relaxed.

'So, Sam, did you inherit this place?' Johan asked.

'Unfortunately not. We bought it a few years ago.'

'But you are so young. Very impressive.'

'Impressive or stupid, I'm never quite sure.'

'I love the rooms. I hope you don't mind, but we looked around. It's very nice,' Monique interjected. 'It is simple but elegant and very comfortable.'

'We are looking to buy something like this too,' Johan added. 'Not really this big, but we want a country house, to run a business, make some income for the maintenance and spend holidays here from time to time.'

We set about talking of the ins and outs of property in France, the idea of a business, the advantages and pitfalls. Monique ran a small B&B in an old townhouse in Antwerp. So they knew what they were in for. Bud joined us in the late morning and she and Monique spoke of design and decoration and shared ideas and creative insights. We spent the morning talking excitedly about the prospects in France. The conversation inevitably tended towards culture and art. This was the very reason I had so eagerly anticipated meeting guests when we first started out those many months ago. I didn't need to be friends with all our clients, just once in a while, I had hoped to meet intelligent, cultured people who could bring energy and interest into our little bit of country.

'So, Sam, how did you go about buying this chateau?' Johan asked. 'Do you have names of agents? We want to visit some houses while we are here. If we find some things we like, we might stay longer.' Very well. It was in my best interest to help them in their search.

'Certainly. I will make some calls and have our agent come here to meet you. It will be great fun.'

Countless cups of coffee later, I called Philippe, our trusty agent. He was ecstatic to have a new client and promised to come over early that afternoon. Meanwhile, Johan and Monique disappeared for the day, off into the French countryside on a titillating jaunt through the region's architectural history.

The next morning I laid out a perfect breakfast for our tired house seekers. I let them eat in peace although I was dying to hear the news.

'So, I want to hear all about it,' I began enthusiastically as they finished.

Johan was subdued but spoke passionately. 'There are so many beautiful castles here. And the prices are still about one half or a third of what we'd pay in Holland and Belgium. We saw one castle, very similar to yours, with 60 hectares, 1,200 square metres, a large lake and more than 30 rooms. Great details. The only problem is it sat very near to a minor but busy *route nationale*. I can't say we like the decor, many outré things and heavy wall coverings and terrible bathrooms, but overall it was very nice and you could easily change those things with some money.'

'That sounds like our house. Very similar. Where was that one?'

'Just an hour west of here with good access to Paris. It's definitely a possibility.'

'I don't understand the decoration, though. It seems to me these old French families have no taste. Perhaps it is a matter of money too. That is why they are selling,' Monique chimed in.

They had seen three other houses that day. That's a lot of chateaux, too many cornices and fireplaces and chimneys and parquet floors, an overload of minutiae and myriad details crowding in on their eager, engaged minds.

'Out of curiosity. That first house, the one with the lake, how much was it selling for? More specifically, after seeing all those houses, how much do you think we could get for this one?'

'They were all over a million euros. I would say, easily, you could sell this, even given the work left to do, which is considerable, for 1.1 or 1.2 million euros.'

'I'm sorry, I didn't understand you. How much?'

'Easily over a million.'

I was speechless. I think I went immediately pale and then bright, glowing red.

'Are you OK, Sam?' Johan said with a smile.

'I think so. I'm not quite sure. So you're telling me a house and property of this size, in roughly the same condition, would go for over a million?'

'Absolutely.'

There are those moments in life where revelation and epiphany come together in a union of inspiration and cast everything one holds dear in a new, shocking light. Right there, I formulated a plan in my head as the words of Johan and Monique seemed to bubble up from underwater. This scrap of information gave me a new idea as to how to push forward, take control of our destiny, and relieve some of the constant burden of a relentless financial situation. Most importantly, this offhand observation gave me what a long, knotty three years had so deprived me of: in a word... hope.

CHAPTER NINETEEN

A Pound of Flesh

Thrown headfirst into a land of need and necessity, urged on by my fortuitous meeting with the exquisite couple from Antwerp, I set about a scheme to extract us from the deep, dark money pit we had so blithely embraced. I would try the banks, armed with my newly discovered equity and, failing that, would consider more drastic measures.

Over the next month, I came up with a seven-year business plan, backdating to 2002. The numbers ran something like this: 2002, income 8,000 euros; 2003, income 16,000 euros; 2004, income (still projected) 57,000 euros; and so on and so on. Given this annual growth, the addition of more weddings, and possibly a freshly renovated additional gîte, in two years, I figured we could bring in over 100,000 euros (£69,000), possibly more if my conservative estimates were low.

Bud and I spoke energetically of the need to begin work on the second floor, renovate one of our large, dormant outbuildings for our personal use and turn the entire chateau over to guests and weddings (at a much higher rate – fewer, more expensive weddings meant more income and less work). We called in our old team of artisans and quickly obtained estimates. A bit wishful, we set the target for all of these projects at 60,000 euros (£41,000). I say 'wishful' because anyone who has ever undertaken renovations knows the double-double rule: determine your costs and the time it will take and double each.

I set up a meeting with our local bank manager and his number two. I prepared our private salon with a roaring fire, made coffee and put out small, refined pastries for their enjoyment. I was filled with doubt as I recalled the *comte*'s insistence that home equity loans were non-existent in France. I brushed this aside by convincing myself that I wasn't looking for a home equity loan but a business loan based on equity. I had to tell myself something.

They arrived in a white late-model Renault Clio, standard issue vehicle for every living, working human in France. The manager walked cautiously to the front door in tight-fitting trousers, a short-sleeved white shirt and a 1980s paisley tie. His minion followed quickly behind, almost stepping on his heels.

I showed them in and led them to the salon. They gazed slowly around, apparently sizing up the place. They seemed impressed.

A POUND OF FLESH

'Thank you for coming today. I believe you've received my business plan. I want to talk to you about the possibility of taking a loan, an additional loan, based on the true value of the property. As you know, I already owe 380,000 euros and I'm looking for 60 more based on the worksheets I sent you.'

'*Alors*, we are very interested in your proposition,' the manager began. 'We have looked at it and find it interesting. But you must understand it is a big risk for us. Do you have a job?'

The entire basis of my project was the fact that I was a small business owner, a serious hotelier with a plan. Perhaps I hadn't been clear.

'I work here and I'm growing this business, as you can see from our past years' numbers and the projections.' I tried not to be impatient. I knew it would be a hard sell.

'This income is not sufficient. It is better if you have a job with a salary.'

'I do have a job – running and owning this business.'

'Yes, yes, but we like for people to have a salary.'

'I hope you will agree there is absolutely no risk for you. If you give me the money, I will be able to make more money and pay you back.'

I actually had trouble believing I was having this conversation. In any other Western industrial civilised nation, if I entered a bank with eight hundred to a million dollars' worth of equity in my home, they would wine and dine me, grovel and compete like hungry jackals for the opportunity to lend me money.

'You see, you do not have a salary. And that is a problem. You need to make more money before we can give you more money.'

'This has absolutely nothing to do with salaries. My chateau is a guarantee; *en anglais*, 'collateral'. I offer something to you of value, this chateau, and you give me money. Did you see the estimate I sent you? The *expert immobilier*, surveyor, put the price – conservatively – at 1.1 million euros.'

'We are very uncomfortable with this arrangement. It is very hard to retrieve a house by default in France.'

'It's actually not. It takes about a year and a half, just like any other country, with some fees. But the value is so great, this is nothing for you.'

'It is just that, it is better if you have a job.'

I thought my head would explode. My cleanly laid plans being shot down by their failure to see the nub of the issue. Or so I thought. Literally and figuratively, we were speaking different languages and our mindsets were universes apart.

'OK, let me make this simple for you,' I said, slowly and deliberately, like a teacher speaking to five-year-olds. 'I have something of value – a chateau, which you see here.' I pointed to all the things around us and out the window. 'I owe you 380,000 euros which I have diligently been paying back for two full years now. The value of this chateau, on the low end, is 1.2 million euros. That's a lot of money.'

I stood now.

'You lend me money based on the value of the house. I do renovations, increase my advertising, increase my income in line with what we have been doing the past two years, and I pay you back. You lend me more money to do this and you make even more interest and money than you are currently making. I'm sure it is the largest private loan you have at your bank. Isn't that true?' He nodded. 'That's how loans work.' I wasn't sure if my slightly too condescending tone was doing the trick. They sat with blank looks on their faces.

'And even better,' I was agitated now, 'if I do not or cannot pay you, you take the house.' I waved my hands like a madman, grabbing big bundles of air and pushing it towards them. 'You take the house and sell it and make one million euros – not one hundred, not one thousand, but one million euros. Then you, *monsieur*, will be the best and most famous bank manager in France. There is no risk. The truth of my proposition is as clear as the sun shining today in the sky.'

I sat down. Stunned silence.

'Yes, yes, we understand,' he stammered. 'But this is not the way we do things in France. It would be better if you had a job.' And that was that. Our plan, as we had discussed it late into the evenings many times, seemed so simple to me and Bud. In fact, I can almost believe that in America or the UK, by law, I would be forced to take an equity loan. It might be a crime, punishable by fines and prison, if I did not seek and take a loan on the greater value of my home.

My pulse was racing. I had exercised myself to the extent that if we continued, I might resort to physical violence.

'I think we are finished. Have a nice day, gentlemen. I'm sure you can find your way out.'

I darted into the kitchen and explained everything to Bud, complete with hand gestures and wild facial expressions.

'I'm so sorry, Sam. It seemed so clear, so simple. What are we going to do?'

'In the short run, I will have to go back to New York. We are on the verge of running low again, the property tax is nearing and you know how costly the winters are.'

'I can't believe you have to leave again. We can't keep doing this. Plus I'm five months pregnant and getting bigger. I won't be able to move very easily as things progress and I have to take care of the kids at the same time.'

'I know, I know. I'm so sorry. But it will be shorter this time because we made a bit of money this summer. I will aim to go for just a month or month and a half. Does that work?'

Bud began to well up and I couldn't bear to look at her like this. We were depleted. Our morale was shot, we were physically, and partly spiritually, defeated. Quite frankly, there are many things in life worse than failing to achieve one's dream. The sickness or loss of a loved one, homelessness, civil war, lack of good drinking water. Of course, we realised this. In the end, we still had a beautiful house worth quite a bit. But dreams and their deaths do trigger the feeling of little deaths in us. It is not the worst thing in the world, but it's deeply disappointing nevertheless. In the end, though, it was clear: 'life has many worthwhile aspects', as my essayist friend was once reminded.

In late October, just weeks after my deeply frustrating meeting with the moneylenders, I made my way back to New York. Again, no job and no place to live. It felt like *Groundhog Day*, different day, different year, same story.

A POUND OF FLESH

I ended up working for ABC News and A&E Network, making a one-hour documentary on the founder of Taco Bell, Glen Bell. It was part of A&E's week of *Super Size Me* documentaries on pop culture icons who changed the way we live today. It was good work and I ended up in California at the beach again while Bud remained in our vast, cold chateau, heavily pregnant with two busy and demanding children. It was over this time that Bud made friends with a lovely, generous couple from England, Tom and Hannah, who lived on a 20-acre farm just north of the chateau. Tom was an ex-special ops man. His missions and experiences were so top secret, we never came to know exactly what it was he had done in his former life before coming to France. Hannah had been a firefighter in England and had the dubious honour of being the only woman in Europe who had more animals than Bud. Animals she too had rescued. They had transported 57 various creatures from England and the number grew every day. Their presence in Bud's life was a blessing.

Through a friend of a friend, they had heard we needed some trees cut and removed, and they came diligently and regularly to stock up for the winter. During their visits, they would call in on Bud and bring her jams, relishes and vegetables, fix things and generally serve the neighbourly role of keeping Bud from going insane.

Every night, Bud and I spoke on the phone. She shared her day with me, the comings and goings of Tom and Hannah and the antics of our busy, *sauvage* children.

We had not yet articulated a way out of our money matters. One night, I began.

'Bud, maybe we should think about selling the house.'

'What are we going to do instead? We have a business here, we've started something. We can't just leave. I'm getting ready to have the baby and I'm organising everything for the birth. I can't believe you're saying this.' She was tearful.

'It's just something to think about. We could make a good bit of money and start something else, something that gives us more pleasure. Something easier. There has to be an easier way to make a living and live a life.'

'I don't want to hear any more about this now. Let's have the baby and see what happens.'

'OK. I won't mention it again.'

I had forgotten. Bud was deep into her period of nesting instinct, something she – and I think most women – embrace as the body's rumblings let a mother know something big is about to happen. So I dropped the subject.

I spent three months in the States, working and crashing on sofas and flying around until late January. I finished my final edit on a Friday and took the next flight out. I had missed my family terribly. I found it hard to accept that I was forced, by our own decisions and dreams, to uproot at least once a year and leave the nest for the never-ending demands of money.

Two weeks after I landed back in France, our third baby was born, Oak. This time we opted for the public health system. Here, we had discovered, only midwives delivered babies. The doctor would only be called in an emergency. After our last experience, we were finished with doctors. The birth was a thing of beauty, and quick too. Bud pushed the little fella out at 2 a.m. and later that morning we were back in our house, cosy and safe with our tiny new gift.

As Bud settled in with Oak, I took to roaming the grounds trying to summon up admiration and joy for this splendid property, but all I conjured was resentment and distrust. With the exception of my family, I couldn't wring an ounce of pleasure out of the place. All the plans, our grand ideals and romantic visions of living like lords in the French countryside, melted away into one monumental case of indigestion.

Something inside of me didn't want to give up quite that easily. We had bought the house four years earlier. We had only moved to France permanently a year after that and we had wrangled our way through only two full summers of running a *chambre d'hôtes*. I wasn't normally a quitter. But the more I thought, the clearer it became that it was ridiculous that we should work so hard, solely for the privilege of living in one small part of a massive house.

Here I was, holding tenuously onto an idea, an ideal, of life in a chateau as lord of the manor. The reality of our life included constant invasions by strangers in a service industry where everyone came before the server. We were both lords and servants, *châtelains et domestiques*. We had created this great romance in the realm of our fantasies, where the world of ideas was disconnected from the everyday life we lived. We had erected through sheer will and hoping a stunning edifice, a sublime castle, a profound theory of how the world worked and how we should live. All the while, we chose to live not in the entirety of this chateau, but dwelled, in our everyday life, in a little, cold room in the basement. OK, not really a basement, but in a small part of the chateau, tending to the needs of others so they could live *their* dream of castle life.

I had a bad case of existential despair. We had sought to become something that we were never meant to be. We sought not ourselves and our own true bliss, but some starry-eyed vision of utopia rooted in seventeenth-century feudal France.

CHAPTER TWENTY

Forsan et haec olim meminisse iuvabit

The Aeneid, Virgil

I n the first chapter of Virgil's *The Aeneid*, the hero and his shipmates are shipwrecked after a wild storm. They have recently been exiled from their beloved Troy. They are hungry, exhausted and drenched. In similar circumstances, another leader – Churchill, let's say – might have exhorted his charges to great feats of courage and perseverance. Aeneas delivers a cold lump of encouragement by simply offering, 'Perhaps some day it will be pleasing to remember even these things.' One day, we'll look back and laugh at all this.

I served Bud breakfast in bed as the baby cuddled close by every day for a couple of weeks. One morning, I ventured into dangerous territory again.

'Bud, I've been thinking. You know how hard it was this winter and last winter and the winter before that? It's just too much. The bank is stuck in the nineteenth century. We will get nothing from them. This summer looks pretty good but it will be a struggle for a few years to come…'

'Sam, stop.' I thought she had forgotten her prohibition against talking about our dire financial straits. Evidently not. 'I know where you're going and I agree. I'm not entirely sure we should sell but I am open to putting it out there, getting it on the market and seeing what happens. My fear is it's too much of a white elephant, too massive. There's still a lot of work to do here, as you well know. The place still, after all our hard work, feels a little cold, austere. There's the heating system, the old roof, the facade and the cornice around the back. I think it might take a long time to sell, if it ever sells.'

'I'm glad you're so optimistic. But I'm very happy you're open to the idea of at least testing the waters.' I was smiling at this point, delighted Bud was open to my latest scheme. She smiled with only the occasional frown as I continued. 'I think it's a great property, despite our intimate awareness of all its faults. But you're right, similar houses like this have taken eighteen months to two years to sell. Let's push ahead with the bookings for the summer and see how the chips fall.'

'I feel much more comfortable with the idea now. It has been difficult. There have been good things too. We've raised the kids here for the past four years. Grim and Oak were born here. It will be hard if we leave.'

I was happy, not because Bud saw it all my way, but because we were coming to some sort of meeting of the minds. Like most couples, our marriage wasn't perfect, but we loved one another and had very similar, almost pitch perfect sensibilities. We had the same threshold for suffering and hardship, the same desire for joy and relaxation, and similar levels of energy. We tended to view our reality and the world around us very nearly the same way. Hugely important when making life's big decisions. It's what had landed us here, our vision of our life, and it's what might just get us out of this mess.

I set about rounding up the usual suspects, the many estate agents I had so lovingly studied for the past seven years. They came running, ravenous for the chance to sell a chateau in the Loire. Even though I didn't have a real sense of the chateau's value before my encounter with the Dutch couple, I had continued poring over the property market for a vicarious thrill. I spoke directly and firmly with them. Bud and I discussed it and set the price at 1.5 million euros, with a little leeway for negotiation. A little, not a lot. That might or might not include the furniture, depending on how long it would take to sell. If we sold quickly, we might be more parsimonious; if it took a while, we'd throw it into the deal.

Although we were in no position to be choosy, I made it very clear: no sightseers. We ourselves had been guilty of this – curious and tantalised by the chance to peek at other estates, we had made appointments with no real intention of buying. Not often, but we had. The indignity of strangers traipsing through our house was one thing, but the indignity of strangers without means on a Sunday outing traipsing through our house was unbearable.

Within a month, our first offer came in. I received an urgent call from one of the agents, Monsieur Challanville. 'Sam, we have an offer from the gentleman who came last week. You know, the man who creates *parfums* in Paris.' Indeed. A robust, tall man with black hair to the middle of his back, a vintage Rolls-Royce and a young, beautiful wife.

'Yes, I remember.' My heart was racing. What was the house really worth, today, on the open market? I could hardly bear the suspense.

'Now, the offer is very good and generous. I think you should think hard. It is a fair price…'

'What's the offer?' I cut him off.

'One million two hundred thousand, including agents' fees.'

'I'll let you know,' I said, cool as a cucumber, while almost wetting my pants.

It was lower than we wanted but I was deeply relieved to hear those numbers.

I told Bud.

'Oh no. That's much too low,' she replied. Mrs Moneybags, evidently.

'I know, I know, but it's still exciting to know we're in the right range.'

'Yes, but we need more than that. It's so soon too, we just put it on the market.' I couldn't tell if this was a ballsy ploy or a resistance to selling.

I wrote to the agent and told him the offer was too low. I countered with the asking price, 1.5 million euros. I instructed him to bring only serious buyers to the house acting the big shot. I was willing to gamble a little. I knew we could soldier through another summer and, if need be, I could always work in New York in the winter. It wasn't ideal but it did give us some flexibility in spite of our poor, church-mouse cash flow.

We had a further dozen or so visits. Many were tourists, some were serious but saw too much work. The pickiest and most demanding were French, even though they were few and far between at this price range. I thought briefly of banning French buyers from the property. Perhaps this was too severe but my feeling was, and anecdotal evidence showed, the French were good up to about 800,000 (£550,000); after that it was all foreigners. We were sceptical about whether or not the perfume guy could actually come up with the money. We had heard through another agent that his real budget was around 800–900,000. This inability to buy the big country house was, understandably, a source of great irritation for the French.

We continued to accept guests, albeit with an air of resignation knowing that we might be rid of the white elephant some time in the not-too-distant future.

We explored the woods, wandered the outbuildings and visited the guest rooms more than we had in the past. We took pleasant long walks up the lane and looped back around on a small hill to gaze affectionately at our stately home. I won't say we were overly sentimental, just appreciative of our opportunity to share in the life of this great home.

One day I received a call.

'Mr Juneau. I want to speak to you about your chateau for sale. Is it still for sale?'

'Yes. Where are you calling from?'

'I am in Italy and I represent buyers who would like to make an offer. We are willing to pay your full asking price plus a small bonus in order to wrap up the sale quickly. Are you interested?'

It sounded too good to be true. 'Of course, we are always interested in serious offers.'

'You must come to Milan to meet my buyers and we will discuss terms. Can you come here this weekend? They are very motivated.'

'That is such short notice. I think it is best if your buyers come to visit the house first. We can meet here, I will show you the property and we can proceed.'

'This is not possible. It is essential you come to Italy.'

It seemed very odd to make an offer on a large estate without having seen it. I spoke to Bud. She was suspicious, but I grew more excited at the prospect of an easy sale and worked out fantasies in my head of how it would all go down. I was walking on air.

I checked flights and trains, suspicions aside, and was about to book something, when Tom and Hannah came by to help out with the woods. We sat in the salon drinking coffee and sampling Hannah's latest country relish. I took the opportunity to feel Tom out on the offer.

'What do you think, Tom? Sound a little fishy? Would you be willing to come with me for the meeting?' I knew Tom would be handy in a tight situation, given his background as a top secret special forces guy.

'Sam, I just read an article on the Web. There is a network of kidnappers working out of Italy and Greece who lure wealthy property sellers away, kidnap them and demand ransom. One man was killed in Nigeria during a similar type of transaction. I can't believe you were even considering it.'

Embarrassed that Bud's intuition was spot on, I dropped the idea. The man from Italy called a few more times and I grew increasingly impatient, even rude, with him as I probed his motives. He was reserved and unwilling to give up any information or any hint of evil-doing. Finally, he went away, on to his next prey.

One weekend in early July, one of our best agents, Patrick from Agence Mercure, called to arrange a visit. He said they were indeed serious buyers, a New Zealand couple living in London. They had contacted him earlier in the week and wanted to come as soon as possible and spend a weekend at the chateau. They would pay for a suite and visit the house.

Ed and Irina Mercy arrived late Friday evening in a minivan straight from the UK–France ferry with two kids and hopeful faces. It struck me how much like us they were. Late thirties, early forties, simply dressed, articulate and curious with small children. We spoke briefly as I showed them their suite. Their first impressions left them smiling and gazing around with wonder. They too were tired of the rat race, wanted more time with the children and wanted to live a simpler life in the countryside. Sounded familiar. I wanted to tell them it wasn't necessarily like that, this life, but I also wanted to sell the house, so I let them dream romantic dreams.

The next morning, I served breakfast in the dining room and we retired to the library for a chat. They had a thousand questions, practical things like schools and transport and heating and electricity bills, taxes and living in France. When a prospective buyer gets down to the nitty-gritty of these details, so I thought, they have made some sort of emotional or mental connection with the place. They wanted to know all about the business and the weddings and precisely how we did things. Bud and I sat and casually shared our experiences; casually but very honestly. They seemed to take it all in. We stressed that the house and business were hard work without putting too fine a point on it. Their tone and attitude reminded me of the first time we saw that castle in Ireland what felt like many years ago. We had driven there looking for a marriage venue. As soon as we saw the house and poked around inside, we looked at one another and said, almost simultaneously, 'This is it.' They were so enamoured with the idea of what we were doing, anything we told them would have sounded wonderful. We could have told them running the property was like being bitten to death by ducks and they would have smiled and thought only that duck was delicious.

Within three days, the Mercys made an offer: 1.38 million euros. We were very pleased about the news but the offer included all the furniture, except for personal things, and the business. We pointed out to the diligent Patrick that the price for the house was *sans* furniture, *sans* business. Of course, we had resigned ourselves to letting the whole thing go, including every stick of furniture and our anaemic business. But we had to pretend, at least, we were driving a harder bargain. We indicated we could do the whole package for one and a half million. Where we found the temerity to insist on such things is beyond me.

They came back immediately and raised their offer to the asking price. That day, Bud and I left the kids with Patricia and drove to a nearby Relais & Châteaux. There we drank cocktails in the garden, giggled and whispered sweet nothings to one another as we plotted our new life. It was a glorious day. We passionately painted our futures and sculpted our hopes for a new life while reliving all the good and hard things that had followed our decision those four years ago.

Normally, the next step after an offer in France is to sign a *compromis de vente*, a contractual agreement to both buy and sell the house. The Mercys were delaying, niggling and questioning the agents' fees (five per cent, but included in the price), the *notaire*'s fees (another six per cent), the state of the septic system. The *compromis* was a big step. The general practice, though not a law, is to put ten per cent down at this first signing. In this case, it was 150,000 euros (£103,000). We had put down the equivalent of 35,000 four years earlier.

Then Irina became alarmed when a cowboy English surveyor told her the septic system would cost 100,000 euros to replace. The number was assuredly closer to 15–20,000

– money we didn't have, but not terrible for someone laying out a million and a half. I calmed their nerves on this and even found them an artisan who could bring the toilet works up to current standards.

Irina rang me one evening. As we were talking, she shared a thought, nonchalantly.

'We are ready to sign but as you know, Ed is a contract IT worker. He makes a very good salary but it is without a permanent contract. We also have our house in London which we need to sell, but this shouldn't be a problem with the way the market is over here. But before we sign and put down the deposit, the French banks have to get their heads around how Ed makes his money.'

That was it. I knew the deal was dead. Our celebration had been premature. There was no way on God's green earth that the banks in France were 'getting their heads' around anything. They had chosen to go with French banks and French banks would block a loan to Bill Gates because he had no salary and was working for charity nowadays. I told Bud about the conversation and she turned white.

'I knew it. It's too big. We'll never sell. What are we going to do?'

'In the short run, we need to continue as if the house is still for sale, live life as usual. I'll have to go to New York again soon.'

It was devastating. One more winter away, the pressures now of three children, Bud alone with them in the house, again. We licked our wounds and forged ahead. We knew the implications and had no other choice.

A week before my planned departure to the Big Apple, we received another call from Patrick. He was always very calm and patient, never overly excited but professional and consistent. He had sold chateaux before – he knew we were in it for the long haul. His last large chateau in our area had taken three years to sell.

'Samuel, we have some more prospective buyers. The Mercys say they are still going to buy the house, but I think it might not happen. How's next Wednesday? It is a Dutch couple. They seem quite serious, but we thought the Mercys were serious too.'

'Of course,' I replied resignedly.

That Wednesday, Patrick showed up with an elegant, reserved couple in their mid fifties, the Van den Redders. She was fashionably dressed, a horsey woman who looked younger than her years and exuded a stateliness befitting a potential chatelaine. He was quite tall with a thick thatch of white hair, dressed in corduroys and tweeds and sensible leather shoes. We said hello and I let them get down to business.

Later that day, as our special guests were leaving with the agent, Patrick said, 'We have another viewing tomorrow morning. Is that OK?'

'That's late notice, but fine. We will be here.'

Bud and I sat in bed that night talking about our latest visitors. Anxiety was the order of the evening as we spoke of my imminent departure. We were not taking my leaving for granted. We had survived the previous separations well but were by no means interested in testing the limits. We both fell into a fitful sleep, bookends in our bed for our three carefree, healthy children.

The next day at nine in the morning, Patrick showed up. With the Van den Redders. What a surprise. He hadn't indicated the visit was with the same couple from the day before. Mrs Van den Redders entered the main gallery with a slightly embarrassed look on her face. Her husband followed closely behind, nodded in my direction and smiled a devious, collegial smile that spoke volumes.

Within a week, we had signed the *compromis de vente* for the asking price, including most furniture and no mention of the business. No delays, no hemming, no hawing: we needed to get out and the Van den Redders had fallen head over heels in love with the place.

Like Frank and Rosemarie from Roundwood House, like Philippe the ruffled agent, like Johan and Monique, the Van den Redders were placed in our lives for a purpose, placed serendipitously with life-changing consequences. *La vie est belle*.

Right away, I started our search for a new house. Why and how we decided to stay in France, a beautiful, thorny and complex country, is another story.

One day in early autumn, as the leaves slid effortlessly to the ground and the sun sat majestically brilliant in the cool pre-winter sky, I darted into the kitchen with a handful of papers splashed with possibilities of a new life, a new dream. We had tried and failed at our endeavour, we had sought happiness and left behind the money and anonymity of New York for a new life. In our seeking, we had gained not the life we hoped for but a new, deeper understanding of who we were and who we could be. We had sought not riches but happiness and, in the end, by luck and pluck, gained more of one and less of the other.

As the clocked ticked away towards the now inevitable exchange, we sometimes grew nostalgic about the place. It did seem odd that someone else would take over something we had poured so much energy and passion into. We envied their new adventure. We experienced the vicarious thrill of having real money to fix up the chateau. Bud and I talked of what we would do if we had a few extra hundred thousand euros. We knew we were doing the right thing. There was never a moment of true regret but there were instances, pangs of 'what if'. There were fleeting moments of panic as we let go of what we had fought so hard to create. The passing of the chateau from our hands to theirs was just another of life's little deaths. But we were steadfast in our hope that the mortality of this venture would give birth to new and engaging challenges.

'Bud,' I yelled as I bounded into the kitchen like an excitable puppy. 'I found this area, it's called the Dordogne. There's this beautiful *chartreuse*, an eighteenth-century manor house. It needs a lot of work but we can pay cash and worry about the renovations later. It says here, the region is known for strawberries, walnuts, truffles and foie gras. And there are hundreds of chateaux and delightful places to visit.' My enthusiasm waned as Bud frowned. I quickly realised the problem. 'Oh, don't worry about the foie gras, focus on the strawberries.'

I showed her the photo.

'Sam, you know what I love about you? You're stubborn but at least you're single-minded. Quite simply, you never learn.'

Filled with a deep, satisfying liberation about our uncertain future, I laughed, and Bud joined in. Indeed, it was already pleasing to look back and remember even these things.